Teaching for Learning Gain in Higher Education

With practical advice that can be immediately applied to a higher education setting, *Teaching for Learning Gain in Higher Education* provides materials and methods specifically designed to improve teaching, learning and assessment for students in higher education through student-centric methods.

Considering how to improve students' learning strategies and thus their learning gain, this book answers key questions about how students can be helped to construct meaning and their own knowledge and knowledge hierarchies. Based on education and psychological theory, it examines nine cognitive approaches that have been tried and tested, and explores how motivation can be both set up and maintained.

Unpacking the concept of learning gain to be both accessible and constructive, this book includes chapters on:

- The nature of higher learning gain and how programmes have achieved it.
- Theories and practice of teaching and learning in higher education.
- Problems and issues for distance and blended learning programmes.
- Strategies to promote learning gain in higher education.

Teaching for Learning Gain in Higher Education fully explores the nature of self-regulated learning and how it can be promoted and maintained to improve student learning. This book is ideal reading for anyone involved in teaching in higher education.

Diane Montgomery is Professor Emerita in Education at Middlesex University, UK, where she was formerly Dean of Faculty and Head of the School of Education.

Teaching for Learning Gain in Higher Education

Developing Self-regulated Learners

Diane Montgomery

Routledge
Taylor & Francis Group

LONDON AND NEW YORK

First published 2021
by Routledge
2 Park Square, Milton Park, Abingdon, Oxon OX14 4RN

and by Routledge
52 Vanderbilt Avenue, New York, NY 10017

Routledge is an imprint of the Taylor & Francis Group, an informa business

© 2021 Diane Montgomery

British Library Cataloguing-in-Publication Data
A catalogue record for this book is available from the British Library

Library of Congress Cataloging-in-Publication Data
A catalog record has been requested for this book

ISBN: 978-0-367-48496-5 (hbk)
ISBN: 978-0-367-48500-9 (pbk)
ISBN: 978-1-003-04129-0 (ebk)

Typeset in Goudy
by Cenveo® Publisher Services

Contents

Introduction

After 600 years of university education in the United Kingdom, there has been a large expansion in the numbers over the last 150 years. Even larger changes took place in the nature of that education in the 1990s that continue to influence today's institutions. It was not just in the UK that such changes were taking place. In the United States, education in its traditional form was also being questioned and for similar reasons. These were expressed in a letter to colleges by college principal, Donald Kennedy. The main points were:

> It simply will not do for our schools to produce a small elite to power our scientific establishment and a larger cadre of workers with basic skills to do routine work. Millions of people around the world now have these same basic skills and are willing to work twice as long for as little as one-tenth our basic wages. To maintain and enhance our quality of life we must develop a leading edge economy based on workers who can think for a living. If skills are equal in the long run wages will be too. This means we have to educate a vast mass of people capable of thinking critically, creatively and imaginatively.
> (Drafted by Donald Kennedy in 1987 and signed by 36 other college principals and sent to all the rest of the colleges in the US as a warning of a national emergency.)

Leaders in the Manpower Services Commission in the UK and the CBI (Confederation of British Industry) were expressing similar views and many university tutors were already ahead of the field from the early 1970s. At that time, the typical university education of the 20th century was one in which the ideal graduate could draw on deep knowledge and understanding of a field of information, extend and deepen it, or by analogy apply it to new areas. It was traditionally an education for personal and intellectual development and to pass on social and cultural values. It was the preserve of a small elite assumed to be intellectually superior.

Then in the 1990s so much of this was challenged. The bilateral system of universities and polytechnics was ended. Mass higher education (HE) was introduced, and students were charged fees; globalisation was rapidly enveloping world economies and the concept of Lifelong Learning began to be absorbed into the education system. At the same time, information and communication technology advanced rapidly and became widespread.

It was in this heady climate of change that the Dearing Report (National Committee of Inquiry into Higher Education, 1997) was published. It emphasised the need for students to develop transferable skills and become flexible learners in all the disciplines. They would have 'soft' skills and become experts at accessing knowledge rather than being knowledgeable. The university programmes needed to develop the students' employability such as in communication skills, teamwork, personal skills and analytical skills (Dearing, 1997, 9.17) and the skills of learning how to learn. The vision was of a broadening of university provision through modularisation, systems of credit accumulation and transfer, and with student Progress Files to recognise achievements in a transparent manner. In fact, many of the polytechnics had already been piloting these initiatives since well before they became universities. But this vision did not appeal to all the educators and observers and this led Blake et al. (1998, 4) to write the following:

> But in this 'vision' it is as if the sense of what a university is for has fallen off the edge. A portfolio of bits and bobs replaces any sense of an institution that could arouse a student's loyalty. But loyalty of a more important kind may disappear also – loyalty to a tradition of enquiry, to the courses that sustain such a tradition, and the kind of commitment that is at the heart of academic endeavour. Without this loyalty and commitment, we cannot but dilute the critical business that is at the heart of higher education.

This resistance had been long in the pipeline. In 1985, a team of professors and educators from the Council for National Academic Awards that approved and conferred degrees in the polytechnic sector initially rejected a proposal for a postgraduate Certificate and Diploma in Special Needs. This was because it was modular and did not contain the theory and research in the theoretical educational discipline spine of traditional programmes. This was despite the fact that in the previous 3 years local inspectors from six surrounding Local Education Authorities (LEAs) supported the work and their teachers had followed the pilot programmes and found them intellectually challenging and professionally effective in updating education theory and practice.

Just 6 years later, a new university accepted a modular MA part-time programme but dithered over an Accreditation of Prior Learning (APL) proposal until 2 years later. This was when a professor from an 'old' university had been appointed to pursue a degree proposal in Work-Based Learning in which he adopted and adapted the original APL documents. These examples show that innovation is hard to achieve in a system that is comfortable with itself and also reflects an elitist bias. However, when the resource base is steadily diminishing as it was at that time, change suddenly becomes possible. Professional teacher training was being largely devolved to schools plus the income needed to support it and so new fields of funding had to be opened up if staff were not to be redeployed, retired or made redundant. The pressures of decreasing funding despite charging student fees arose because the overall university funding formula was designed to increase student numbers at reduced cost.

In the current era, new institutional challenges have emerged and these centre on Virtual Learning Environments (VLEs), and blended learning versus 'face-to-face' provision. The set-up costs of VLE may be extraordinarily high but can become more economically viable over time. But there can be other running costs in management and technology, and no indication that learning gain is any better than in the normal range. Most institutions have adopted or begun the journey with Blended Learning or Open learning, that is, a mixture of distance-supported technology with E-learning and contact time with tutors.

The changes however have not yet resulted in the bleak vision conceived by Blake et al. (1998), at least not in most institutions. This was because the employability skills and Lifelong Learning techniques could be used to motivate the students and also broaden and deepen their academic studies. It raised the standards in many cases of some rather mundane programmes and led to learning gain although the administrative costs of modularisation and random choices that students might make were more difficult to manage. A million trees have however been saved since student handbooks and study guides went online.

Learning gain is the difference between what students know and can do when they enter HE and when they leave. The general assumption is that it is the quality of teaching that is the key to promoting this learning gain. However, this is not always the case. Instead, research shows that it is the quality time that students spend on learning, reduced class sizes, high-quality resources, increased student-staff contact and regular and prompt feedback on assignments that increases learning gain (Gibbs, 2015). However, there is normal learning gain and higher learning gain, and this difference will be explored and exemplified in the chapters that follow.

Universities with high reputations can attract well-qualified students and their outcomes will be in the superior range but this will be because of the selectivity of their input not necessarily the process in between. Some students may know little more when they leave than when they entered the institution others make normal gain. Other universities may take in a much wider range of students with varied qualifications but achieve equally high learning outcomes and this is some evidence of learning gain intrinsic to the academic process.

Another factor that has to be considered is retention. Having recruited the students, if a course does not meet its objectives and confer student satisfaction then many will opt out, become disaffected and do the minimum of work. Others will transfer to another course or university or leave HE altogether. This is a waste of resources, personal and financial.

Access to resources can be a highly significant factor in promoting or decreasing learning gain and retention. Large numbers of students put a strain on access to library and other resources such as laboratory time or theatre and studio work-shop areas and technical support unless there is a complementary investment in them. Increasing the number of students makes courses viable and increases the funding available but the money is not always allocated to the resources that promote learning gains.

Research shows that it is what students do that makes more difference than what their tutors do and students learn more when they have 'self-efficacy' or are self-regulated learners. It is thus student time on task that predicts the highest learning outcomes. Gibbs has suggested that this ratio needs to be 10:1 student hours to tutor contact time. In these hours, it is important that students engage in deep learning and understanding rather than adopting superficial or surface approaches. How deep learning can be facilitated and student time on study can be increased will form topics for consideration and example.

Are tutors or lecturers effective teachers in their contact time? One factor that is shown to improve their effectiveness is teacher training. This is offered now in long courses such as the Postgraduate Certificate in Teaching and Learning Course in HE that lasts over 200 hours. Even then some of these courses are more effective than others. It is thus the nature of effective teaching and effective learning that need to be investigated so that good practice can be more widely disseminated. It also raises questions such as what constitutes 'good' practice, and can lecturing and the role of lecturer be equivalent to teaching and the role of teacher? Is lecturing teaching? Some people think so. Outside the training for new recruits to lecturing, there yet remains the large cadre of the untrained and though they may seek updating in their subject specialisms through research and conferencing they may not be part of any in-house CPD (Continuing Professional Development) in teaching the subject. This is a weakness in the system.

To cut down running costs, many courses recruit part-time tutors and postgrad-uate students to undertake parts of the work. These are usually also untrained and so it is found that it is the full-time faculty members that can reliably teach and integrate the programme content and have a grasp of the issues, assess-ment procedures and expectations. These problems are widely identified in the annual National Surveys of Student Evaluations and Satisfaction and yet there are issues to be considered in these too. For example, students' satisfaction can be heightened in easy study programmes and assessments, whereas challenging programmes and assessments may lower it.

Significant amounts of university funding accrue from research and the 'top' universities are known for their high research profiles but highly qualified researchers are not necessarily highly qualified teachers and their communication and management skills may also be weak. It thus becomes a challenge for a uni-versity to maintain a high profile in both research and teaching. In fact, some of the universities with the lowest research profiles may have the highest profile in quality of teaching. Yet teaching in some institutions is regarded as of low status.

In the present era, other concerns have re-emerged and a major one is 'elitist Britain'. The Sutton Trust and Social Mobility Commission (2018) found that

5,000 people in the top jobs in the UK were five times more likely to be privately educated than the average. Their jobs were in business, politics, media, public organisations and the creative industries. They found that 39% of the elites were privately educated compared to 7% of the population. Things appear to have improved slightly from 20 years previously when the privately educated occupied 42% of the top jobs in politics, the Law, the Church, universities, medicine and business.

The Sutton Trust (2018) research found 19% of the working population had not been to any university and 24% of the elites went to Oxbridge. Oxbridge recruited more students from 8 private schools than all the 3,000 state secondary schools. Findings such as these have caused universities to revise their admissions procedures and it is to be hoped the situation will improve. The main concern is how to improve access to HE for disadvantaged populations when their school records are not strong. High ability and high learning potential may go unnoticed in the presence of poverty, and linguistic and cultural disadvantages, it is a waste of a country's resource.

DfE (Department for Education) funded research by Cullen et al. (2018, 57) on *Research to understand successful approaches to supporting the most academically able disadvantaged pupils* found the following problems or barriers:

- Pupils' fear of failure
- Fear of the costs of HE
- Pupils not knowing what they are really interested in academically
- Lack of awareness on the part of pupils and their parents of the wider world, leading to low aspirations
- Pupils' fear of leaving home, and mixing with people not like them
- Low aspirations and not working hard at home after school
- The difficulties schools face in trying to raise the aspirations of parents and pupils
- Hard to reach parents with low aspirations for their children
- Bright pupils hiding the fact that they are able to avoid being isolated
- Lack of self-confidence
- Attendance issues
- Pupils refusing to accept help because they feel a stigma attached to the help

One interviewee summed all this up saying that it was 'aspirations at home – that's where the attitude to education comes from – schools can't change this', (School 29, Interviewee 17). Many schools and universities have sought to improve access for these students but there is clearly more to do in both spheres.

A different emphasis has recently been adopted in the US instead of 'underachievement' (UAch) they research 'excellence gaps'.

'Excellence gaps' are the differences in rates of advanced achievement between various groups of students. The excellence gaps usually focus upon the percentages of students achieving advanced scores on international, national and state assessments in maths and reading/language arts but test scores are a narrow view and UAch goes wider than this. Plucker and Scott (2018) decided to focus on high-end achievement gaps to redress the lack of improvement that was observed across the ability range because it was felt it would gain more attention from the legislators. Getting the right term or label was important.

> We don't have enough high achievers in the US and the ones we do have come from a shrinking piece of the population pie. If you are from a Caucasian or Asian background, or from a relatively high socioeconomic background, then the schools are doing a pretty good job of developing your potential. But simply developing the potential of this segment of the student population isn't enough.
>
> (Plucker, 2018, 66)

We can recognise this situation in the UK and we use the same international assessments to identify the gaps between our students and those in other countries. These assessments are the Organisation for Economic and Co-operative Development's assessment surveys – PISA (Programme for International Student Assessment), TIMSS (Trends in Maths and Science Studies) and PIRLS (Progress in International Literacy Study).

When our results have been poorer than those of Estonia and Finland in Europe and China, Singapore and Hong Kong policymakers have tried to move our education system and pedagogy towards those in these countries. However, this has taken no account of the different lengths of study time spent by the students in these different cultures – 17 hours a day for some in South-East Asia (Paik et al., 2002) on learning and extra classes and extensive homework times in the European high scorers. A major distinction is in the attitude to the ways in which achievements may be attained in Western versus Eastern cultures. The East tends to emphasise persistence and hard work as the route to excellence rather than high ability (Freeman, 2010). In 2019, the UK results have risen a little to place us at 14th in the 2018 PISA tests league tables or perhaps the others are regressing?

In English, we have a larger vocabulary than most other languages and tend to splice concepts in many ways. For example, experiential learning has been continually translated as 'experimental' learning in several European countries and the difference between the two terms seems hard for the other to understand. Similarly, teaching method is translated as 'didactics' but we have assigned it to a particular type of teaching method known as the traditional transmission mode. As Plucker points out, getting the right term is important but then it takes a long time for it to be widely adopted however apposite it might be. Unfortunately, when the term 'achievement gap' framed conversations about race and education teachers in the US placed less priority on doing something about it than when it was framed as inequalities in provision (Quinn et al., 2019).

In the early chapters of this book, a theory and practice for engaging students in deep learning will be expounded and show with practice examples how high learning gain may be achieved across the HE curriculum following the idea that what students do makes more difference to learning outcomes than what their tutors do.

What this has illustrated is that a system that was prone to inertia had found itself in several decades of rapid change with the outlook of further change to come. Dewey's (1938) thoughts on education cited by Tinkler (1990) at the first Learner Managed Learning Conference in London showed that this was already a known problem:

> The gulf between the nature of adult products and the experience and abilities of the young is so wide that the very situation forbids much active participation by the pupils in the development of what is taught. Theirs is to do and learn that which is taught is essentially static. It is taught as a finished product with little regard either to the ways in which it was originally built up or to the changes that will surely occur in the future. It is to a large extent the cultural product of societies that assumed the future would be much like the past and yet it is used as educational food in a society where change is the rule not the exception.

The traditional methods are still being followed in schools and universities worldwide as research will show and are unlikely to change until the models being developed in HE are more widely disseminated and promote the change. New technology cannot be relied upon to solve the problem if it is designed to repeat the old models and merely concentrates on producing virtual forms of a face-to-face and transmission methodology, and it will not lead to higher learning gain.

Can we change things this time round and close the excellence gaps before climate change overcomes us all? It would appear so if we follow the 95-5 rule. This comes from Management Studies of change and used to be the 80-20 rule. It is found that in order to produce change, it is only necessary to focus on and make significant changes to 5% of the processes, technology or the people to make a real difference.

Chapter 1

The nature of learning gain and how programmes have achieved it

Introduction

Learning gain is the difference between what students know and can do when they enter higher education (HE) and when they leave. However, some gains are more extensive and secure than others, and particular programmes have been found to achieve these better than others. Three learning gain examples are discussed below that adopt different perspectives. They are followed by some strategic approaches that have been claimed to achieve higher learning gain.

The principles of learning show that the learner who is an active participant will learn more than one who is not but even the passive learner in an educational environment will learn something. This learning gain is frequently achieved by incidental learning, by being present when students discuss relevant topics or attending seminars and lectures when a small amount of the contents will be absorbed. In such environments, we also imbibe a hidden curriculum of attitudes, ideas and values but may not think to raise questions about them.

It has been recorded that many schools are not promoting self-regulation skills in their learners and instead are cramming them with facts to pass examinations. There appear to be a range of causes for this such as over-filled syllabuses, the nature of some subjects, examination board requirements, government expectations and regulations, league tables for schools and even coaching and close tutorial support in the private sector none of which fit the young person for an education at many modern universities. By comparison with schools, universities have low contact hours except perhaps in the sciences and performance arts subjects where extensive practical work is required.

It is therefore of considerable concern that many students arrive at university unable to cope both with the more advanced work requiring critical thinking and abstract thought and with the lack of skills and experience to engage in independent study. This is especially problematic in first-year students transitioning from school to university and also to independent living in most cases. An additional factor has been the impact of social media as a major occupying activity also competing with independent study time.

Faculties and researchers that are aware of these problems have tried to find out more about individual student needs and perceptions using self-report inventories and changing the style of working to develop some of the necessary skills. These approaches have been developed more in HE than schools not least because of the independence of thought and action that is still permitted to tutors in the HE sector. Traditionalists will of course always maintain the 'usual practices' but there has been significant room for trialling new ways of working and some examples are set out in this chapter.

Many students may have built up a history as a passive learner. It becomes a habit and they do not read around the subject or prepare any work for which there is no assessment. They remain passengers in seminars and have always lived on their wits in this way and succeeded because they have good memories and will engage in a few days cramming for examinations. To get the best out of these students is a regular challenge in HE when there can be so many more engaging social activities to distract them.

Another major concern is that in the transition year from school to university, family and friendship groups and the security of a known school timetable and routine are all abandoned. There are now no rules to follow and if there are, they have to be learned and new social groups formed. This is easier for the students residing on the campus rather than those living outside in rooms and flats. Thus, in some universities, it is a policy to expect all first-year students to live in the 'halls of residence' to help their integration. If they live at home, as is becoming an increasing feature, integration is less strong.

Some individuals can develop anomie and alienation in this transition period, and retention rates are lowered as a result. If the course does not provide the stimulus and interest that it promised, then motivation to learn and stay is lowered. If there is too much competition for limited resources, journeying in may easily be given up for other pursuits. Students who live on campus tend to gain better results in the assessments than those who do not.

Another effect on retention is an extensive modular course structure. To counteract some of the effects of loneliness and anomie, the organisation and development of teams or groups can be promoted who arrange to select their modules on a group basis and so can keep together throughout the course.

In consideration of all of these negative factors, there is one underlying feature that links them all and can turn them round and this is motivation. Motivation to learn needs to be intrinsic to the programme so students want to attend and participate despite all the difficulties. Some will respond to the extrinsic motivators such as rules, assessments and awards but most learning gain will come from the wish to learn for its own sake and the achievement of self-regulation as a learner and for it to be lifelong.

These are some of the issues underlying learning gain and will be discussed at greater length in the subsequent chapters. In the present chapter, three different systems are outlined to show how some of the problems have been overcome.

1. The Oxbridge University tutorial system

The essence of the Oxford and Cambridge system is that with the lowest of staff-student contact time, in the order of 6 hours per week, a high level of student time on study task is generated. The student and tutor meet on a one-to-one basis or sometimes with two and three on a weekly basis. This amounts to about 50 hours of staff-student contact time over the 3 years and even the terms are short. The weekly assignments given out in the tutorials are estimated to generate about 10 hours of student out-of-class study time (Gibbs, 2015).

This makes the Oxbridge students the most hardworking in the UK. The assignments also generate large amounts of personalised feedback and feed forward. Oxford University spends much more than other institutions on library and learning resources (Gibbs, 2015) although it has the advantage over other universities of choosing to receive free copies of all published works along with Cambridge and Dublin under copyright laws. The Oxford courses also have less summative assessment than other courses, in the ratio of 1:10. Finals are preceded by a long period of revision in the order of 2–3 months so the students have time to 'get it altogether' rather than a few weeks for cramming and question spotting.

In other universities, the contact time can be 12 hours per week and generate very little out-of-class study time although students are expected to spend up to 15 hours in further study. Science, professional and performance courses generate much more contact time and in addition laboratory, internship and workshop time. The problem is that many of the students are not equipped to use their free study time in useful ways and others have very little to spend. Many also have to juggle part- or even full-time work to pay for their course.

A brief analysis of what is involved in the Oxbridge tutorial system can help in thinking about these strategies. A programme of lectures is available to the student but there is no obligation to attend, the sciences include extensive laboratory work and all the studies are backed by extensive library and other first-class resources. The tutors are experts in the subject fields and the tutorial system, often having been through it themselves. An essay topic is set and the student goes off to prepare and write the essay. This involves reading round the subject, maybe whole works or a selection of research papers and critiques have to be studied. Notes are made, key issues highlighted, points of interest noted, lines of argument developed and a first draft is produced. After the tutorials, it soon becomes clear that several drafts are needed before the essay is fit to be read and shared with the tutor. During the tutorial, arguments and evidence are considered and critiqued and act as a running commentary of formative and diagnostic feedback and feed forward, at the end there might be a summative grade. This grade is shared along with the criteria that show what standard the essay has reached with feed forward that indicates how improved grades might be obtained and other works that might have been read or ideas considered.

It is not therefore surprising that the Oxbridge student spends at least 10 times the amount of time on independent study as in face-to-face contact and the retention rates are high. Compared with the lecture-seminar model in which a student may or may not read the study papers and can easily be a passenger in the group of 12–16, the tutorial system by comparison is very effective in training students to write literate reports, pass essay examinations and communicate effectively in vivas or later in job interviews.

Mass education and funding limits have come to HE and the systems and techniques have not always been adapted to these changes although the Open University (OU) found its way through.

2. The Open University 'correspondence' course

The OU courses are essentially Distance Learning programmes with high quality and extensive resources on easy access. There is little class contact time and none at all now in some programmes. In addition, there is a highly systematic and structured assessment system with a work force trained to administer it. Each tutor may not have high qualifications but is trained to assess and support the work of a personal tutor group of about 30 students. This relationship is maintained over a specific course and so the tutor can get to know them and be known.

The initial few tasks the students are set are graded and increased in difficulty, and although feedback is given on them, there is no summative grade. The purpose of this is to give the students who may never have engaged in advanced study the confidence to continue and get to know the ropes, improving their confidence and self-efficacy. The feedback is thus formative and feeds forward. The amount of written feedback the students get is 10 times the amount that other students get on conventional courses.

Assessment generates student work and time on task. The assessments are phased so that they occur at regular intervals across the course rather than appear as one large summative assignment at the end. Mixed methods are used so that there may be multiple choice assessments as well as essays and projects. There are however more techniques than this that may be used in assignments to generate student time on task.

As can be seen both the Oxbridge tutorial and the OU systems emphasise resource-based and assessment-driven programmes to generate student time on task and are acknowledged to produce higher learning gain. The next example shows what can be done with limited funding and a bit of creativity.

3. A 'Walking the talk' experiment in a polytechnic

Radical staffing cuts were being made in the teachers' colleges and Faculties of Education in 1987/9 to meet the CATE (1983) criteria and prepare students in Initial Teacher Training for the new National Curriculum (NCC, 1991). It was clear that only a few Education (Philosophy, Sociology and Psychology) staff would be left by the end of 1988. In this particular organisation, the prospect to be faced was 70 or so students returning as fourth-year BEd students who would have only one tutor to teach them instead of at least three. This was thought to be a magnificent efficiency by the polytechnic, now university directorate who believed that it was only necessary to lecture in the 4 hours per week assigned in the 108-hour course as was the habit in many of their other subject programmes.

Innovations are known to seldom take place in a period of stability. In times of perturbation, major changes in programmes can take place and pass under the radar, as everyone else is absorbed with their own problems, especially the leaders in the hierarchy. This was how the experiment began in the last year of life of a Year-4 BEd Learning Difficulties (Special Needs) programme.

The rationale was derived from the student feedback in formal and informal sessions. They said they enjoyed the programme and found it useful in practice. It was strongly academic and more difficult to understand than their main teaching subjects such as history or science. But they often wondered why our teaching methods were not those that we preached such as problem-based approaches and practical activities. They said that their secondary education had set them to follow the old transmission model tradition with lecture and seminar which was also that used by their main subject tutors. This made it hard for them to move to our problem-based type of learning and teaching, or make it inclusive for all pupils, which they could see was needed.

The course was set, a totally new form of programme had to be invented that met the students' needs but with just one tutor available. The outline plan was drawn up as follows:

1 A 1-hour lecture giving a Cook's tour of the area under study
2 A 1.5-hour follow-up in semi- or independent practical workshops with a problem base
3 A 1.5-hour seminar starting with feedback from the workshop, followed by a critical analysis of a relevant research paper

The lecture was necessary because it had been found in earlier years that when tutors did not provide this students became distressed and confused and begged to go into classes where there was some knowledge given out. The workshops would be set up in advance with the help of a part-time technician.

The seminars would take place with groups of 12 students. This would mean one seminar per student group every 6 weeks. A little problem to present to the management! The result was that this part of the plan caused such a fright that payment for two part-time tutors was made available for the afternoon seminars so that all the students could have a seminar on alternate weeks. The tutors recruited were teachers who had already followed the in-service BEd programme. They were interested enough to attend the lecture and programme for the whole day and regarded it as their personal CPD.

Over the length of the programme, the final phases would be developed so that student specialist groups took over 1-day's planning and tuition. The subjects agreed upon were Reading and reading difficulties, Maths and mathematical difficulties and Co-ordination difficulties and remedial PE. One or two local special needs and disability experts were also invited to give a lecture during the course.

During the previous summer holiday, seminar papers for each topic were identified and copyright clearance was obtained by library services. Special shelving was set aside in the library for the handbooks already developed in the LDRP (Learning Difficulties Research Project) since 1981 as study guides. Copies were also put on sale to students for £1.00, and there were multiple copies of them and key research articles that every student was required to read in the library.

In order to motivate them to read the articles, there was a set format for the seminars as follows. No student was identified in advance to 'give the paper'. Instead, in the seminar two students were randomly identified to tell the rest what it was about and the main ideas but without consulting their notes. All could then chip in and fill out further details and ask questions. Then all would consult their notes and the tutor would help the group go over the main ideas and findings, and apply them to practice. Anyone who had not read the paper was asked to leave and do so at the outset of the session. Nearly full attendance was secured each week, no passengers.

Early in the programme one particular day proved especially effective. The day began with a 1-hour lecture on 'What makes a good test?', for example, for reading or IQ, etc. The workshop room was set out with a range of educational tests and students were asked to look at the tests laid out, select one and individually or in groups of two and three decide if the test chosen was a good one. They should write a one-page summary giving reasons for their decision and hand it in at the end of the 1.5 hours. The session was not supervised and about half the students left and went to the refectory after half an hour, all finished within an hour.

The lecturer marked the papers over the lunch period. All but one paper were given grades of D+ to C–. D+ was the failure grade. All the students had been given a 12-point criterion referenced assessment scale for marking education essays at the beginning of the course. The papers were handed back in the afternoon debriefing and seminar session. On receipt, there was uproar and anger. The grades were 'the lowest they had ever received' so the tutors must be blamed for this, 'the task was not defined properly', etc. It was explained that the lecture had contained all they needed to do the task, for example, standardisation facts, the meaning and need for high correlational values and types of validity and reliability. They had listened and taken notes. The students insisted they must all be allowed to do the workshop again the following week and we agreed. The next week's seminar paper was set and consisted of a simple flow chart for them to complete based on a research article by Leach (1983) on 'Early Screening Techniques'.

Of course in the second workshop, they understood exactly what to do to get the higher B+/A–, etc. grades and did so. Honour was satisfied. But this was not all a wave of new interest had swept over them. The next week the tutor arrived at the lecture hall and instead of students waiting around and some coming in a bit late, every single one was already in the hall, pen poised, in utter silence

5 minutes before the lecture was due to begin. This continued for the rest of the series. The feedback was that they did not know what the tutor might get up to next and so were ready, alert and waiting just in case.

The flow-chart exercise went well too! None of them could identify the main point (validity) and some groups said they had spent 5 hours or more going over it and yet it was all too obvious once they had been led towards it and then the three subordinate points became crystal clear. All the students had managed to identify the final point. Once again they had not used the lecture to lead them to the main idea, they had sat passively taking notes and not reflecting during or afterwards. They had not actioned or applied their new knowledge to a different situation. But they began to catch on and so new strategies needed to be developed to 'keep them on their intellectual toes'. By the end of the programme, the groups took over the teaching for a day on their other subject specialisms. They gave the lectures, designed and organised the workshops, found the study papers and led the seminars. Teaching is 90% effective for learning (Race, 1992) with assessment (95%) even better and they did that too when they marked a good Education essay and a poor one using the course criteria. One was an A– and the other was D+ standard. The students had copies of the essays and were individually required to give a summative assessment of the standard using the 12-point course assessment criteria but then were required to write teacherly comments at the end of each essay explaining how the student could improve the standard next time, formative feed forward. Feedback was then given on the feedback explaining how the comments should and could have been constructive and couched in positive rather than negative ways. The criteria included the following:

An A score essay. Valid theoretical framework outlined and discussed, concepts in topic examined and defined and good critique of relevant research. Practical and professional implications discussed and evaluated. Makes lucid argument and uses good referencing techniques.

D+ Borderline fail. Lacks coherent structure, is mainly anecdotal and lacks sufficient relevance to topic. Much undigested, regurgitated material, possible indications of plagiarism and poor or absent referencing.

In another session on more able pupil's needs students were asked to assess the levels of the school curriculum learning materials using Bloom's (1956) taxonomy. They then assessed the levels in their Learning Difficulties programme and main subject studies.

Later in the programme, another profound effect was created by some experiential or simulation-based educative experiences. There were lectures and seminars on Physical and Sensory difficulties and impairments, and the issues for schools and a guest speaker from RADAR gave a personal perspective. The workshop involved something that can be controversial. Students were invited to choose to wear earmuffs, or blindfold goggles, and two wheel chairs were made available in case someone chose to simulate physical disability. Others were able to choose silence – simulating an inability to speak!

Examples of all the disabilities were represented among the group, and their partners and peers were asked to look after them for the rest of the workshop and through the lunch hour. All were to meet in the afternoon symposium for the debriefing. In this session, they shared their experiences and insights, and some very telling issues and experiences emerged about disabilities and other people's responses. They also found that 'Access' to rooms and services for all of them was a key issue and became sensitised to it for their schools. The problem was posed that if given a budget of only £500 what could they possibly do to improve access in a particular school, what should such a small sum of money be spent on. What else could be done?

The controversial aspect of this simulation was also discussed. It is not always approved of among those with disabilities and those caring for them. This was because that at the end of the simulation, the participant can always remove the 'disability' whereas the person with the disability has to live it. It is not a real or valid experience to them. The students however were moved to a greater understanding of the needs of children with SEND (Special Educational Needs and Disabilities) and some had become upset for them and how they were treated. They said they could not forget it. The issue of access was very clearly demonstrated to them in real terms and the one known as 'Does he take sugar?' The debriefing after experiential learning is essential in both emotional and cognitive terms, and this was evident in the plenary.

In the final term, students took over some of the teaching and leadership of the programme, the planning, workshop design and provision of research papers for the seminars. This course was adopted because as the Learning Difficulties programme progressed the students had begun to find papers the staff had not read and were citing these as better or more recent and so on. They also contributed to lecture points in the seminars and so it seemed time to give them their heads. Teaching something to someone else is a very strong way of learning the material and it had proved highly successful with GCSE students in schools volunteering to teach for 5–10 minutes on biology topics in their final year.

At the end of the programme, the students took a 3-hour examination paper and came out smiling. Many said that it was the first time they had ever really enjoyed an exam. The results showed that instead of the usual 1–2% gaining a mark in the first-class category, there were 23.61%, many more 2.1s than 2.2s and no 3rds. There was then a difficulty in explaining to the Examination Board that the students had not been told the questions in advance. It was just the result of changing the teaching and learning methods. The external examiners were able to question the students and did confirm the grades.

The increase in grades reflected the higher learning gain that had been achieved by changing the teaching-learning methods. They had increased the students' independent learning time on task, helped in team-building skills, increased opportunities for student communication of ideas and knowledge and increased the amount of formative feedback and feed forward that they received.

The course was closed in July 1989 so that subject led specialisms based on Foundation subjects in the school curriculum could expand to fill the time. The other applied course in Reading was also closed!

Some HE teaching developments

1. PGCTLHE

Some things have changed in the UK for university and college staff. Programmes leading to awards of a Post-Graduate Certificate for Teaching and Learning in Higher Education were developed in the 1990s and new lecturers are obliged to follow them in some UK universities. Prior to this, a researcher or subject specialist could obtain a lecturing post with no prior experience or training in teaching or lecturing to students. They might read their lecture notes badly or well to a class of students and depart appearing to have no responsibility for the students' learning outcomes. This may still be observed in its more modern form at national and international conferences when the 'speaker' reads the Power Points to the audience often in a monotone.

2. IT-based learning

A leading proponent of the information technology (IT) solution was Sir Douglas Hague, who warned of the demise of universities if they failed to embrace the new ITs and engage in IT-based learning.

> It is because I am keen that the universities should survive both as competitors and complements of the knowledge industries that in the paper I try to identify for universities the challenges which they will meet in the coming decades. I do so not in the hope that they may fail in meeting them, but that they may succeed. (Hague, 1991, 9)

Technology has changed approaches in most courses and institutions since then as Open learning. Power Points have replaced acetate slides and the whiteboard the chalkboard. Students can remotely access lectures, power points and videos of the lectures online and join webinars. *The Psychologist Guide to University Life* (Rhodes, 2017) stated that the lecture has changed and we no longer see the 'sage on the stage'. Instead, there are attempts to engage the learners and in doing this students may vote on their mobiles to check their understanding, use clickers and use live Twitter feeds to ask questions. Chat rooms and webinars are also common phenomena.

A group of Slovakian students (Bratislava, 2016) developed an Application that EU conference attendees could contact by their mobiles and as the lecture(s) proceeded they could ask questions. These questions were shown in rank order on a screen in the lecture room and could be dealt with by the speaker as and when convenient. In addition, the lecture could be accessed in individual rooms around the campus and beyond. Thus, ideas and questions were also be added by other delegates and students from these remote locations. In addition to these developments illustrating Blended learning, some Colleges have invested in Virtual Learning Environments (VLE). Instead of setting up a branch of their university in another country or district, they establish themselves in the virtual environment.

3. Resource-based learning

The leading proponents of 'resource-based learning' were at the Oxford Centre for Staff Development led by Graham Gibbs where they argued the case primarily in terms of 'teaching more with less', that is, a declining unit of teaching resource. The OU system and the Walking the talk experiment above are also both examples of resource-based learning.

4. Action learning

Revans (1976) was an early advocate of Action learning based on his initial work with coal miners in 1945 and he regularly promoted the concept at British Association of Commercial and Industrial Education (BACIE) conferences at Cullum laboratories. It was also part of developmental work in Further Education by Gibbs (1988) and by Zuber-Skerrett (1992) in HE. Since then, a number of universities such as Salford, Brighton and City have adopted it particularly with post-graduate, Masters level students and part-time researchers to support self-managed learning.

Action learning sets are independent student working groups and they plan and question each other about a project in hand and have been used to support the learning from project work at different levels. It has been used on modular courses to help students integrate the learning at each level by, for example, producing a report showing how the modules taken so far relate to each other and to the student's learning needs and career aspirations. A similar strategy is used in Work-based learning programme portfolios. Groups of five or six students can contribute ideas from different mindsets and question each other about the topic and reflect together on the process and products.

It can be used as a means of supervising students on sandwich placements to help them to get more learning from the experience and used with final-year students to develop a learning contract containing a plan for their continuing professional development and lifelong learning.

Action learning sets have also been used to enable students to get more learning from the experience of preparing portfolios of evidence for the accreditation of prior learning (APL). The independent workshops in the BEd programme above could also be regarded as examples of Action learning sets.

5. Prior knowledge effects – priming – flipped learning

Despite technological innovations described above, they do not amount to more than attempts to gain and maintain attention and interest in lectures and perhaps they create a feeling of personal involvement and engagement. In *The Psychologist* guide, we are given an example of 'flipped learning' a new term for an old technique. Instead of the lecture being the first introduction to the topic, the students are given tasks to complete and then the lecturer reflects on these in the talk and presents further issues.

If the students do the tasks then this will increase their readiness and ability to incorporate the new information into their existing schemas and exemplifies the High Prior Knowledge (HPK) condition that Kalyuga et al. (2003) found was more effective than Low PK. The lecture first condition would be the Low Prior Knowledge (LPK) condition. They found that students with LPK were better at learning from examples than solving them and those with HPK were the reverse, they were better at solving problems.

Even if learning does takes place, the learner does not return to the same point as in the Kolb cycle each time but at each turn progresses further. It changes the processes and the understanding in an additive way. This learning process can best be described as a Cognitive Process Learning Spiral or an Action learning cycle (Kemmis et al., 1983).

Flipped learning. This is akin to priming experiments in perception when showing or hearing a key word or seeing a picture can enable the listener or observer to hear or read the correct 'message' in a garbled stimulus. The HPK strategy ensures there is some prior knowledge in all the students that can link to and enhance the reception of the new information. It is a more sustained and active form of using advance organisers or lecture objectives.

As with all things, there can be disadvantages. If every topic begins in the same way with a task to investigate prior to the lecture, the novelty may soon wear off, curiosity and motivation may not be sustained and the task is not completed. Flipped learning is a racy title to catch the interest of students and staff alike but is usually known by the more mundane title as 'front-loaded' and 'prior knowledge' learning. It is based on the psychological principle of 'priming' to improve readiness and increase learning.

Before a new topic is introduced, teachers in some schools working with more able pupils in the UK (NACE, 2019) give out resources and readings ahead of lessons so knowledge can be applied, analysed and evaluated during the lesson. These readings and tasks for independent study prepare the students' minds for the teaching session that is to follow. The students are in the gifted and talented 'challenge programmes' and this has been found to enhance their learning outcomes in later examinations. The independent aspects of this work begin to prepare them for university. As these students are likely to be highly motivated, they are likely to do this preparatory work, whereas disadvantaged learners may not know where to begin or will not have the motivation to bother to do what they would see as extra work. They may also regard it as the teacher's job to 'tell them' the knowledge. Other strategies will need to be found for them when they bring these attitudes into HE.

Flipped classrooms. This technique involves the teacher or lecturer giving a lecture online. The students can view this at home and can replay it as necessary. At school or college, the teacher uses the class time to engage with the students in more activities and give individual support 'the flip'. Although this technique has become popular in the US, its benefits appear to be short term. It is possible that the novelty effect soon wears off. It is likely that many students do not watch the whole lecture or attention falls off and cannot be re-awakened because there is no teacher to notice this and draw them back in. Given other competing interests and more exciting videos, students may only watch half the lecture and when they feel they have the gist, turn to something else. Even watching the lecture twice, as is possible to try to understand difficult content does not result in learning gain even in university students.

Elizabeth Setren (2019) randomly assigned more than 1,300 West Point Academy students to one of two different conditions in their introductory maths and economics courses. In the flipped learning condition, the students were assigned a video lecture before each class and engaged in interactive problem solving during the class. In the traditional version, the teachers gave a standardised lecture covering the same material and assigned as homework the problems that the other group had worked on during class. The classes were small, on average 16–18 cadets all highly motivated to do their course work.

No differences were found in the economics classes but the maths 'flipped' classes showed one third of a standard deviation better results in the flipped classes. But by the end of the course both groups performed equally well. Setren concluded that the differences observed were perhaps due to the greater enthusiasm of the maths staff about the flipped learning and their greater engagement with practical activities than the economics staff. She also found that the cadets in the 'flipped' classes on average only watched about half the video contents and spent no more time on preparing for classes than the other students did.

The short-term maths improvements also appeared to be driven by white male students who had entered with scores in the top quartile on tests before entering the Academy. Women and Black Asian and Minority Ethnic (BAME) students as well as cadets who had performed in the bottom quartile for maths on entry gained no benefits from the 'flipped' learning and the achievement gaps tended to widen and remained throughout the course.

Although she still supported the model, Setren suggested that more attention should be paid to equalising the support given to individuals in class and especially to those who did not like to 'bother' the tutor. This help-seeking behaviour tended to be more reserved in 'working class' students and such behaviour can reduce learning gain as they obtain less information appropriate to their needs. This is typical of disadvantaged students who are in the excellence gap.

A similar phenomenon has been noticeable in distance learning courses in which particular students spend large amounts of time in Chat rooms, on the telephone to the administrators and in E-mailing questions and needs about support and further information. Even when all the details are set out clearly, they seem to need to be talked through it. This is an aspect of learned helplessness that is not uncommon and needs to be overcome early in a course.

Another problem arises from the students who have sailed through the school years and gained the highest grades without much effort. They often have very good memories and have never really been challenged or failed in anything. They may have developed a 'perfectionist' attitude as in the BEd Learning Difficulties course example above. When they meet challenge and failure in HE, it can be for the first time and they can quickly succumb as they have few coping strategies. Some can become overanxious and depressed and drop out of the course. They need support and resilience building especially at the beginning of programmes to increase their self-efficacy as in the OU example.

6. Simulation-based education

Simulation-Based Education (SBE) has appeared in many different forms in the history of disciplines. In law, the practice was to hold Moots. In Business Studies, problem-based group work was engaged in using case studies of real and simulated organisations. History students work on facsimile documentation and teacher undergraduates may engage in micro-teaching and small group teaching.

Other approaches have been immersion experiences in Modern Foreign Language programmes and social anthropology where the student goes to live and work in another country for a year. Geographers and biologists go on field courses and intending archaeologists work on digs. Technology students and engineering students design and make things and scientists work on laboratory experiments. Medical students practice on models, cadavers and pigs. Despite these experiences back in the university lecture rooms, there may have been little change to the transmission model.

7. The learning cycle approach

The learning cycle is the process whereby knowledge is created through the transformation of experience (Kolb, 1984). Students relate these new ideas to their experience and place them into a framework for understanding (Bransford et al., 2001) and thus it is argued that the learning cycle is a critical learning process in improving students' self-regulation. It shows better retention of concepts, improved reasoning ability and superior processing skills than would be the case with traditional instructional approaches (Beeth et al., 1999).

Gerber et al. (2001) found that students taught via the learning cycle scored higher on a test than students taught with the traditional style. Learning cycles have varied over time containing from three to five elements. In more recent research, Zanaty and Kitama (2015) described their Form-Inform and Reform (FIR)-6E cycle in Education for Sustainable Development. This stands for three core phases FIR and 6E conceptual learning elements – experimentation, exploration, explication, elaboration, evaluation and extension. The links between FIR and 6E run as follows:

(1) Forming – the self-experimentation and self-reflection, (2) Informing – self-achievement in a longitudinal learning environment and (3) Reforming – the dissemination of students' information to the community in sustainable local and international environments.

The students were creating digital learning materials with the support of teacher facilitation. The FIR phases were supported by qualitative and quantitative assessments of self-achievement. There was informal evaluation after each phase in the students' learning (a) performance card, (b) a self-achievement step-by-step card, (c) teachers' questionnaire and (d) interviews.

Zanaty et al. (2015) concluded that the experimental group who will be exposed to the FIR-6E could develop their self-regulation skills, such as problem-solving, goal-based scenario, higher-order critical thinking and active peer-educator approaches through the dissemination of their information to the community.

8. Learning styles

One of the most popular models widely applied in management training courses was based upon the work of Honey and Mumford (1986). They claimed to have identified four 'Learning Styles' corresponding roughly to four stages in the experiential learning process defined by Kolb (1984). The cycle can be entered at any point but must be followed in sequence. Kolb recognised that not all individuals are equally well equipped to handle each stage of the cycle. He argued that learning occurred not in the doing but in the reflection and conceptualisation that takes place during and after the event.

Honey and Mumford (1986) developed their Learning Styles Questionnaire (LSQ) to access four learning styles equating with the four stages in the cycle:

a   Activists involve themselves fully and without bias in new experiences. Concrete experience.
b   Reflectors like to stand back and ponder experiences and observe them from many different perspectives. Reflective Observation.
c   Theorists adapt and integrate observations into complex but logically sound theories. Abstract Conceptualisation.
d   Pragmatists are keen on trying out ideas, theories and techniques to see if they work in practice. Active Experimentation.

The management 'coach' does not have to be highly knowledgeable or skilled to help a learner adopt a more balanced style. It is done by helping the learner review, explore the 'models', create an action plan and implement it.

There is however a lack of evidence to support such styles perhaps because the questionnaires do not appear to be sufficiently sensitive. A review of recent research showed it was still a persistent misconception to believe that learning styles existed and matching any task to them would improve learning (Coffield et al., 2003; Rayner, 2007; Martin, 2017). Unfortunately, adopting learning styles approaches has led to a serious restriction to learning experiences in schools when learners were labelled as, for example, kinetic, visual or auditory learners and input restricted to the one modality.

In a meta-analysis of research on Cognitive and Learning styles, Riding and Rayner (1998) found that we do not really have multiple cognitive styles but a preference for or bias towards the ways in which we deal with situations. These apparently all boil down to this orthogonal model as shown in Figure 1.1.

The renewal of interest in learning styles was encouraged by studies of right and left hemisphere processes. The left hemisphere in 95% of the population is dominant for language and processes information sequentially. The right hemisphere processes information simultaneously or in an 'all at once fashion'. It tends therefore to be more involved in creative and perceptual activities such as facial recognition, music and drawing and painting. In fully functioning brains, both hemispheres are operating in unison and cooperatively sharing and analysing information. Although we may have learning style preferences, we need to be able to use either or both strategies effectively and in its appropriate setting.

Most of us adapt our styles to the situation but have a preference for using an analytic or holistic approach to, for example, problem solving and some like to tackle problems in an ordered analytical and sequential manner following instructions, rules and protocols. Others like to take a more holistic approach, for example, shake the pieces out of the box, look at the picture and start the construction and only read the instructions when their strategy runs into difficulties.

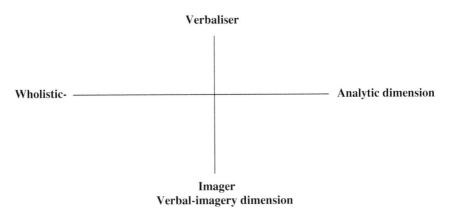

Figure 1.1 Orthogonal model of cognitive style.

Source: Riding and Rayner (1998).

Similarly, we have preferences for verbal versus pictorial material and methods. As can be imagined those who have difficulties with reading and writing such as dyslexics are going to be obliged to practice holistic and imager (iconic) styles and show a preference for them.

Learning style is held to be the composite of:

- Cognition – people perceive and gain knowledge differently
- Conceptualisation – people think and form ideas differently
- Affect – people feel and form values differently
- Behaviour – people act differently

Styles are said to serve as relatively stable indicators of how a learner perceives, interacts with and responds to the learning environment.

It is necessary to use the abilities associated with each of the four learning styles in turn if students **are** to learn effectively. It **is** important to be adaptable and operate in the style appropriate to the stage of experiential learning in a learning task. Even if the students **have** style preferences, it **is** helpful to arrange mixed style groups.

9. Management initiatives

A number of other initiatives that have influenced the methods of teaching and learning in HE have been operating since 1996. Teaching Quality Assessment (TQA) visits have been carried out by the Quality Assurance Agency (QAA) and Total Quality Management (TQM) and Quality Assurance Boards set up with universities to develop and manage change. There have also been programmes aimed at encouraging changes in teaching and learning methods such as Computers in Teaching Initiative (CTI), the Teaching and Learning Technology Programme (TLTP), the Fund for the Development of Teaching and Learning (FDTL), the National Teaching Fellowship Scheme (NTFS) and the Learning and Teaching Support Network (LTSN) and staff appraisal. This latter has had a chequered career not least because of the complexity of the roles that university staff undertake.

Conclusion

The three main programmes discussed have features associated with higher learning gain that increased the amount of student time on task and predicted the higher learning outcomes. The Oxbridge model with one-to-one tuition giving immediate feedback and feed forward caused extensive student time on task. The resources are extensive.

The OU distance system keeps one trained tutor with a group of no more than 30 students over the period of the module. The feedback and feed forward is prompt and regular. Initially, it is designed to build self-efficacy. The resources are extensive, excellent and easily available.

The BEd fourth-year course was structured to use problem-based tasks to induce motivation to want to learn and encouraged collaborative working in small student groups. The resources were good and readily available. The seminars once a fortnight gave students time in the other seminar slot to access the resources and engage in independent study. There was little opportunity for this in the rest of their high contact time course. Feedback and feed forward was regular and structured. The students reported spending many hours outside the programme working on the tasks individually and in their groups.

Not surprisingly, higher learning gains have also been shown when HE staff are actually trained to do their job. In addition, lecturing staff have been creative in designing new techniques or remodelling old ones such as in using Kolb's experiential learning cycle and using priming to promote interest and attention as well as learning gain and more examples in subject areas can be found in the *Handbook for Teaching and Learning in HE* by Fry et al. (2015).

An overview of the area suggests two major issues for future concern and development, these are the following: (1) that there needs to be shared cross-curricular theory for teaching and effective learning across HE and there are some references to critical theory, meta-cognition and active participation of learners and (2) many learners arrive at university lacking self-efficacy and self-regulation and therefore systematic strategies need to be in place to deal with this as students can quickly become demotivated or distracted. Students from disadvantaged areas can become doubly disadvantaged when support for learning to learn independently is not in place. These topics will be the subject of analysis in subsequent chapters.

Chapter 2

A theory and practice of teaching and learning in higher education

Introduction

Since the 1990s, higher education in the UK has been expanded from a service to about 7% of the student population to 47%. Charging students fees has become part of this development in England and Wales. At the same time, government funding has been reduced and so have staffing levels in ratios of staff to students in many institutions. It is thus that wide-ranging levels of student abilities, needs and experiences in HE come into sharper focus and the methods needed to support them have to be constantly under review.

Originally, students went to university to 'read for their degrees' and it was assumed that they had the necessary independent learning skills to do this. Over time and change in the student population, it is apparent that many, even those with the highest ability and school achievement, are not self-regulated learners. Tuition and more support for learners at all levels is needed but especially for those from disadvantaging environments and poor-quality schools if they are to achieve what they are capable of and what society now needs. Training in self-regulated learning (SRL) is seen as one way to achieve this and both schools and universities need and want to play a part.

Government and employers' needs of this new millennium to compete in world markets were identified by the Department for Employment (2001) in consultation with employers as follows:

- Good communication skills
- Problem-solving skills
- Creative-thinking abilities
- Flexibility
- Good listening skills
- Ability to learn from experience
- Ability to learn from others
- Cooperative abilities

Although these skills and abilities might be implicit in some teaching programmes, it was thought that there must be more deliberate teaching of the skills if widespread competence was to be achieved. None of them were being explicitly taught in most schools or university programmes except perhaps in Business Education. The list of millennium skills appears to be intimately related to lifelong learning and SRL and also indicates that methods of effective training in SRL need to be reconsidered. It was evident that the traditional model of the lecturer transmitting knowledge to passive rows of student listeners taking notes was far from any model of effective teaching or millennium objectives. Learning was not such a simple acquisition process. Lecturing or telling was not teaching and only about 5% of the knowledge being told was actually acquired (Race, 1992). Thus lecturers in HE began to think about the theory and practice of what they were doing. This process was also underway at the same time in the US where HE was privatised (Kennedy, 1987; Resnick, 1989; Paul, 1990).

In the UK, Stones (1983, 68) discussed 'the dominant place of expository verbal teaching in most teaching institutions' and argued that it was

Deleterious to student learning.

He proposed that greater attention to pedagogy was essential to break out of transmission modes of teaching. In particular, it was crucial to develop teaching for conceptual learning and for problem solving, and he suggested that there was information from learning psychology that could be fruitfully related to practical teaching to achieve these developments. He suggested that teachers should not merely apply learning theory but that they needed to explore its relevance and mode of application to real teaching situations. In teacher education, he found a serious problem of a lack of pedagogical understanding in supervisory staff of student teachers. This was a vital deficiency that would need to be repaired before advances in teacher preparation could be realistically expected.

Despite Stone's recommendations, the transmission model of 'effective' pedagogy appealed to policymakers in England because of the way in which it could be translated into lists of competencies to help develop a 'technology of teaching'. The English Teacher Education Agency appears still to be rooted in this 'technical rationalist' view because it can be defined, identified and reduced to a set of descriptors and prescriptive recommendations. Ofsted (the Office for Standards in Education) then uses these as criteria for school inspections thus ensuring the cycle is complete and that directive teaching is maintained. At no point when the system was introduced from management education was this methodology investigated to test its evidence base in creating effective learning especially in the complex interactive processes involved in teaching at any level. Thus for the last 35 years, UK teachers have been trained to teach in a didactic transmission mode that is inimitable to SRL and that Weikart (1967, 1998) had already found was the least effective as a method of promoting learning in his longitudinal Perry Pre-school (Headstart) programme.

Models of teaching and learning

Paul (1990) identified two pathways in teaching and learning – the didactic and traditional route involving direct transmission of knowledge to the learner and the critical theory route. This latter involved critical questioning of what was to be learnt. Paul summarised these as learning *what* to think (didactics) as opposed to learning *how* to think (critical theory). The following outline of Paul's work shows summaries of 3 categories of 17 that he discussed in Table 2.1 below.

According to Paul, most education worldwide was still geared to inducing monological thinking that is single track and context defined because of the overuse of didactic methods whereas critical thinking is what was needed. Critical thinking is:

- The art of identifying and reversing bias, prejudice and one-sidedness of thought.
- The art of self-directed, in-depth, rational thinking.
- Thinking that rationally certifies what we know and makes clear where we are ignorant (Paul, 1990, 32).

Table 2.1 Contrasting pathways in teaching and learning suggested by Paul

Didactic theory	Critical theory
The fundamental needs of students	
To be taught more or less WHAT to think not how to think; are given details, definitions, explanations, rules, guidelines and reasons to learn.	To be taught HOW not what to think, that it is important to focus on significant content but accompanied by live issues that stimulate students to gather, analyse and assess content.
The nature of knowledge	
Knowledge is independent of thinking that generates, organises and applies it. Students are said to know when they can repeat what has been covered. Students are given the finished products of someone else's thought.	All knowledge of content is generated, organised, applied and analysed, synthesised and assessed by thinking; that gaining knowledge is unintelligible without such thought. Students are given opportunities to puzzle their way through to knowledge and explore its justification as part of the process of learning.
Model of the educated person	
Educated, literate people are fundamentally repositories of content analogous to an encyclopaedia or a data bank, directly comparing situations in the world with facts in storage. This is a true believer. Texts, assessments, lectures, discussions are content dense and detail-orientated.	An educated literate person is fundamentally a repository of strategies, principles, concepts and insights embedded in processes of thought. Much of what is known is constructed as needed, not pre-fabricated. This is a seeker and a questioner rather than a true believer. Teachers model insightful consideration of questions and problems, and facilitate fruitful enquiry.

It is this critical thinking approach that was widely disseminated and found its way into HE especially in the performance arts and the humanities, and emerged at the same time in several different theatres of education and research. For example, it was developed and promoted in the UK among others by Graham Gibbs (1988, 1990) at the Oxford Brookes Polytechnic Centre for Staff Development, by Alex Fisher (1988, 1991) at UEA and John Biggs (1991) and Paul Ramsden (1991) in Hong Kong and Australia. It meant that their work had begun at least a decade earlier before their key publications began to emerge.

Didactics

The situation according to Skilbeck (1989), Rogers and Span (1993) and Wallace and Eriksson (2006) more recently was that education worldwide was still stuck in fact transmission mode. They all found that 90% of education worldwide was didactic. In other words, most teachers and lecturers engaged in a lecture style, teacher-led mode, impolitely termed 'content ramming'.

Wallace and Eriksson (2006, 361) summarised the main points in their book from a galaxy of contributors worldwide concluding that although educationalists were full of hope and optimism there was:

- A universal stubborn adherence to a content curriculum
- A dominant culture that sought to preserve itself
- Bureaucracies resistant to change
- 19th-century education systems based upon authority, didactics and authoritarianism (p. 361)

High-stakes assessment-driven systems researched by Gregory and Clarke (2003) in England and East Asian schools were shown to generate an elite of winners and an underclass of losers. Singapore, one of the top countries in the academic stakes, was found to produce teenagers who:

> exhibit a narrow mindedness, tend to be smug and egocentric, and see the paper chase as the means to a good life' – 'they make good employees, but few can think out of the box, much less lead.
>
> (Cited in Heng and Tam, 2006, 172)

While politicians hold these systems up as models to be followed, these societies are becoming aware of the problems created and are trying to move to a more learner-centred approach both in the schools and universities but progress has been slow. Even those who seek to improve the self-regulation skills of students tend to do so in a highly structured didactic format that demotivates the disadvantaged learners (Fischer, 2014).

Reception learning. This is a traditional didactic format defined by Ausubel (1968) in his explanation of effective learning. He believed that learners learnt more effectively by 'reception'. The term 'advance organisers' was coined by him to describe the short outline of the whole material introduced before the lesson or lecture begins, now called 'objectives' or targets. In this method, the teacher or lecturer presents the whole content of what has to be learned in its final form. It places a great emphasis on the presenter's skill in structuring the content to be learned. The learning is considered meaningful if it allows reproduction with understanding at a future date.

Such analyses are common in that the investigator observes and defines the best and most-effective practice that is in operation at the time and describes it. However, what is going on is not necessarily what should be going on even though it is effective in achieving defined learning outcomes. This is especially so in education when the intended learning outcomes may be narrowly defined in terms of subject content rather than the wider realms of intellectual, personal and cultural development.

Reception learning does not meet the effective learning criteria established by De Corte (1995, 2013) below. Instead, it is a highly structured form of didactics and the methods are likely to lead to superficial or 'surface learning' and memorising. This means that the material needs frequent revision to make it available for use. It is also likely to have a low degree of transfer to new and different situations and remains relatively inert. The question it raises is that if we have to keep revising knowledge can it have been effectively taught and learned in the first place? It reflects Blagg et al.'s (1993) 'Bo Peep theory' of transfer (leave them alone and they'll come home by themselves). In this model despite the millennium needs, the skills and knowledge will be unlikely to be transferred from reception learning lecture rooms to the workplace.

Effective learning

Extensive research in instructional psychology by De Corte (1995, 2013) has shown that in order to be effective, learning experiences needed to be:

- **Constructive.** Obey the constructivist principles that learners must be given opportunities to construct their own learning. Students are not passive recipients of information, in order to learn they have to participate in making meaning and constructing their own knowledge and skills.
- **Situated.** Be connected in time and place and have relevance to other meaningful learning events. It means that learning essentially takes place in interaction with the social and cultural environment not the confines of regular classrooms.
- **Cumulative.** It is on the basis of what they already know that people construct new knowledge and derive new meanings and skills.
- **Self-organised.** Learning is best when self-organised. This is related to the metacognitive nature of effective learning especially the managing and monitoring of learning activities – self-regulation.

- **Goal-oriented.** Learning is generally goal-orientated, although a small amount of learning is incidental. An explicit awareness of and orientation towards a goal facilitates effective and meaningful learning especially when the learners can choose the goal and define their own objectives.
- **Individual.** Finally, learning is individually different. Individual differences in ability, skills, needs, interests, learning style, etc. mean that we each construct our learning of the same experience in different ways.

Learning can be facilitated in **collaborative activities**.

These requirements for effective learning are a significant advance upon the early studies of learning that concentrated upon Repetition, Contiguity and Reinforcement, the principles underlying Behaviourist approaches. Cognition, knowing and understanding is the cognitivist approach that De Corte's list of effective learning strategies fits into. It can be used as a checklist to evaluate learning provision within lecture programmes. There is perhaps one caveat and that is that not all advances in learning and understanding are necessarily cumulative and straightforward. There can and often need to be innovative leaps based upon divergent and inductive approaches or by analogy.

It was found that when De Corte's criteria were applied to over 1,250 lessons observed in schools and universities (Montgomery, 2002, 2017b) the sessions did not meet most of these criteria. In addition, students regularly complained that they could not see the relevance of the lecture or lesson content to the programme they thought they were following.

Table 2.2 Contrasting models of teaching, educational leadership and evaluation in higher education

	Model I: 'Disseminating knowledge'	Model II: 'Making learning possible'
Epistemological assumptions	Knowledge exists separately from the people who possess it. Knowledge can be conveyed. Concepts and facts are prerequisites for problem solving in a field of study. Theory and practice are separate domains.	Knowledge doesn't exist apart from people. Knowledge must be reconstructed by learners. Facts and concepts are learned as they are used. Problem-solving concepts and facts are mutually dependent, in learning as well as in expert practice.
Academic and social environment	Of little importance: Knowledge is created through a social system but is learned through individual study and practice; other students provide competition but are otherwise marginal to learning.	Of central significance: Effective learning occurs in an environment that mimics social systems of inquiry; social interaction and cooperation are essential to the negotiation of understanding.

(Continued)

Table 2.2 Contrasting models of teaching, educational leadership and evaluation in higher education (Continued)

	Model I: 'Disseminating knowledge'	Model II: 'Making learning possible'
Student learning	Teacher focused: Practice procedures produce correct answers, reproduce knowledge accurately. Infer methods of inquiry from knowledge organisation and texts.	Learner focused: Responsibly regulate inquiry, construct personal understanding and emulate experts' methods. Abstract concepts and principles from experiences.
Teacher's role	Ensure that the ever-expanding content is covered. Organise and present knowledge well. Arrange suitable teaching activities including lectures, tutorials and labs as appropriate. Rely on students to understand and absorb presented knowledge and procedures.	Limit the content to essentials. Model the methods of practice and scholarship in the field. Design diverse tasks strongly related to learning goals. Challenge misconceptions and build understanding through dialogue. Constantly monitor student understanding and intervene whenever necessary.
Desirable learning and assessment tasks	Well-structured problems and standard exercises with high reliability. 'Decontextualised practice': parts are studied separately and only brought together towards the end of the course. Tasks provide feedback at end of unit or not at all.	Poorly structured problems and realistic tasks requiring student decision making. 'Situated practice': Tasks of increasing complexity that incorporate essential skills and knowledge. Tasks provide continuous feedback.
How is teaching improved?	Mainly through practice; driven by extrinsic rewards.	Mainly through repeated cycles of reflection and action; driven by intrinsic interest.
Approach to management and leadership of teaching	Essentially transactional: Assigning tasks and rewarding their successful completion.	Essentially transformational: Creating an enabling environment and pursuing a moral vision.
Evaluation and audit	Measurement focused, externally directed and value-free. Preferred indicators are quantitative, such as pass rates and student ratings.	Process-focused, user-directed and permeated by values. Preferred indicators are qualitative, such as student comments and evidence of changes in conceptions.
Educational effectiveness	Essentially technical: A problem to be solved.	Essentially problematic: An enduring human dilemma.

Table 2.2 is based on Bain (1993) 'Towards a framework for more effective teaching in higher education: Some experiences based on a new Graduate Certificate in Higher Education'.

It is similar to the model produced by Paul comparing Didactic and Critical Theory of Education. It is interesting to note that they appeared about the same time reflecting developments and new thinking in that era.

Critical theory

Critical theory was born in the universities derived from courses in logic and reasoning (Fisher, 2006) but it was as informal not formal logic. It can be seen to have permeated the thoughts and practices in HE as described in the *Handbook of Teaching in HE* by Fry et al. (2015). As these things go, some secondary schools have begun to adopt the model just as they copied the 19th-century university didactic model (Barnard, 1963).

The essence of critical thinking theory is thinking about our thinking or metacognition. It is this that Flavell (1979) found increased intelligence. Shayer and Adey (2002) also found evidence of this when in secondary science education courses they reserved one lesson each fortnight for such metacognitive processes. They found the experimental groups had significantly better science examination results than the controls but there was also a transfer to better results in their English and maths at GCSE (General Certificate of Secondary Education).

Meta-teaching is the understanding and reflection on teaching just as metacognition is reflection on cognition. Stones (1983) refers to meta-metateaching as the understanding and reflection on teaching about teaching a third-order set of representations. Effective teaching however is more than just encouraging reasoning and thinking. The wider frame of reference is constructivism. In this, it is known that learners build their own internal structures and systems of knowledge by thinking and problem solving and incorporating new information and protocols into their existing frameworks.

Constructivist theory

Constructivism originated in the early 20th century in the work of Bartlett (1932) in the UK and Piaget, Rey and Inhelder in Paris at about the same time. Essentially, it emphasised that in order to learn individuals have to participate in and construct their own knowledge. They are meaning-makers by the processes that Piaget (1952) termed Accommodation and Equilibration. Because the theory was initially applied to young children's learning its application to adult learning was overlooked. Critical thinking theory as proposed by Resnick (1989) and Paul (1990) as in the Table 2.1 above belongs to this realm.

According to Brookes and Brookes (1993), there are 12 guiding principles in the approaches of constructivist teachers/lecturers, they:

- Encourage and accept student autonomy and initiative.
- Use raw data and primary sources, along with manipulative, interactive and physical materials.

- Use cognitive terminology when framing tasks.
- Allow student responses to drive sessions, shift instructional strategies and alter content.
- Inquire about students' understanding of concepts before sharing understanding of them.
- Encourage students to engage in dialogue both with the teacher and each other.
- Encourage student enquiry by asking thoughtful, open-ended questions and encourage students to ask questions of each other.
- Seek elaboration of students' initial responses.
- Engage students in experiences that might engender contradictions to their initial hypotheses and then encourage discussion.
- Allow wait time after posing questions.
- Provide time for students to construct relationships and create metaphors.
- Nurture students' natural curiosity.

As can be imagined, teachers once versed in these skills find it hard to work in didactic environments.

Learners in this new millennium need to be self-starters, self-regulating and self-motivated. They are stimulated and extended in situations that offer such opportunities and it is constructivist methods that can facilitate this. It can be seen that constructivism forms a platform for the development of SRL. The good news is that Nicol and MacFarlane-Dick (2006) suggested that over the previous two decades, there had been a shift in the way teachers and researchers wrote about student learning in HE. Instead of characterising it as a simple acquisition process based on teacher transmission, learning was more commonly conceptualised as a process whereby students actively constructed their own knowledge and skills and programmes should become 'student centred'. They argued that feedback and assessment however was still dominated by the transmission culture and was tutor controlled. They identified a set of principles of good assessment for learning (AfL) that can be undertaken by students and lecturers demonstrating the essential role of their feedback in SRL. The details can be found in Chapter 4.

What has to be recognised is that it will be those in the forefront of teaching development who will be writing and sharing their expertise but there will always be pockets of 'resistance'. Change can be emotionally unsettling and may create unwanted extra work.

Pedagogy and andragogy

In some spheres, pedagogy is considered to be the art of teaching in which the classical approach is in teaching school pupils in the traditional or didactic mode. Andragogy on the other hand was defined as the art and science of teaching adult learners (Edosomwan, 2016). This is a philosophical perspective. In andragogy, the role of the teacher is to facilitate the learning process by providing guidance and resources and an extension of this was defined by Hase and Kenyon (2000) as Heutagogy! This is the study of self-determined learning in which the teacher facilitates the learning process but fully relinquishes the ownership of the learning to the learner. The learner negotiates the learning and determines what will be learnt and how it will be learned. This is typical of the graduate student undertaking the dissertation or the learner engaging in certain forms of distance and online learning.

Blaschke (2012) defines the key construct in heutagogy as 'double-loop' learning and self-reflection. In double-loop learning, she describes the process in which learners consider the problem, the effects and outcomes and in addition reflect on the problem-solving process and how it eventually influences their own beliefs and actions.

Self-directed learning, one of the central ideas of andragogy is fast becoming not only an adult phenomenon, but also childhood practice. Many children are also becoming self-directed learners with developmental changes in their curricula. It is evident that pedagogy and andragogy need to be applied in learning situations simultaneously depending on the learning objectives and outcomes. But we also need to consider whether giving them separate terms is really necessary to describe pedagogy and its different teaching methods or different learners.

Deep and surface learning

Marton and Säljo (1976, 1984) identified HE students who engaged in either deep or surface learning and found that in order to secure deep learning, the learner must be an active participant not just in childhood but throughout life: They reported that students with a deep approach achieved better results than surface learners.

Gibbs (1990) defined the characteristics of surface learning as follows:

- A heavy workload
- Relatively high class contact hours
- An excessive amount of course material
- Lack of opportunity to pursue subjects in depth
- Lack of choice over subjects
- Lack of choice over methods of study
- Threatening and anxiety-provoking assessment systems

All these surface characteristics are implicit in high-stakes education systems and transmission models. Fostering a deep learning approach rests on the obverse of surface approaches:

- Relatively low class contact hours
- Intrinsic interest in the subject
- Freedom in learning in content and method or scope for intellectual independence

- Experience perceived as 'good' teaching
- A positive and supportive assessment system

Ramsden (1994, 121) reported that departments using deeper approaches to learning had a number of characteristics in common: They showed a concern for and availability to students; had enthusiastic and interested tutors; had clear organisational goals; provided feedback on learning; encouraged student independence; promoted active learning; constructed an appropriate workload; used relevant assessment methods and offered a suitably challenging academic environment.

Independent learning and capability

In 1974, a Diploma in Higher Education studies by Independent Learning was given academic approval by the CNAA (Council for National Academic Awards). The North-East London Polytechnic, now the University of East London designed a Dip. HE that had no specified content, no programme of studies, no prescribed reading lists; no timetable and no formal examinations. It did have a rationale, a set of procedures and criteria for validating programmes of study prepared by students and arrangements for the provision of specialist supervision and basic skills support. All tutors across the institution might be recruited as mentors to the School of Independent Studies students. The students had to plan and negotiate approval for their own programmes leading to the award. It was a radical innovation at that time, the ultimate in self-regulated or learner-managed learning. Later successful degree and masters programmes were developed and could include work-based learning.

Higher Education for Capability

John Stephenson with a like-minded group of colleagues saw the need for change in university programmes following the success of the Independent Studies programmes and they initiated a new movement to try to effect this – Higher Education for Capability. It incorporated many of the qualities that would promote self-regulated learners equipped to make a strong contribution to any field of employment that they entered. In his inaugural speech at the Royal Society of Arts launching the Challenge of Higher Education for Capability, the Project Leader (Stephenson, 1988) outlined the following agenda:

> ... Employers of graduates ... had said that capability consisted of 40 per cent specialist knowledge and skill and 60 per cent personal qualities. Qualities of being continuously prepared to learn and adapt, being self critical, self starters, able to communicate in speech and writing, initiative, empathy, self awareness, commitment to what they are doing, team-working, problem analysis and solution, ambition, and a sense of purpose. Higher education was not doing enough to foster these qualities.

The theme of the new Higher Education for Capability project which we are launching today is to do just that – to encourage the development of the qualities of capability through the process by which students learn. (p. 1)

The general capabilities identified were as follows:

- Acquire and apply knowledge
- Communicate ideas and information
- Listen to and collaborate with others in mutually planned activities
- Set achievable and relevant goals
- Assess the effectiveness of their actions
- Be critical of and creative in their thinking and actions
- See both success and failures as opportunities for learning
- Show respect and concern for others and take account of their feelings
- Reflect on their values

The specific capabilities identified were those that referred to specific subject or job competencies. Both general and specific capabilities have elements in common in the promotion of core skills in oracy, literacy, numeracy, information and communication technology and key skills in problem solving, communication and creativity. For capabilities, we could substitute 'SRL strategies and outcomes'.

Two years after the launch, they made a similar declaration about Capability in Secondary Schools but that seemed to gather little momentum. The effect of the implementation of the Education Reform Act and the National Curriculum no doubt stopped schools from becoming involved. This was when content on a substantial scale had been loaded into the curriculum and process was downgraded.

After 10 years, John Stephenson, leader of Independent Studies, obtained a research grant. His project was to search out former students and collect their evaluations of the effects of the programme in personal, capability and career terms. By then, there had been over 1,000 students on degree and masters' programmes.

The Capability in HE organisation was established at Leeds University and promoted the work from there. After conferences to promote Capability in the UK and then in Eastern Europe at Opava recruiting interest and showing developments across the sector the movement appeared to falter and as before individuals rather than institutions kept up the work. Yorke (1995), for example, published papers from the Manchester conference on capability research and development and continued the work.

Lifelong Learning

In 1998, Dr Kim Howells produced a White Paper on Lifelong Learning that envisioned access to the National Grid from cradle to grave. He wanted to break down the barriers between schools and colleges and universities, and give everyone access to their knowledge and expertise. He wanted to set up large regional colleges linked to regional learning networks. He wanted schools with sixth forms to become part of a coordinated post-school planning and funding regime with a regional dimension. Making post-school education demand-led and student-driven alarmed the Treasury and the Prime Minister (Gordon Brown) agreed that the paper lacked rigour and coherence and there was too little in it about standards and exam qualifications (Low, 1998). The status of the paper was downgraded to green (consultation) then to blue and disappeared. This is another example of the 'elites' who are nervous about the redistribution of opportunities for lifelong learning to the least educated and trained.

Considerable interest has been taken in the subject of lifelong learning by researchers in giftedness and talent looking at the life histories of many talented people who seem to retain a lifelong interest in a favourite subject or indeed in many subjects and may go on researching lifelong when others would retire. Even ordinary workers who retire take up new interests or visit places and do things they would never have dreamt of doing before. Others draw up a 'bucket list' that they determine to complete before they die. These examples illustrate the stimulus-seeking nature of human beings.

The Perry Pre-school Project (Weikart, 1967, 1998) showed the positive impact of a 'cognitive' curriculum on classes of pre-school disadvantaged learners as opposed to two other more typical early education programmes. Although the differences did not show up as academic advantages in school, in later life the experimental groups went back into education and continuing development, they had become lifelong learners and had stayed out of prison much more than peers not in the cognitive classes.

Fiedler (2015) reviewing the life stories of talented individuals identified a series of phases or stages that they appeared to go through (SENAC) that could be typical of all humans given the opportunities. They began in the early years as Seekers after knowledge and moved in late adolescence to become Explorers of the environment and its possibilities. In middle age, they became Navigators as they settled on and pursued their career pathways and later became Actualisers as they achieved and enjoyed their goals. In the final phase of their lives, she said they were 'Cruising', living out the life and enjoying the results. Hers is a developmental perspective on the competence theory of motivation.

Knapper (1995, 15) identified five strategies that had been found in lifelong learners as follows:

- Capacity to set personal and realistic goals
- Ability to apply existing knowledge and skills effectively
- Ability to evaluate one's own learning
- Skill in locating information from different sources
- Capacity to use different learning strategies in different situations

These are the classic competencies also found in self-regulated learners. The critical problem is how can these skills be developed in those who do not have them and how can they be honed and improved in those who do have them.

Effective teaching

It was surprising to find that in the 1980s, there was no agreed definition of what was 'good' teaching. In teacher education, there seemed to be a rule of thumb that 'you know it when you see it'. It became essential to develop some criteria by which good and effective teaching could be described and shared with students and became a significant topic for research as the appraisal movement began. However, the foundations begin long before that as we have all been to school and experienced both good and bad teaching. As teachers, we would have tried all sorts of different techniques and strategies, and as teacher, educators observed hundreds of students and experienced teachers teaching. From this experience, a theory and practice of effective teaching was developed and tested.

Changes in teaching methods over the 19th/20th centuries had moved from rote memorising and drills in basic skills and a few other more domestic subjects to a broader content-filled curriculum. This included humanities, geography, science, maths, music, arts and so on. Eventually, most of these subjects depended on the teacher finding interesting ways in which the pupils would commit the essential information to memory to be tested in exams. Nevertheless, many of the pupils were not much motivated to go on learning in these ways and responded better when they had problems to solve and challenging questions and things to do.

These teaching methods were by analogy likened to changes in the stages of intellectual development of children defined by Piaget (1952). These were from pre-operational intuitive thinking (Rote era) to concrete operations (Content/product learning era) to abstract operations (Investigative problem-based learning). This enabled the two central objectives in teaching in the 'new era' to be defined as:

- To enable students to think efficiently.
- To express those thoughts succinctly.

These were to be the core theme in every subject and skills area of the school curriculum and at each of the age levels beginning in pre-school through into degree programmes. The methods and problems would take account of the children's level of intellectual development in the social context and provide a curriculum of strategies that could be used to train teachers. These were termed 'Cognitive Process Strategies' (CPS) or 'brain engage' techniques (Chapters 6 and 7).

The developmental context referred to development in perception, emotion, personality, physical, intellectual, language, thinking, motivation and social skills. It was evident, for example, that many individuals entered the adult world without having developed beyond Piaget's concrete operational level of thinking and still do. It makes them vulnerable to prejudice and stereotyping as coping strategies. It means that not all students in HE are capable initially of abstract thought although they may have prodigious memories.

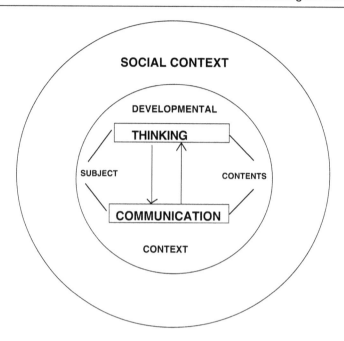

Figure 2.1 A model of modern teaching.

Source: Montgomery (1981).

The aim to teach for thinking and communication is set in the construc-tivist realm. Once established, it was possible to develop a set of strategies to achieve these learning goals that were cross curricular and followed constructivist principles.

Boiling theory down to bare essentials illustrated in Figure 2.1 in this way was necessary because teachers in their daily decision-making do not have time to rif-fle through a series of research abstracts in the mind, they needed some overarch-ing principles or key constructs to guide their daily teaching activities. It becomes essential that teachers in HE also have the opportunity for CPD in which they are able to reflect on their personal theories of teaching and student learning to help them make changes in practice.

Critics in the period of the 'Traditional versus Progressive' debate argued that process methods advocated by the 'Progressives' were empty of content and there-fore useless. The same argument has been made about the skills approach in HE. There is a whole range of methods that can be content free but have specific purposes for dealing with social skills, mediation, team building, interviewing and problem solving. But equally need not be so they can be content dense when they are built into the curriculum as ways of learning. In Chapter 1, the 'walking the talk' experiment was the first opportunity to apply these constructs in HE in real time. It was in a time when officials in charge of education were proclaiming 'A good man knows his subject and teaches it in a lively manner' (!!!).

Quality in teaching

Astin's (1993, 383) research examined the quality of teaching perceived by 20,000 students and 25,000 staff across 200 institutions in the US. He found that staff-student interaction had a positive correlation with every area of self-reported intellectual and personal growth. A similar positive effect was shown for student-to-student interactions. The sheer number of hours devoted to lecturing/teaching was unrelated to cognitive development.

Quality is frequently assessed in HE by using student satisfaction survey questionnaires among other techniques. But it can become a weapon so that staff can feel a threat to their tenure. Recent studies have shown that these surveys are not so reliable as administrators have assumed. For example, courses with lax standards that are easy to follow and to gain high grades in are frequently given high satisfaction scores by many students, High-quality, challenging courses can receive low grades from these students. Another simple measure used is the number of first-class degrees obtained by students and these have risen over time and have been termed 'grade inflation'. Between 1994/1995 and 2011/2012 first-class grades doubled from 7% to 15.8% and have now increased to 26% in 2018 according to the Guardian newspaper.

This has led to the conclusion that standards in universities have fallen but it may indicate standards of teaching and learning have risen, or methods of assessment have a broader remit to include course work portfolios, criterion referenced assessments, not just memory test examinations. In addition, students may be working harder now they have to pay their own fees and/or they may be more demanding of their universities.

Simple measures give simplistic responses and often the wrong answers. A survey is currently underway in HE to establish the top quality universities across the world. The first question involves the respondent listing the top 15 universities for teaching in the country/world, then listing the top 15 in terms of quality in research. How many have studied or taught in 15 universities even in one country to know the answer to this? Who would not include their own university despite it having four faculties that operate lower standards? Even in them there may be several high-quality departments/schools or individual tutors that are excellent.

Even the quality assessments made by CNAA visitation panels in 3-day investigations in the past were unable to plumb the real depths of the institutions or their heights but made a passable evaluation after lengthy interviews with staff and students and examination of documentary evidence. The same might be said of Her Majesty's Inspectorate visitations when they did sit in on lectures and meet the students. Even so biases were implicit in the processes that were difficult to challenge.

Assessment

The model of evaluation linked to the modern model of teaching in Figure 2.1 was that it should be an AfL. Evaluation was to be a part of teaching and learning and seek to:

- Improve quality continuously as an everyday activity.
- Help individual students learn better.
- Focus on process as well as product.
- Be collaborative.
- 'Engage brain' rather than rely only on memory recall.
- Promote deep learning.
- Operate in the main at the three higher levels of Bloom's (1956) taxonomy of educational objectives (analysis, synthesis and evaluation against external or internal criteria).

For example, in the Distance Learning MAs and full-time degree programmes all set tasks were to be assessed and three types of AfL were undertaken, for example, Formative, Diagnostic and Summative. It will be noticed that all these developments in education theory, research and practice were taking place in and around the 1990s. It is well understood that advances in various fields do not necessarily become incorporated into the mainstream and it usually takes 30–50 years for even the best of them to become widely implemented (Cooper, 1999). A glimpse of the future in HE (now) during that period was given by Bourne and Flowers (1997) and it ran as follows.

The glimpse of our future from 1997

Because of the decrease in the unit of teaching resource lecture and seminar groups would have to become much larger and modular courses would become more common. Small tutor groups and one-to-one tuition would fall away. High-financial-yield courses would increase and low ones would decrease or have to be changed. The low-yield courses were final-year options; masters level work; research degree work and innovative teaching and learning initiatives. They predicted that a two-tier system such as had developed in the US community colleges would prevail. This would mean that after 2 years in HE, students would take their portfolios and complete their degrees in 'senior' universities.

Because of the need for large student numbers and closer monitoring of quality standards, technological communication and distance learning would increase especially in the information dissemination (didactics) model. There would be an expansion of Open Learning from prestigious universities via the internet and most universities would not survive this competition.

> Globalisation – if there is a single learning aim of dissemination of facts and ideas it will eliminate most universities. (Bourne and Flowers, 1997, 3)

From our position post 2020, we can now judge how far their predictions have become a reality and if there is further to go.

Bourne and Flowers (1997) listed 10 teaching methods then in operation but these do not really qualify as pedagogy they are formats for the presentation of information.

1 Lectures
2 Up-to-date textbooks
3 Reading
4 Handouts
5 'Guest' lectures
6 Use of exercises that require students to find up-to-date knowledge
7 Developing skills in using library and other learning resources
8 Directed private study
9 Open learning materials
10 Use of the Internet

If the aims in HE were broader than just dissemination of facts and ideas then a wider range of methods was required to support them. For example:

> 'Disseminate knowledge' and develop the capability to use ideas and information, develop the student's ability to test ideas and evidence, develop the student's ability to generate ideas and evidence, facilitate the personal development of students, develop the capacity of students to plan and manage their own learning'.
>
> (Bourne et al., 4)

Even so, this is merely a wish list not a teaching methodology and they moved on to tabulate more lists of presentation methods that could be used to meet the different aims. They included the following (their overlaps removed):

Case studies. Practicals, Work experience, Project, Demonstrations, Group work, Simulations (e.g. computer based), Workshops, Discussion and debate, Essay writing.

Seminars and tutorials. Supervision, Presentations, Feedback on written work, Literature reviewing, Examination papers, Open learning, Peer assessment, Self-assessment.

Research projects. Workshops on techniques of creative problem solving, Action learning, Lateral thinking, Brainstorming, Mind-mapping, Creative visualisation, Coaching, Problem solving.

Experiential learning. Learning contracts, Role-play; Self-assessment, Profiling, Mentoring.

Reflective logs and diaries. Independent study, Portfolio development, Dissertations.

Only in the latter part of the list do they begin to distinguish some teaching methods.

All of these techniques are still widely in operation in some courses and in some departments but obviously not all of them. The list itself has the quality of a shotgun scatter or pick and mix bag. There appears to be a lack of a coherent rationale for the place and purpose of each technique within a programme. The chapters that follow will try to provide the underpinning for the choice of cross-curricular teaching and learning methods in forms and fields of knowledge.

This has to begin with a question about the teacher-lecturer role. A person giving a lecture cannot claim to be teaching because to teach carries with it the assumption that someone has learnt a significant amount of it (Hirst, 1975) and its main themes and ideas. Lecturers 'tell' information to students, they lecture. Telling is not teaching although it is widely used to impart knowledge to students when they could equally well read it in a book, listen on audio CD or watch it on film. To reserve the term 'teacher' for more appropriate use and for professionally trained personnel, the term 'tutor' will be more frequently used to describe the lecturer's role.

The second point is that the lecture, seminar, workshop and tutorial are the formats or structures within which teaching methods may operate. Each lecture may be situated on a continuum as in the following examples from recent conferences. Assume each lecture has the following format – advance organisers or objectives – introduction – main content – summary or conclusions. The methods chosen:

1 The lecturer reads the lecture notes to the audience.
2 The lecturer tells the lecture to the audience.
3 The lecturer reads the Power Point presentation to the audience.
4 The lecturer talks to the audience with the support of the Power Points.
5 The lecturer talks to the audience and uses diagrams and/or video examples and Power Points to reinforce main ideas.
6 The teacher talks to the audience supported by the Power Point and engages the audience in some participative activities to reinforce main ideas and give insights and learning experiences.
7 The teacher talks to the audience as in the above sixth point, but also raises questions and poses problems to take away and think about or try.

There can be similar continua in relation to the presentations in seminars, workshops and tutorials. Only 5% of a lecture will be remembered according to Race (1992), that is, unless the students do some further work on the subject by themselves. It is their time on task that is crucial for higher learning gain. It is also important for them to make their own handwritten notes rather than word-process them or photograph them (Mueller and Oppenheimer, 2014). Even when the Power Points are available to download later unless the student does work with them soon afterwards, there will be little gain although they might feel more secure because the notes are somewhere safely captured and filed.

Corrardi (2015), a lecturer at Bath University, described her work in Experimental Sciences at the University. Her example is clearly a case of a lecturer teaching. She was engaged in Just in Time Teaching (JiTT), providing blended learning experiences. She was teaching protein crystallography to second-year students.

> The students read through some course notes on line before the lecture, answer a comprehension quiz and some open-ended questions to explain what they had found difficult. When the quizzes closed she had half a day to read the results. The class consisted of some explanations, some clicker questions and linked peer discussions, 1-minute papers on concepts and some demonstrations with props and movies. (p. 222)

The students reported that spending twice the amount of time on learning in and out of class enabled them to retain the material when they came to revise it. While a few students preferred formal lectures and others criticised the quality of some of the questions, this feedback enabled the whole process to be improved and developed. The feedback was especially valuable because it was going in both directions. It did involve a lot of commitment and additional work for the tutor.

The students: Dual and multiple exceptionality (DME)

It has been recorded that in the era of mass HE when nearly 50% of the population enter the universities a much wider range of students has entered the programmes from the elites to the disadvantaged. The disadvantaged students are known for their underachievements in school due to a variety of circumstances not of their own making such as low expectations, poverty and BAME when they can become high achievers with the right support. The excellence gap for them is now well known and has already been pointed out.

However, there are many more students who may be overlooked, who also exhibit excellence gaps and these are those with learning difficulties, disabilities and learning disorders. This does not mean they are intellectually limited but have certain skills deficits that provide barriers to academic achievement if not dealt with or circumvented. There are many famous examples among writers, artists and actors, and many others have become leaders in politics and business as entrepreneurs when poor school grades or disaffection prevented them from going to university.

Students with sensory and physical disabilities may use vision and hearing aids or a wheelchair and can be regarded as intellectually limited when this is far from the case. The disability can however act as a barrier to some people seeing beyond the disability to the high learning potential and creative gifts. A main issue once high ability is recognised is gaining access to services and resources especially in buildings and sites not originally designed with them in mind.

Equally of concern are those whose disabilities are hidden and who are frequently blamed for their underachievements rather than the difficulties they experience and the lack of appropriate support on their learning journey. They also fall into the category of Dual and Multiple Exceptionality. They have dual exceptionality in that they are 'gifted' and/or talented with a special educational need or disability (SEND). In fact, many of them will have more than one special need, for example, a dyslexic may also have a handwriting problem-making essay writing and note taking especially difficult. The dyslexic may also have some Asperger Syndrome or attention deficit hyperactivity disorder (ADHD) characteristics making multiple exceptionality. Dyslexia is the most prevalent of the learning disabilities at 10%, Asperger Syndrome (High Functioning Autism) 1% and ADHD 2.5% amongst students in HE. However, it is males who are more likely to be identified with these conditions in a ratio of 4:1 for dyslexia, for example. These numbers tend to be based upon referrals to help centres but in the population at large, the ratios are more likely to 3:2 men to women (Rutter et al., 2004; Montgomery, 2017a). Similar hidden populations of girls with Asperger Syndrome and ADHD are just beginning to be discovered (Gould et al., 2011).

Because English is not a transparent language, the numbers of dyslexics in the UK is high, 10% of the population (British Dyslexia Association, 2019), and 4% of the cases are regarded as severe. The condition is found across the ability range so there are plenty of dyslexics in HE. In fact, there are many more than has been thought. For example, the numbers in disadvantaged inner city areas and coastal towns can rise to nearly 20%. Others have never had reading difficulties and even learned to read self-taught but like all adult dyslexics have residual spelling problems (dysorthographia) especially when meeting new vocabulary and they can have compositional shortcomings (Montgomery, 2015).

Word processors have to some extent alleviated the problems of those with handwriting coordination difficulties (dysgraphia) but in schools, they will have been blamed for their illegible scribble or failure to write neatly. This alone can put many off an academic career. They often also have locational and organisational difficulties. There is also a hidden population who are slower at writing for a range of reasons and this can consign them to a lower class of degree (Connelly et al., 2005). Over 90% of those with Asperger Syndrome also have some writing difficulties and although they may be very bright are lacking in social and life skills. They need careful support and protection from bullying and social isolation. Living on campus is also a help to them.

The good news is that things are improving for some of these students so that it was possible for severely dyslexic James unable to read or write, when given an amanuensis passed GCSEs and A levels, and obtained a BSc without ever having actually read a book or written an essay. He now teaches music technology and maths at a secondary school.

Conclusion

Changes in society and in views about education have moved in the direction of 'student-centred' or 'learner-centred' teaching and learning. Employers too have redefined their needs for the workers in this new millennium and these appear to be strongly embedded in self-regulatory learning approaches.

Rosenshine's (2010) widely quoted research on effective teaching carried with it the implicit assumption that didactic, direct instruction was at its heart. The recommendations for this pedagogy, a transmission model, are predicated on a behaviourist, stimulus-response theory and on particular assumptions about what was to be taught. It was an illustration of research that shows what is going on, not necessarily what should be going on. In this chapter, a different perspective was offered that is based in critical thinking theory and constructivism with associated AfL.

The methods associated with them need to be designed to increase student time on task and these involve strategic and problem-based learning activities. Details of these methods will be discussed and illustrated in Chapter 6 on Study Skills and in Chapter 7 on Problem-Based Learning.

The next chapter considers the nature of SRL and what skills and competencies are involved for students and also the barriers to learning that may stand in their way.

Chapter 3

Self-regulated learning
Theory, research and practice

Introduction

Interest in self-regulated learning (SRL) stems from 19th-century educators with more formal research on the topic beginning in the early 20th century. Stronger research and theory emerged in the 1970s and 1980s, which form the platform for research at the present time. Over the decades SRL appears under many different headings. Frequent titles have been as follows: Autonomous learning (AL), Self-managed learning (SML), Learner-managed learning (LML), Self-organised learning (SOL), Independent learning (IL), Self-directed learning (SDL), Independent research strategies (IRS) and Independent study skills (ISS).

In 1972, the international committee, the Organisation for Economic and Co-operative Development (OECD), noted that the changing role of the teacher in modern society emphasised the importance of the transfer of responsibility for learning to the learner, while the teacher became less of a transmitter of knowledge and more a manager of the learning environment and the central organiser of supports for the learner. The goal was that schools and universities should be producing Lifelong Learners with the capacity and motivation to learn for themselves throughout life. Changing the role of the teacher from lecturer to facilitator was seen as the way of accomplishing this.

After an initial flurry of research, mainly in schools, interest in the topic in the UK appeared to decline. This was probably because of other major initiatives such as the Education Reform Act (1988) and the imposition of a National Curriculum (NCC, 1991). Because this curriculum had an over-filled content in 10 separate subject areas for ages 5–16, it placed the onus back on the teacher as a transmitter of knowledge and skill with the learners as passive recipients and according to Gibb's criteria (1990) surface learners.

By this time, concern for independent and lifelong learning had moved into tertiary education, the colleges and the universities. Departments and faculties were being renamed school/faculty of Lifelong Learning and even Lifelong Learning and Education! The position at the time in the UK was summarised in collections of papers by Graves (1993) on LML; Gibbs (1994, 1995) on theory, research and assessment and Yorke (1995) on Assessment of Capability and a Post Graduate Certificate for Teaching in higher education (HE) was in development. In the US, Weinstein et al. (1988) published papers on Study Skills and Learning Strategies, showing the developments there.

Two decades later there appears to be a reawakening interest in SRL in HE not only in the UK but also in Europe and South East Asia. The aim is to encourage methods that induce lifelong learning and self-regulation in students of all ages. In the interim, there has been an immense technological change making information available on a vast scale that was estimated to double every 8 years and now every 2 years. This causes a major challenge for students and their tutors in how to manage such a large body of information and has put a simple transmission model under threat.

The topic of SRL has also become an important area of research and development. It is very much related to future scenarios and managing the increasing numbers of students entering HE and with decreasing budgets. As larger numbers of students have entered HE, the needs have widened and strategies for teaching them have needed to be developed. In the past, 7% of the UK population entered HE and students were expected to 'read for their degrees' and manage their own learning. The former polytechnics that catered for a wider range of students took it upon themselves to engage with more teaching and learning strategies, but now it is a widespread concern across tertiary education.

There is also a recognition now by schools with pupils applying for university places that there is a need to prepare them for an independent style of learning and how to manage their study time. But only some schools with more forward looking leaders are beginning to focus on developing self-regulated learners to prepare them for HE.

New technology has also played a significant role in these changes. It has enabled universities to develop satellite centres in other countries and also build virtual colleges and courses. However, the main model appears to reproduce the status quo and to develop a face-to-face system in a virtual or blended form. Thus, questions need to be raised about the lecture-seminar model as an effective system for inducing student learning whether virtual or in real time. It will be proposed that independent SRL is a more effective method in constructing meaning and developing competencies. This does not mean that there is no role for lectures and seminars, although it is possible to manage without them in some circumstances.

Self-regulatory activities

SRL activities were defined by Brown et al. (1983) as planning, predicting outcomes and scheduling time and resources, monitoring and evaluation. Monitoring included testing, revising and rescheduling. Evaluating outcomes involved using criteria developed by the individual and also those that were externally defined. These are higher-order executive intellectual functions (Gagné, 1973).

The value of SRL was shown by Wang and Lindvall (1984). They found that the self-monitoring and self-regulatory activities not only contributed to improved acquisition of subjects but also to improved generalisation and transfer of knowledge and skills. SRL also gave students a sense of personal agency, a feeling of being in control of their own learning.

When SRL was involved, we found from the university feedback sessions and questionnaires that undergraduates enjoyed these activities most of all. In their formal and informal feedback on the courses, they said the dissertation was the most interesting, creative and motivating part of the course. Some spent an inordinate amount of time working on it, but it was time pleasurably spent.

Independent project work was recommended by Reis and Renzulli (2008) as the highest level in their School-wide Enrichment Model but found that even gifted achievers destined for HE did not necessarily develop the necessary self-regulatory skills especially in didactic systems, they needed some training and they produced modules that gave training on separate sets of SRL skills.

Self-directed learning and/or self-regulated learning

Knowles (1975, 15) defined SDL as learning in which:

> Individuals take the initiative, with or without the help of others, in diagnosing their learning needs, formulating learning goals, identifying human and material resources for learning, choosing and implementing learning strategies, and evaluating learning outcomes.

It is also characteristic of real-world problem-solving in which the initial problem is essentially 'fuzzy' (Gallagher, 1997). Knowles suggested that there was an increasingly profound psychological need to be independent as humans develop and mature; naturally developing the ability to take on more and more responsibility for one's life and to be increasingly self-directed. He equated learning to living, and said that every experience in life was a 'learning experience'. He put forward three concepts for SDL: proactive learner, learner initiative and psychological development. He believed that human beings who take the initiative in learning as proactive learners learn more things and learn better than reactive learners. The predictor variables were motivation to learn, learner independence and intellectual curiosity.

According to Garrison (1997, 18), SDL was:

> An approach where learners are motivated to assume personal responsibility and collaborative control of the cognitive and contextual processes in constructing and confirming worthwhile learning outcomes.

More recently, Ramdass and Zimmerman (2011) defined SRL as a pro-active process in which individuals are expected to organise and manage their thoughts, emotions, behaviours and their environment to fulfil their academic objectives.

> SRL is thus an active, constructive process in which learners set their own goals and then seek to monitor, regulate, and control their cognition, motivation, and behaviour, in accordance with their goals and the contextual features of the environment.
>
> (Pintrich, 2000, 453)

Thus, the construct of self-regulation refers to the degree to which students can regulate aspects of their thinking, motivation and behaviour during learning (Pintrich and Zusho, 2002, 64). It involves developing knowledge, skills and attitudes that can be transferred from one learning context to another. It promotes learners' self-competence and also predicts academic success and athletic involvement (Zimmerman and Kitsantas, 2005). It involves the setting of, and orientation towards learning goals, the management of resources, the effort exerted, reactions to external feedback and the products produced (Nicol and MacFarlane-Dick, 2006). It is surely essential to equip disadvantaged and underachieving learners with such skills to improve their future prospects.

> Self-regulated learning involves developing knowledge, skills, and attitudes which can be transferred from one learning context to another and from learning situations in which this information has been acquired to a leisure and work related context.
>
> (Boekaerts, 1999, 446)

Widely known models in the literature are as follows:

1 Zimmerman's Social Cognitive Model of Self-Regulation (1990, 1998),
2 Boekaerts' Model of Adaptable Learning (1999),
3 Winne's Four-Stage Model of Self-Regulated Learning (Winne, 1996; Winne and Hadwin, 1998),
4 Borkowski's Process-Oriented Model of Metacognition (1996) and
5 Pintrich's General Framework for SRL (2000).

Pintrich's General Framework for SRL includes cognitive, motivational, sensory and biological individual processes. Pintrich's (2000) self-regulated model has four stages: (1) forethought, planning and activation; (2) monitoring; (3) control and (4) reaction and reflection.

Self-regulated learners in school according to Niehart (2011) do well but may not be in the top 10% of achievers on leaving. She found they handled stress well, were persistent, self-directed, self-regulated, self-motivated, tended to be risk-takers and good self-advocates. This indicated they would be good at handling their experiences of HE and be successful in their studies as they will have self-efficacy and resilience and will be unlikely to drop out.

It appears to be especially important that throughout the education sector SRL needs to be developed and increased. It is especially needed to enable students to become more effective learners in HE and their subsequent careers.

Over the last two decades, there has been a shift in the way some teachers and researchers write about student learning in HE. Instead of characterising it as a simple acquisition process based on teacher transmission, learning is now more commonly conceptualised as a process whereby students actively construct their own knowledge and skills (Barr and Tagg, 1995). Students interact with subject content, transforming and discussing it with others, in order to internalise meaning and make connections with what is already known. Terms like 'student-centred learning', have entered the lexicon of HE and are one reflection of this way of thinking. Even though there is disagreement over the precise definition of student-centred learning, the core assumptions are active engagement in learning and learner responsibility for the management of learning (Lea et al., 2003)

Stoeger (2018) identified seven SRL skills that her research had been addressing. These were as follows:

- **Self-assessment.** This was related to self-efficacy, academic performance, persistence and extrinsic motivation. How competent individuals were in assessing performance well was related to their ability. The less able were poorer in self-assessment.
- **Goal setting.** She found a positive relationship between goal setting and achievement. It directs attention and mobilises effort, increases persistence and motivates strategy development.
- **Strategic planning.** This predicted student achievement and explained 10% of the variance in student results.
- **Strategy implementation.** Rehearsal was the least effective method, whereas organisational and elaborative strategies were more effective. Organisational strategies consisted of restructuring and grouping and elaboration involved in mind maps and topical groups. The learning strategies that related to performance involved how competent students were in using them. They might only have declarative knowledge or miss the procedural knowledge they needed.
- **Strategy monitoring.** This had a positive effect on learning strategies and main ideas.
- **Strategy adaptation.** This was important in maintaining attention to and direction in responding to the needs of the task.
- **Outcome evaluation.** This means assessment criteria need to be shared with and without the support of external assessors such as tutors.

Stoeger and her colleagues found that the gifted are not necessarily better than the average at all of this but the skills can be taught. Ziegler and Stoeger (2005) found that it took 6–7 weeks of daily training to improve students' SRL skills and it took 2–3 full days training to enable staff to understand and promote them. The learning outcomes for their students were significantly improved if the tutors were in the SRL-trained group.

Perspectives in SRL

There is a range of theoretical perspectives from which models and theories of SRL have developed and these according to Zimmerman and Schunk (2002) are as follows: Operant behaviourist, Phenomenological, Social-cognitive, Information Processing, Volitional, Vygotskian and Constructivist. Several of the more relevant perspectives will be identified and mixtures of the influences will become apparent. Phenomenology and the social-cognitive theory warrant the more detailed treatment as they focus on wider human behaviour and try to explain it in SRL.

According to Boud (1986), human function involves reciprocal interaction between behaviours, environmental variables and cognitions and other personal variables. Learners have a range of ways of learning, for example, Enactive Learning involves learning by doing and is embodied in Experiential Learning. In Vicarious Learning, students learn by watching what happens to others and the reinforcements they are given. They may also learn vicariously via secondary sources such as in reading, listening to audio broadcasts or watching TV and film. In Modelling, cognitive and affective behavioural changes can occur as the result of observing symbolic or real models. Implicit Learning, for example, occurs by the learner being in the presence of 'a word-filled world' in the case of language learning. Social skills, cultural beliefs and values can also be absorbed in a similar manner.

During these processes and in educational activities, learners also acquire Declarative Knowledge of facts and events. They acquire Procedural Knowledge – concepts, rules and algorithms and they also acquire Conditional Knowledge – when to apply them. Students arriving at university are thus packed with knowledge in its broadest sense and have many ways of learning that can be engaged that the traditional lecture format does not reach. The students themselves may not realise how they can learn in so many ways if they have been subjected to a rigid didactic information filled curriculum. This can make some of them resistant initially to more exploratory and independent learning techniques. They lose the sense of security if they have to leave their comfort zone. Paying large fees can tend to make them demand to be spoon-fed the course contents because that is the way in which they have been successful in the past. Such an attitude does not help them when they move into employment especially in cognitively and socially challenging environments.

This problem was exemplified by Ken Booth (2015) from the Department of International Politics at Aberystwyth University. The course was titled 'Behind the Headlines' and was designed to introduce new students to the key skills contained in the Dearing Report (1997), including those related to their future careers.

> We attempted to reach beyond the usual litany of news information sources by raising awareness of historiography, writing styles, 'reading', TV and the press. (p. 281)

The topics were introduced in four sessions mixing traditional lectures, debates and video clips and role-playing. The final session was in the format of BBC Question Time. Self-managed student working groups formulated comments and questions in advance to help group members intervene and cope with a large public meeting.

The assessment was a reflective log produced by the group on a self-chosen topic and a 3-hour open book examination. Booth reported that the course had a mixed response from the students. Some liked it and the variety, others preferred traditional modules with one lecturer and less variety, and they resented the 'free riders' in the collective log task. The tutors found the BTH course very labour-intensive in advance and week by week. It also had to be delivered in dual language format – English and Welsh – and so it closed after six semesters. The role-plays and simulations however did continue. What the students also missed was a single tutor to identify with and relate to and a course textbook. However, it is a valuable experiment to learn from. The lessons are the need to overcome student mindsets and learning histories in a more gradual manner; the importance of a course tutor to relate to and an assessment process that is seen as equitable. It is however an imaginative course design that should be developed with iterations that are able to capitalise on the work already done with course texts made from it to back it and perhaps the module could be contrived to occur later in the course when the students are more settled.

In the 'Walking the Talk' experiment, described in Chapter 1, lectures were very much part of the planning process as the effects of no lectures versus lectures in other programmes had been observed. The daily 'Cook's tour' lecture of the area under consideration and the main facts and issues was essential to preserve student confidence, comfort and self-efficacy. There was one tutor giving the lectures until the second semester and three regular tutors assigned to undertake the six seminar groups. The assessments were formative until the final 3-hour written examination. The two part-time tutors were new to the programme methodology and there needed to be weekly meetings to keep them on target so they would know how to manage the seminars and how not to tell the students the 'answers' and give them their own notes!

1. Phenomenology

In this perspective, the self is the primary phenomenon. Phenomenology is the study of the development of human consciousness and self-awareness of perception, cognition and emotion (Mish, 1988). Introspection is the primary source of investigation and data collection and there are three phases of it – intuiting, analysing and describing. It was a popular method of investigation in the early years of psychology until the rise of Behaviourism suppressed it. But in the 21st century it is relevant to the newer person- and learner-centred models of education. It values agency in motivation, cognition and behaviour. The 'authentic' self selects and defines the external influences that are 'best' for self. It is an active transitional model in which individuals change reality and these changes affect the behaviour of individuals in a dynamic developmental process (McCombs, 2002).

Self-perceived identities are a key phenomenological component of a learners' self-system. The following are two examples.

a. Mindsets about intelligence and performance

Mindsets are gaining significance in research about SRL and it has become necessary to consider both student and staff mindsets (Dweck, 2011) in relation to it. Dweck (1999) identified implicit beliefs held by learners about learning. She termed them 'entity and 'incremental' theories. Those who held entity theory believed that intelligence was fixed and that you only had so much of it and nothing much could be done to improve it. They also assumed that education could have little effect on it.

Teachers/tutors who held entity views encouraged performance goals, believed the products of learning were important and in feedback encouraged students to compare their work with the standards of others. This theory seems to be held throughout many education systems and by those administrators and politicians responsible for it.

On the other hand, she did find those who held incremental theory beliefs and they behaved differently. They believed that intelligence or ability was something that could be developed through learning and that it can change and people can become more intelligent. Thus, the more students learn, the more they become capable of it and education can make a significant impact on intelligence. Teachers and tutors holding incremental theory beliefs encouraged learning goals. They focused on the process of learning and used assessment and feedback to encourage improvement based on individual progress.

Freeman's (2010) research showed a distinct difference between the western and the eastern mindsets. The eastern and in particular the Chinese mindset was that it was not high ability – the western perspective – but persistent work effort that produced high achievement. We see this in their Olympic successes in Diving and in world-class Piano and Violin performance.

Changing a student's entity beliefs can be considered to be an important part of their learning experience in HE, but it is not easy and needs systematic and constructive developmental work in each domain. It has been shown that systematic strategy training facilitates expert performance and the same seems to apply to incremental theory. We need to believe that appropriately directed effort will enable us to succeed and achieve higher learning outcomes, then this will assist in the motivation to persist even through failures especially if the feedback is constructive. The ability to learn from failures is a key component.

According to the research of Stoeger (2006, 36), the epistemic beliefs of students in German gymnasia were better predictors of their achievement than quantitative cognitive abilities. The psychological aspect of epistemology deals with individual beliefs about the nature of knowledge and how different beliefs can affect cognition, motivation, emotion and behaviour.

b. Typology issues

Holland (1997), based upon his research, found that most students could be classified into one of six personality types (Realistic, Investigative, Artistic, Social, Enterprising, and Conventional). Definitions of the salient attitudes, interests and competencies of each personality type were developed over four decades by Holland. He found, for example, that Investigative types tend to be critical, intellectual and reserved, to possess strong mathematical and scientific competencies, and to value scholarly and scientific achievements; while Enterprising types tend to be self-confident, pleasure-seeking and sociable, possessing strong public speaking and leadership competencies, and valued political and economic achievements.

Holland claimed that a variety of qualitative and quantitative methods could be used to assess these personality types. One of these was the expression of vocational preferences for, or actual employment in, an occupation that was characteristic of a type. Using methods such as questionnaires, an individual's personality type was defined by his or her preference for or selection of a particular occupation or academic major that had been shown to be representative of the respective personality types.

Whatever developmental and experiential profiles lead to mindsets and types choices, it can prove problematic for academic achievement and learning gain. Dweck demonstrated this limitation for those with entity mindsets. In the case of inferred personality types, the problems are subtle. The most innovative and creative people of the past appear to have been knowledgeable, even expert, in several or many fields. This enabled them to draw analogies and metaphors from different disciplines and fields of knowledge.

While it is possible for students to bury themselves in one narrow field and gain high achievement at university, it may not lead to some form of productive creative outcome in later life. The typology they 'adopt' can narrow their interests and will prevent some from learning from others in different disciplines or parallel fields or even 'reading around the subject'. Schools are expected to offer a broad and balanced curriculum, but universities expect many students to focus on a narrow pathway.

In contrast joint honours, subsidiary subjects and supplementary studies can be intellectually broadening and enriching. It has also been shown, for example, that learning a second language and becoming bilingual can increase cognitive capacity and intellectual functioning. Although not proven yet, it is likely that the same benefits can be obtained from a wider experience in forms and fields of knowledge and make a secure platform for later achievement. Medical research teams with different profiles have reported finding creative developments more likely to be achieved in such teams in interviews on BBC Radio 4, 'The Life Scientific'.

2. Social-cognitive theory

Schunk and Zimmerman (1997) and Zimmerman (1998) identified a three-phase cyclical model of SRL in the development of self-regulated competence. It begins with forethought in which there is goal-setting and social modelling. In the next phase, there is performance control in which there will be social comparisons, attributional feedback, strategy instruction and self-verbalisation. In the final phase – self-reflection – the learner obtains progress feedback and self-evaluation and there are self-monitoring and reward contingencies (Schunck, 2002, 134). The model suggests that academic competence develops from social sources and moves to self-resources through a series of steps. The steps are as follows: Observational – Emulative – Self-controlled – Self-regulated. The social influences that affect the first two steps are models, verbal descriptions and social guidance and feedback. The second two steps are influenced by internal standards self-reinforcement, self-regulatory processes and self-efficacy beliefs.

At the final level, learners are able to adapt their skills and strategies systematically as personal and contextual conditions change. Social factors influence behaviour and personal factors that in turn influence behaviour in the social environment. Not all learners move through the steps in a predicted order. They may observe, internalise and implement the strategy immediately, others may observe and need coaching or extended practice to emulate the strategy.

The social-cognitive models convey optimal forms of goal setting and can increase learners' sense of self-efficacy to undertake difficult learning tasks. They give a verbal index of later performance and use cognitive, affective and social judgments, and so are not just a proxy for behaviour.

The self-organised learner

> Terms like 'independent learner' 'self-paced learning' 'independent study skills' 'autonomous learning' and so on … misrepresent what they are about. Most of them are about successfully submitting to being taught. They are about how to accept instruction at a distance or how to rote learn some of the tricks and short cuts … from those who have been through the system.
>
> (Thomas and Harri-Augstein, 1983, 1)

This statement summarises their findings from a range of learning-to-learn studies not only of undergraduates in training, but also of employees in a range of companies. They were able to identify the characteristics of those who were self-organised learners and those they described as in 'robot mode'. The companies had been concerned about workers' inflexibility and unwillingness to change their traditional ways of working to adopt or adapt to new methods and techniques.

These researchers found that self-organised learners had the inner freedom and skills to identify the resources available to them and define their own goals and purposes and how they would plan and proceed. They were the ones who were best able to make use of the occasional insights and 'tricks' that came their way. Three basic principles were identified that self-organised learners possessed or needed in order to be self-organised. They were concerned with enabling personal learning and the sharing of personal meaning. This places their frame of reference in constructivism, SRL and self-efficacy theory. The three basic principles were:

1 An ability to use oneself as a test bed of personal validity and viability and the construction of internal referents.
2 An ability to monitor the construction and reconstruction of personal meaning over time.
3 Shared meaning as against public knowledge must be truly negotiated.

In order to develop self-organised learners special awareness, training techniques were required and for this they designed a 'Conversational methodology' in which the learner also becomes a personal observer of events, experiences and the metacognitions arising from them. The technique and theory that most influenced them (Thomas and Harri-Augstein, 1983, 5) was George Kelly's (1955) Personal Construct theory and the repertory grids system. This system asks the learner to list some concepts about a topic of interest, then three concepts are selected and in turn the learner says how two are the same and the third is different. They systematically go through this cycle for each concept and the arising metacognitions. Finally, a construct emerges that the learner is using as an organising principle that is available for inspection and discussion. They termed the metacognitive processing going on inside the person's head as a 'Learning conversation' and it was the role of the tutor/trainer help set up these learning conversations.

> – while the occasional lucky learner may unconsciously hit upon some successful strategies for learning, the disabled majority of learners only become more fully functioning as they learn how to reflect upon their own learning activities. In the learning conversation they become able to recognise, represent and control their own processes.
>
> (Thomas and Harri-Augstein, 1983, 11)

Their contribution seems to be central to concerns about SRL. It suggests that the internal representations, metacognitions, inner speech or learning conversations are the core or crucial component in planning, monitoring and regulation, etc. It was a construct adopted in teacher appraisal research to mentor and coach unsuccessful trainees and failing professionals into becoming successful, competent teachers (Montgomery, 2002, 2017b).

Learning conversations

Pauline Perry (1984), the Chief HMI for in-service education, opening a conference on teacher appraisal pointed out that in teaching there was not a shared language that could be used to lead to improving and improved performance. At the same conference, the first pilot experiments in this respect were then shared (Montgomery, 1984). A research grant was later obtained to appoint a research assistant to further the investigations and the 5-Star appraisal outline below explains the conversational technique and results.

In competency-based teacher education, doubts were raised as to whether skills practised and then tested transferred to the real classroom (Elliott and Labett, 1974; McIntyre, 1980; Tuxworth, 1982; Burgess, 1990). The connection between the checklist summative system and competency-based approaches was clear. In this connection, Scriven (1986) proposed four dimensions of merit for summative teacher evaluation, these were as follows:

- Quality of content taught (not the quality of content known).
- Success in imparting or inspiring learning.
- Mastery of professional skills, for example class control.
- Ethics seen in the avoidance of racism, sexism, classism and so on.

He found that 'good' lesson plans were not critically related to these dimensions but they were often in evidence and that poor teachers could not make up in subject knowledge for their inability to control a class. In 1990, McIntyre's summary of the situation was:

> … there are no general theories of teacher competency which could provide a basis for summarising accounts, and it is not plausible to expect any such theories will be developed. (p. 71)

This was wrong then and it is wrong now, but the mindsets are difficult to change.

Teachers engaged in teaching can be taking over 200 decisions per hour and dealing with many complex phenomena. They cannot refer to specifics of research and practice to guide the general thrust of their actions. They need a simple but coherent frame of reference to refer to and on which to base their decisions. This was not the '10 quick tips to teaching' usually offered. It is illustrated in the following '5-Star sampling frame' and each aspect is only the tip of an iceberg. Separate books of research and practice underpinned the constructs (Montgomery, 1989, 1990, 1996, 1998, 2002).

The constructs were **CBG, 3Ms, PCI, TLP** and **AfL** (Montgomery, 1983b, 2002, 2017b). The CBG initials stand for 'CATCH them BEING GOOD' and the students would learn that the task was to increase the positives over desists and reinforce social as well as on-task behaviours. They studied the research, discussed the implications and observed the outcomes on practice visits. They tried it themselves and analysed the outcomes. The supervisor gave feedback and discussed the outcomes in a coaching session.

3Ms stands for Management, Monitoring and Maintenance. Each had a set of techniques, successful teachers were observed to use to gain and maintain classroom control and attention. In the appraisal research, CBG and 3Ms were crucial and about which failing teachers' mindsets needed to be changed. After this, it was necessary to get them to attend to PCI – Positive Cognitive Intervention (challenging and open questioning, problem-based learning and other 'brain engage' strategies).

TLP stands for Tactical Lesson Planning. This put the learners first so that at each phase of a lesson, the learners were given different tasks to do to maintain attention and to switch to if they began to lose motivation, for example listening, think-pair-share, writing, discussing, role-play, plenary, etc.

AfL stands for assessment for learning that was positive supportive and gave cognitive feedback, formative, diagnostic and summative, both verbal and written.

The research project was with control and experimental groups (Montgomery and Hadfield, 1989; Montgomery, 2002). But it was disrupted by Union Action against Government appraisal proposals; however, wider interest in the technique was generated and schools began to refer failing teachers to the project. Thus over time, sufficient numbers were built up to test the technique (Montgomery, 2017b). The College 24-point criterion referenced summative scale was used to judge performance before and after intervention and was also completed by the subjects.

The mean performance of the failing group was 7.23 before intervention and 13.7 afterwards. The satisfactory competence level was 12 points. The difference between these sets of scores was significant at above the 0.01 level of confidence. However, of more importance was the effect, the improved performance was noted by the schools and the disciplinary procedures were cancelled.

There was considerable variation between the original failing scores from a base of 4 of 24 to what appears to be a marginally poor performance at a score of 9–12. The observation records contained qualitative evidence of these changes as well as the teacher performance itself. In relation to the successful teachers, the pre- and post-test results were not significantly different and this is accounted for by the fact that we were looking at some excellent teaching and the College instrument was not sensitive at this end of the scale. In fact, any instrument that has been evaluated would put the 5-Star experienced teacher DP and the other top scorer probationer as excellent on any scale.

However, what they and the others were intrigued by, and many were very experienced teachers, was how their excellence and their success was constructed. They had never had this revealed to them before and were not only pleased with the result of the observation but also delighted with a self-improvement and continuing professional development tool and a learning conversation strategy, which they now knew how to share with others.

Scott MacDonald (1971) had indeed found that the performance of some very good teachers could not be analysed in terms of the effectiveness models and rating scales then in use. This 5-Star System, however, does appear to be able to do so. It is also a system that others have been trained to use, many of them teachers in schools and on the MA programmes. With minor modifications in relation to the 3Ms, it was also used in staff appraisal sessions in HE and FE.

The observers and the teachers in difficulties also recorded their summative assessments of the pre- and post-intervention lessons. After the intervention, it was noted that each teacher was seen to have made a significant amount of improvement. All their performances had improved to a basic satisfactory level. Several years later all were still functioning satisfactorily. The NQT (Newly Qualified Teacher) had passed the probationary year comfortably and the one with the most serious difficulties had become the schools' 'star' teacher. The inter-observer reliability coefficient was very high in the use of the checklist – 98.4% in the 'Before' condition and 95% in the 'After' condition. The failing teachers in each case rated themselves considerably higher than the observers. This is not untypical and their misperceptions and mindsets are frequently contributing factors to their problems.

In one series of evaluations, over 200 experienced teachers on in-service training courses were shown unedited extracts of randomised before and after running records and video extracts of lessons from the research, and were asked to judge in which extract the teacher had been more effective. In 99.5% of cases, they were correctly able to identify which was the more successful lesson and this correlated precisely with the second lesson after the appraisal feedback. The procedure in appraisal training sessions has been to show extracts of the pre- and post-written and video records and with more than 1,000 teachers, the results have proved to be the same. The subjects have been seen clearly to have improved.

Other quantitative studies on the written records showed in a conceptual analysis that the number of positive constructs after intervention far exceeded those in the first record. The teachers and their mentors confirmed the accuracy of these records. It became clear that as in all consultancies, there needs to be a necessary element of coaching if change for the better in performance is to be achieved. The extent to which a consultant has the necessary developmental teaching skills therefore becomes crucial and Edgington (2015) in her research showed how appraisers were so often deficient in these skills and damaged the relationships and motivation of the staff involved.

A deputy head trained to use the **5-Star** method became an appraisal advisor to Local Authority probationers. Their feedback showed they valued being made to feel relaxed and at ease. The classroom observation was felt to be supportive and unobtrusive and there was a general feeling that the experience was positive and helpful. They welcomed the detailed observation and time given to offering specific supportive feedback. Very few positive statements were made about the majority of their inspectorial appraisals. Similar results were obtained when the MA students in their appraisal reports and reflections compared the system with the Ofsted inspections and school appraisal systems in their schools.

What was concluded was that the five variables lodged themselves in the appraisee's heads and they could use them as a personal learning conversation and metacognitive checklist about their own lessons and had a shared language to discuss issues with colleagues. They had names for the key components of success and had seen it work and knew there was a literature to refer to and follow up if they wished. In some schools, they would put messages on the inside of the staffroom door such as 'CBG Darren today, please'!

3. The Vygostskian view and SRL

Lev Vygotsky (1978) argued that self-directed speech could guide and improve performance in children and adults. It can be internalised 'inner speech' and used as a conscious strategy. He found it was especially used when tasks became difficult and may at that point even be externalised or actually voiced. High-functioning SRLs used it twice as much as low achieving SRLs in difficult problem-solving tasks (Berk and Winsler, 1995).

Vygotsky also coined the term Zone of Proximal Development (ZPD). This referred to

> The distance between the actual developmental level as determined by independent problem solving and the level of potential development as determined through problem-solving under adult guidance, or in collaboration with more capable peers.
>
> (Vygotsky, 1978, 86)

When students were in the ZPD, providing the appropriate help could enable them to achieve the goal that they could not readily attain by their own efforts.

Scaffolding. This help would involve scaffolding. It meant providing hints or clues, modelling a skill, adapting the material or activity. It also involved social interaction, assessing the learner's current knowledge and experience, relating the content to what the student already knows and understands and can do and breaking the task into smaller steps or sequences.

Metacognitions. It is the learning conversations, the inner speech and the scaffolds that can form the substance of metacognitions.

Expert performance and high ability

Universities widely accept the students from the schools and colleges who have achieved the highest scores in tests and examinations relevant to the field of study that is on offer. The most prestigious universities attract and give offers to those applicants with the highest achievements or predicted performances although recently more consideration is being given for wider access. This would include more students from disadvantaging backgrounds and from schools with poorer standards of results.

By recruiting the students with the best school results, it is an underlying assumption that they are the most gifted learners and are likely to achieve most during and after university life. They probably have not only a supportive background but are also perceived to have some innate potential or high intelligence (often measured with an IQ test) that gives them advantages over other candidates. They are judged suitable based on the learning outcomes they have achieved at school or other programmes in relevant areas of study and recommendations and reports from their former teachers or coaches. It is expected that they are the most likely to go on to become experts and that some will even achieve eminence and international recognition and prizes in the chosen domain.

But is all this true? Does innate high ability lead to expert performance and even Nobel prizes? The research shows something very different. The children with the highest abilities do not necessarily grow up to become eminent (Terman, 1954; Freeman, 2001; McCoach et al., 2017). Lykken (1998) and Simonton (1997) argued that exceptional performance was not predictable from similarity with other family members and thus cannot be accounted for by simple independent genes. The research has shown that expert performance is no direct consequence of the same genetic endowment and environment. When identical twins engaged in extended practice in the same domain, the twins' performance was not always the same – in some cases it differed significantly (Ericsson, 2015).

According to Bloom (1985), the international-level performers did not show any evidence that would meet the criteria for clearly superior performance before the start of training. Their superior performance emerged as the result of training. More generally, research is increasingly questioning claims that some highly talented individuals can attain high levels of performance in a domain without concentration and deliberate practice. Even the well-known fact that allegedly more 'talented' children improve faster in the beginning of their musical development appears to be in large part due to the fact that these children spend more time in practice each week (Sloboda et al., 1996), rather than naturally learning faster per unit of time. The age at which experts typically reach the peak performance of their careers is the mid-to-late 20s for many vigorous sports, and a decade later, in the 30s and 40s, for the arts and sciences and games such as chess and music (Charness et al., 2005).

The critical role of deliberate practice in attaining expert performance was first proposed by Ericsson et al. (1993). They reported a study of three groups of expert musicians who differed in level of attained music performance and studied how these musicians spent their daily lives by interviewing them and having them keep detailed diaries for a week. They found that by the age of 20, the most accomplished musicians had spent over 10,000 hours of practice. It was 2,500 and 5,000 hours more than two less accomplished groups of expert musicians and 8,000 hours more than amateur pianists of the same age (Krampe & Ericsson, 1996).

The same type of solitary deliberate practice was closely correlated with the attainment of expert and elite performance in a wide range of domains. Those considered 'talented' trained and practiced extensively, and this practice was necessary for the development of performance. Evidence showed that engagement in domain-related activities is required for high levels of performance and that even individuals who might be the most 'talented' needed around 10 years of intense involvement before they reached a level where they could consistently win at open adult competitions in sports, sciences and the arts (Simon and Chase, 1973; Ericsson et al., 1993). Effortful training was required for all individuals, even those who might have gifts and the evidence indicated that the most successful individuals engaged in the most deliberate practice despite the popular idea that some individuals enter a domain and rapidly reach high levels of performance with little effort.

However, deliberate practice is a very special form of activity that differs from mere experience and mindless drill. Unlike playful engagement with peers, deliberate practice is not inherently enjoyable. It also differs from the successful performance in front of an audience, which is rewarded with applause, acclaim and receiving prizes. Unlike execution of already acquired skills, solitary practice is not immediately rewarded with monetary prizes or social acclaim. Deliberate practice does not involve a mere execution or repetition of already attained skills, but repeated attempts to reach beyond one's current level that is associated with frequent failures. Aspiring performers therefore concentrate on improving specific aspects by engaging in practice activities designed to change and refine particular mediating mechanisms, requiring problem-solving and successive refinement with feedback (Ericsson, 2015).

Even in cases of famous legends, such as chess prodigies like Bobby Fischer, the time required to reach grandmaster strength was still around 9 years, and it took another two decades before Fischer played for the world championship. Charness et al. (2005) found that the amount of solitary chess study was the best predictor of performance during chess tournaments, and when this factor was statistically controlled, there was only a very small benefit from the number of games played in chess tournaments.

Similar findings of the unique effectiveness of deliberate solitary practice were reported by Duffy et al. (2004) for dart throwing, and a study by Ward et al. (2004) demonstrated that elite-level youth soccer players spent less time in playful activities than less-skilled control participants and accrued more time spent engaged in deliberate practice. This was typical of the youthful behaviour of David Beckham.

The National Commission on Excellence in Education (1983) in the US reported that up to half of all gifted students, the top 3–5%, were not performing up to their expected abilities. As a result, there were proposals for a wealth of strategies similar to those offered to underachieving non-gifted students to 'rehabilitate' these gifted students (Gallagher, 1991; Schultz, 2002). But Ma (2005) found that early acceleration in mathematics benefited regular students even more than gifted and honours students and concluded that all students should receive challenges and feedback appropriate to their own current level of performance. Remedial interventions and acceleration programmes designed for gifted students should be offered to all students.

The single most important difference between the amateurs and elite performers is that the future elite performers seek out teachers and coaches and engage in supervised training, whereas the amateurs rarely engage in similar types of practice. Ericsson (2003) was unable to find any reproducible evidence that would limit the ability of motivated and healthy adults to achieve exceptional levels of memory performance given access to instruction and supportive training environments. For example, ordinary individuals with the standard working memory capacity of 7 units plus or minus 2 (Miller, 1956) were capable of achieving 80 units after systematic strategy training and there seemed no limit on their capacities. They were also able to transfer the memories to long-term storage. However, it all took a considerable amount of time and effort. A review by Wilding and Valentine (2006, 546) concluded that the most striking examples of superior memory were strategy dependent.

Larson and Verma (1999) found evidence that studying was viewed as challenging with low intrinsic motivation across cultures in spite of the differences in the duration of engagement. The differences in studying were large – Paik et al. (2002) estimated that Asian students spend almost twice as much time on practice-related activities during their first 18 years of life. They attend additional classes after school and engaged in individual study making their day's work 17 hours long.

Research in the UK showed that the achievement gap at 16 is 18 months behind the rest of the class if students are disadvantaged. Westminster students were 4 months behind and in Blackpool, Portsmouth and Peterborough, they were almost 2 years behind whereas Chinese students were 2 years ahead (Education Policy Institute, 2019). Recent Ofsted reports have found that students from coastal area towns in England have poorer standards of achievement than the national average; these also tend to be economically poorer areas. While quality of teaching and learning may be problematic in these areas, lower student time on task is also likely to be a contributing factor because of a lack of tradition and knowledge about study time advantages.

Research by Cullen et al. (2018, 57) found fear of failure, low aspirations and lack of self-confidence significant among disadvantaged groups. Schools have a big responsibility for changing these attitudes and must clearly change their teaching and learning approaches and give more appropriate and supportive feedback. But universities also need to be prepared to find and accommodate these students. For example, the students need to be shown early in their introductory studies how they can succeed. They need to have their self-efficacy promoted and experience success as the Open University programmes showed can be done. Their mindsets have to be changed.

Overall, the general finding from expertise and novice versus expert performance is that IQ does not predict higher levels of achievement among participants. For virtually all domains evidence shows that individuals with average or even below average IQ scores can achieve extremely high levels of performance. Generally, Gardner's (1993) multiple intelligence and other conceptions of intelligence lack explanatory power given that,

> … neither the multiplication of intelligence nor its enhancement through additional psychological variables was able to procure more than a partial clarification of what gifts or talents 'really' were and what role they played in the emergence of achievement excellence.
>
> (Ziegler, 2005, 412)

Ericsson (2015) however considered that strategic approaches to teaching and learning and deliberate practice could enable the development of expert performance in the widest range of students. It involved problem-solving, iterative refinement and at higher levels of skill, the development of internal representations for planning, evaluating and monitoring mental representations – the metacognitive learning conversations and strategy use. Sustained deliberate practice throughout development needed to be motivated by the outcomes of continued practice such as the improvement of different aspects of performance.

'How do people get good at stuff?' was a question posed by Bailey (2003). He concluded that there is a view that high ability is the result of effort, but there are particular environmental factors such as having a supportive middle-class family as well as being motivated and fit that can make the difference as well of course as having the lucky genes! He suggested that there are three pillars of excellence needed to ensure success.

1 **Deliberate practice.** This is more than simply just practising. Everyone who wants to excel in a particular field needs to receive **feedback** on their efforts – a coach or teacher suggesting ways to improve and consolidate their practice. It needs to be in the right **context**. Deliberate practice requires **variation** and **observation** and needs to be done with **mindfulness** – in other words paying very close attention, being purposefully aware of what and why you are practising.
2 **Having the right mindset.** A person with a fixed mindset sees criticism as negative, while someone with a growth mindset values criticism and sees it as a positive way to help improvement.
3 **Real learning.** It is a form of problem-solving. It is not about learning out of context. Real learning begins when a problem is identified, then tentative solutions (guesses) are made, next error elimination (testing) occurs and finally a new problem emerges. This pattern of real learning will continue for the rest of our lives.

Conclusion

SRL is once again becoming an important topic for research and in the literature on learning and futures scenarios in education at all levels. In summary, it appears to be that it is the self-regulation of the learner with strong motivation, a persistent personality and self-efficacy that leads to high achievement and potential eminence. This learner may or may not have a very high IQ.

Three methods of achieving learning gain were discussed – student time on task, positive supportive feedback and strategy training. In this chapter, these conclusions have been reinforced and in addition it has been argued that particular metacognitions in the form of inner speech or 'learning conversations' and the strategies required to set them up underpin the learning gain. These are crucial components that mediate the learning gain.

Most successful approaches to improving learning in a permanent way use reflection or metacognition (thinking about our thinking) to support them. Barriers to learning gain were also outlined and these are inappropriate mindsets, narrow typologies and lack of motivation and student independent time on task.

A concept analysis of SDL/SRL by Grandinetti (2015) identified three factors as the primary antecedents. These were motivation to learn, learner independence and intellectual curiosity. The problem that needs to be addressed is how these three antecedents can be promoted when a learner arrives at university without them or without a strong study capacity. The next chapter will therefore pursue the topic of motivation and shows ways in which it may be understood and promoted before and during learning. It discusses the nature of higher-order executive function skills and motivation, and will show how particular forms of assessment can support them.

Chapter 4

Executive function skills

Motivation and assessment

Introduction

The executive functions (EFs) are also known as higher-order cognitive skills (Gagné, 1973) and it is useful to consider them as targets for development and training at all age levels from pre-school onwards. There are four areas that invite intervention based on the early research of Brown et al. (1983), these are:

1 **Self-management.** This is the ability or lack of it to manage time, plan and prepare for deadlines and easily engage in other goal-directed behaviours.
2 **Self-Organisation and Problem Solving.** The ability to organise thoughts, actions and writing as well as thinking quickly to solve problems.
3 **Self-motivation.** The intrinsic motivation to work and complete projects, without it we may be called 'lazy' and need supervision or bribery to do tasks.
4 **Self-regulation.** Of emotions and impulsiveness, self-control.

The distinction made by Gagné (1973) between intellectual and cognitive skills is critical to the design and development process for education programmes. The cognitive skills he described are the higher-order EF skills and his analysis is summarised as follows:

Intellectual skills. These are about knowing 'that' and knowing 'how'. They include converting printed words into meaning, fractions into decimals, knowing about classes, groups and categories, laws of mechanics and genetics, forming sentences and pictures. They enable us to deal with the world 'out there'. Mostly these are taught in schools and universities within subject areas and also make up items on IQ tests.

Cognitive skills. These are internally organised capabilities that we make use of in guiding our attention, learning, thinking and remembering. They are the **executive control processes** that activate and direct other learning processes. We use them when we think about our learning, plan a course of action and evaluate learning outcomes. These are seldom explicitly taught in schools or universities or given value there. They form the basis of wisdom and are not usually tested except in real life situations. It means that developing strategic approaches and problem-based learning in higher education (HE) programmes can contribute to the development of these EF skills.

Optimal cognitive and intellectual challenge in the HE programmes must introduce new information, concepts and skills for students to learn but in the process teach them how to develop the EF skills and invoke their curiosity and interest. The methods need to be more carefully constructed so that they induce strategic approaches and strategy learning to carry forward to new tasks. It cannot be assumed that students will develop strategic approaches implicitly although some may do so. It helps if they can be made explicit as in the 5-Star plan outlined in Chapter 3. The tasks need to enable students to apply what they have learned in some simulated or real-life active settings. The general approach is to create 'engage brain' programmes with the techniques based on cognitive process methodology. Examples of this methodology are set out in Chapters 6 and 7.

Following the various initiatives such as those involved in student centred learning (OECD, 1972), lifelong learning (Dearing, 1997), transferable and flexible learning skills (CBI, 2001) educators are widely aware of the importance of teaching for self-regulation as well as immersing students in challenging content and skills in their fields of knowledge. The danger is that delivery by VLE (Virtual Learning Environments) and internet Blending of programmes may cause us to take our eyes off the real goal that is constructivist development and real learning and revert only to content and skills memorising.

The executive function continuum

At one extreme, demonstrating very poor EFs and a disordered system Barkley (1998) gave the example of ADHD – Attention Deficit Hyperactivity Disorder. He identified the central role of three factors in ADHD these were genetic, attentional and executive dysfunctions. There were also co-morbidities to consider such as learning disorders, and environments such as unstructured settings and parenting styles that could exacerbate the problems.

Studies suggest that the incidence of ADHD in children has risen from 3% to 5% and in adults, it is 2.5%. The incidence in first-year undergraduates is estimated to be 5%. The data on adults is difficult to collect because those with definite clinical symptoms tend to under-report and those with less problematic conditions tend to over-report. The nature of the condition in adults is less clear than in children because there are fewer opportunities to collect the observations of parents, teachers and siblings and self-report has to be relied upon (Bender and Privitera, 2016). It can be suggested that students are on a continuum of EF skills with those with ADHD, learning difficulties and disadvantage at the lower ranges across all the four SRL categories of skill. A constructivist and cognitive approach to their needs such as training in skills for self-regulated learning has been shown to be an effective way of helping them (Montgomery, 2015).

When students apply to join HE programmes their level of EF skills are not assessed but are relevant to their potential to dropout or the potential to achieve the award. The variability in the nature of levels of EF skills arises from an ecosystemic heritage, genetic, developmental, academic and social. These result in the current competencies and arise from external and internal motivational factors that have driven them.

When thinking about designing programmes for learning it would seem that most HE students will have acquired some skills in self-control, self-management and organisation and a pattern of motivations. The key construct is self-motivation. It is likely to be difficult to maintain even in face-to-face courses where many other social and living experiences compete. In distance programmes it is even more problematic without fellow students and a tutor on hand for support especially if things become difficult, hence the special consideration given to Distance Learning in Chapter 5.

A time, a place and a plan

There are a number of top tips given in management courses for time management and planning. The place is usually the workstation but in SRL, the place may well be home or the transport system and moveable timing. It is however a good idea to encourage new students to build habits of place and time and develop a schedule for completing assignments. The most naïve may imagine that just by turning up to lectures and being at the university immersed in academia will confer knowledge upon then.

The tips suggest they begin with the purchase of an open calendar on which the key assignments and dates can be written and hung in the study area. At home or student flat a particular spot needs to be selected where all the necessary materials, books, papers, laptop, printer and study chair can be set up and ready for use at any time but not available to anyone else. Other comfort spots may also be chosen where necessary for study reading. Developing the habit of study in a specific location especially when writing an assignment is an important stabilising factor.

Timing is more difficult to control in the self-directed study system and it is a good idea for students to map their usual activities over a typical week or two to find out where there are 'dead times' and opportunities to move activities to set aside times for study. The map can be set out over 7 days as hourly blocks of time from 6.00 a.m. to 10.00 p.m. In the spaces, a note can be made to show what was going on. 'Early birds' might set aside a time from 6.00 a.m. to 7.00 a.m. for a regular programme of study. 'Night owls' might choose an early evening time before going out on a spree. The important factor is for students to learn to study 'little and often' rather than promise themselves to do a big catch up at the weekends or on a free afternoon. Procrastination is the big danger to achievement.

The next task is for them to study the course handbook to find out what elements are crucial and necessary to the typical student and make a list of the 6–10 most important things to know and remember. They need to keep these near at hand for easy reference not enclosed inside the computer. A hard copy of the summary curriculum/syllabus and key objectives can be added to this list. These will keep their minds on the core tasks and objectives.

After the settling down time a plan needs to be made to find a time each day to 'read for the degree'. This means reading the course study guide and materials, reading the course text(s), reading relevant research papers and reading around the subject plus making some notes and recording references to show where the subject may be found again when writing up any assignment. One of the daily study periods may be the journey on the bus or train. Another may be to arrive early at work or college and spend the half an hour on personal study. Leaving later after a study hour can be an advantage on public transport.

The task most students find difficult is writing the summative assignment. This is so often because they delay starting until they feel they know what is needed and what it is all about. Others accumulate copious notes and thus also defer actually starting the task. Instead the strategy should be to begin the assignment several weeks before the deadline, read the task many times and list all the items it contains.

It is then advisable for them to plan to write 250–500 words about the topic on a regular basis throughout the following week without consulting any notes but from what is left inside the head after any lecture or readings. After several sessions, about 1,000 words will have been built up and then it is important to leave the topic for a few days and then do a first proof reading edit after checking the task assignment again. This enables the mind to bring a fresh perspective to what is written and find the flaws and missing elements and rejig the whole thing. The next task is to go back to the notes and original sources and fill in some of the missing pieces. There is thus always something to work on and correct.

The cycle of writing, rewriting, editing and redrafting can go on until a satisfactory response has been produced or until the time runs out. At all events, there will be something cogent to hand in for assessment. The novitiate and even the experienced writer need to go through several such cycles, it is rare to expect to produce an A class answer in one go. Unfortunately, many students do not learn this in their secondary education and accounts in part for the excellence gap.

Motivation

Motivation is seen to arise from internal factors or needs within the individual that determine actions in some way or from external factors or pressures. At the most basic response level we see it as flight or fight responses but there appears to be a hierarchy of needs that determine our motivational responses according to Maslow (1987). These range from the basic need to satisfy hunger and thirst, to the need for safety and belonging, the need for stimulation and self-esteem and at the top of this hierarchy we become a self-actualised learner although not all of us are thought to achieve this higher status.

In education we find that students lose autonomy and self-regulation in response to extrinsic motivation and that intrinsic motivation is fostered by a consistent, positive, supportive climate and positive constructive feedback (Ryan and Deci, 2000). It is destroyed under pressure to reach and maintain standards in the high stakes summative testing regimes typical in education at present. Thus we require one sort of creative, supportive and therapeutic educational regime but can too easily set up the opposite, a coercive one (Mongon and Hart, 1989) that will increase the excellence gap.

What causes intrinsic motivation after our basic needs for sustenance, safety and belonging are satisfied? It seems that this is the need for social contact and self-esteem and the stimulation and satisfaction of curiosity but what elicits these? Kelly (1955) showed that from birth we act as scientific explorers 'man the scientist' and suggests as Leites (1971) did that this exploratory capacity is innate and could be found in all of us. What appears to happen however is that our upbringing and schooling can cause this natural exploratory behaviour to be suppressed and may even train it out of us. It is therefore essential that university programmes are designed to retrieve this position not endorse it. In this respect, it can often be the administrative procedures and assessment system that can be repressive.

The theory of cognitive dissonance by Festinger (1957) offers an explanation of the mechanism underlying intrinsic motivation. He suggested that when we observe a mismatch between what we see, hear or experience and what we expect or know then it makes us curious to investigate or resolve the cognitive conflict or dissonance we feel. It follows from this that if education offers cognitive challenge, questions and sets learning experiences, as problems to resolve then intrinsic motivation in students will be increased. Festinger identified three factors that reduced cognitive dissonance and these were (i) a change or a move in attitudes or beliefs; (ii) new information is acquired that outweighs the dissonance and (iii) a reduction in the importance of the attitudes or beliefs that resolves the dissonance.

A number of theories and models have been put forward to explain intrinsic motivation's origins, aside from this underlying mechanism by Festinger. Instead, they tend to regard the motivation as arising from particular contexts or as a result of experience that then structure or guide it. These additional directive mechanisms are competence motivation, self-efficacy theory, attribution theory, and perceptions of self-control, metacognitive development, and strategy use.

In simple terms motivation means to put in motion to do something. Over several decades, Robert Ryan and Ed Deci have been researching and theorising on human motivation. They developed the Self-Determination Theory (SDT) in 1985 in which they distinguished between different levels of motivation beyond the two traditional motives, intrinsic and extrinsic drives to action of the early Behaviourists such as Hull (1943) and Skinner (1953). A later concept analysis of self-directed learning (SDL) by Grandinetti (2015) identified motivation to learn, learner independence and intellectual curiosity as the primary antecedents of this phenomenon.

Some motives students give to engage in further study:

- To obtain a 'ticket'.
- To gain further academic knowledge and skills.
- To gain professional skills.
- To research an area of interest
- For personal interest and stimulus.
- For acclaim.
- For job prospects.

As can be seen they can have mixed motives both intrinsic and extrinsic for following advanced study.

Intrinsic motivation is when we are driven to do something because it is enjoyable or inherently interesting or perceived as necessary. Extrinsic motivation is where we do something because of externally determined pressures such as threats, rewards or directives. The suggestion is that we have a basic need for feelings of competence. Rewards, optimal challenge, communications and supportive feedback that increase feelings of competence increase intrinsic motivation. However, Deci and Ryan (1985) found that the increase in intrinsic motivation was only achieved if the behaviour is perceived as self-determined by the learner. Thus competence and self-efficacy were essential to its development. This means that HE programmes must provide those optimal challenge experiences, give expectance-promoting feedback and freedom from demeaning evaluations and this will lead to feelings of competence. At the same time, experiences must provide for student autonomy. In attributional terms, autonomy is an internal perceived locus of control and causality.

The programmes therefore need to be interesting, provoke curiosity, offer intellectual challenge but be supportive and give constructive feedback. To meet the need for autonomy there will need to be the element of choice and opportunities for learner decision-making especially in the more significant tasks.

Intrinsic motivation is fostered by a consistent, positive, supportive climate and positive constructive feedback and is destroyed under pressure to reach and maintain standards. Students lose autonomy and self-regulation in response to extrinsic motivation (Ryan and Deci, 2000, 6). They confirmed that virtually every type of expected tangible reward made contingent on task performance does, in fact, undermine intrinsic motivation.

Extrinsic motivators are tangible rewards such as prizes, payments and promotions but so are threats, deadlines, directives, negative feedback and competition pressures. They diminish intrinsic motivation because people experience them as controllers of their behaviour. On the other hand, choice and the opportunity for self-direction appear to enhance intrinsic motivation, as they afford a greater sense of autonomy.

The significance of autonomy versus control for the maintenance of intrinsic motivation has been observed in studies of classroom learning. For example, autonomy-supportive in contrast to controlling teachers increased their students' greater intrinsic motivation, curiosity and the desire for challenge. Students who were overly controlled not only lost initiative but also learned less well, especially when learning was complex or required conceptual, creative work. Similarly, studies showed students of parents who were more autonomy supportive were more mastery orientated and more likely to spontaneously explore and extend themselves than those of parents who were more controlling (Grolnick et al., 1997).

Intrinsic motivation only occurs for activities that hold intrinsic interest for an individual. These are those that have the appeal of novelty, challenge, or aesthetic value for that individual. In schools, for example, it appeared that intrinsic motivation became weaker with each advancing grade (Ryan and Deci, 2000) and this can be observed in the UK as pupils move through primary and then secondary schools and education becomes increasingly formal and directive. The introduction of league tables and publication of school SATs and GCSE results have increased extrinsic pressures and induced anxiety in students, parents and teachers alike. The workforce and HE student that 18 years of such directive parenting and schooling can produce will not be self-regulated and self-motivated. This means the HE programmes must cater for this by weaning them from directive to more autonomous learning approaches. The weaning process can provide the necessary comfort and security while building their self-efficacy.

Levels of extrinsic motivation

Extrinsic motivation applies whenever an activity is done in order to attain some separable outcome. As part of SDT, Ryan and Deci defined four increasing levels of extrinsic motivation before arriving at intrinsic motivation. These are significant for the design of HE programmes and examples of their four levels follow:

1 **Amotivation.** This results from not valuing an activity, not feeling competent to do it, or not believing it will yield a desired outcome. This is typical of students from difficult and disadvantaging homes, environments and schools, raised in adversity. It may also arise because of persistent learning failures and learning difficulties that have not been addressed or from coercive schooling and classroom regimes that are punitive and negative rather than supportive of learners.

2 **Introjection.** This represents regulation by contingent self-esteem. A typical form of introjection is ego involvement. Here the student performs a task in order to enhance or maintain self-esteem and feelings of self-worth. Although the regulation is internal to the person these introjected behaviours are not experienced as fully part of the self and the perceived locus of control is external. Introjected regulation was positively related to expending effort, but was also related to more anxiety and to poorer coping with failures.

3 **Identification.** This is regulation through identification. Here, the student identifies with the personal importance of a behaviour and has thus accepted its regulation as his or her own. When we memorise tables and spelling lists because we see them as relevant to money exchange, or reading and writing and regard them as useful life skills, then we have identified with the value of those learning activities. In university, the programmes need to have per-ceived relevance or their relevance needs to be carefully explained. Identified regulation was associated with greater enjoyment of school and college and more positive coping styles.

4 **Integrated regulation.** The most autonomous form of extrinsic motivation is integrated regulation. Integration occurs when identified regulations have fully assimilated to the self the different types of extrinsic motivation.

Using these four definitions of extrinsic motivation they showed that the more students were externally regulated the less they showed interest, value or effort, and the more they indicated a tendency to blame others, such as the teacher or tutor, for negative outcomes. Intrinsic motivation was correlated with inter-est, enjoyment, felt competence and positive coping. Other researchers extended these findings showing that more autonomous extrinsic motivation is associated with greater engagement and better performance. There was also less dropping out, higher-quality learning and greater psychological well-being.

In classrooms, students who felt respected and cared for by the tutor were more willing to accept the proffered classroom values. In support of this, Ryan et al. (1994) found that relatedness to teachers (and parents) was associated with greater internalisation of institutional rules and behaviours. In disadvantaged areas it can be seen how important it becomes to have respectful and caring teachers willing to 'go the extra mile' for their students. They need the best teachers. These same values can be applied to students in HE – an autocratic, overbearing tutor, who is rules orientated and lacking in empathy can increase feelings of student alien-ation and anomie and cause dropout. Equally the perception of favouritism to some and hostility to others will reduce motivation in the wider group.

If we adopt as our own an extrinsic goal we have to feel efficacious with respect to it. Students will be more likely to adopt and internalise a goal if they understand it and have the relevant skills to succeed at it. Supports for competence such as offering optimal challenges and effectance-relevant feedback facilitate internal-isation. Deci et al. (1994) experimentally demonstrated that providing a mean-ingful rationale for an uninteresting behaviour, along with supports for autonomy and relatedness, promoted internalisation and integration. The facilitation of more self-determined learning required conditions that allowed satisfaction of three basic human needs—the innate needs to feel connected, effective, and feel personal agency when exposed to new ideas or in the exercise of new skills.

A mixture of both extrinsic and intrinsic motives can be seen in the reasons why students choose to join the HE programmes and similarly a mixture of reasons related to the theories of motivation also apply. For example to obtain a 'ticket' or for acclaim the underlying purpose may be to gain self-esteem, whereas to gain further academic knowledge and professional skills will be related to competence motives and self-efficacy. If the motive is to improve job prospects then self-efficacy and competence are also involved. All these are related to extrinsic motivations. Whereas wishing to research an area for personal interest, stimulus and curiosity is intrinsic motivation and linked with autonomy and metacognitive theory.

Theories that seek to explain intrinsic motivation

Competence theory

This theory by White (1959) illustrates an effectance model that is directed, selective and persistent that satisfies an intrinsic need to deal with the environment. Successful efforts lead to feelings of efficacy that maintain continuing interest. It brings the environment under control and the individuals become more self-determining. In education, this can be domain specific competence. General feelings of self-worth are primarily based on discrepancies between domain-specific competence evaluations and attitudes about the importance of success in particular domains. This causes them to seek out or avoid particular learning activities.

Self-efficacy theory

Self-efficacy was defined by Bandura (1986) and also emphasises competence (self-efficacy) and perceived self-control (personal agency) in motivation and performance. Self efficacy judgments according to Bandura come from (1) performing the task successfully, (2) watching others perform successfully (vicarious learning), (3) being able to assess one's own stress level, fatigue, or other arousal and (4) being able to adopt standards against which to evaluate performance – self-regulation.

The fulfilment of the standards results in feelings of satisfaction that lead to interest, feelings of self-efficacy and motivation. Important contextual influences on efficacy judgments include specific attributional feedback strategies, goal-setting, social comparison strategies and reward contingencies. This shows how internal standards can be affected by extrinsic factors and be influenced by training (Zimmerman, 1990).

Attribution

In this theory, Weine (1980) assumes the motivation of human behaviour as the search for the underlying causes of failure. The sorts of explanations that people give for their failures are – inability, bad luck, lack of effort and task difficulty. Higher performance and motivation are said to be due to regarding success as personally caused, likely to recur and under one's control. A contrary view was proposed by Ames (1987) that students who engage in self-regulation and are strategy-based are mastery orientated and attribute failure to the variable and controllable factors such as lack of effort or inappropriate strategies used. A related concept is locus of control in which some learners project blame for failure outwards on others and some, more often women blame themselves for failures.

The conclusions derived from attribution theory are that programmes for achievement change need not only to address student performance attributions but also help them view life experiences as under control and result from their efforts. Failure can also be viewed constructively and treated as problems, analysed and strategies developed for change in actions and perceptions. Such strategies can help overcome learned helplessness.

All three theories thus far can be seen to be intimately related to and arise from the competency/effectance theory and dissonance analysis based on success, perceived success and control and the analysis of failure.

The self-control theory

According to Hansford and Hattie (1982), it had been shown that learners' perceptions of themselves and their perceptions of control over learning had a consistent relationship with educational achievement. This led them to use deep learning strategies focusing on the content as a whole and the interrelationships between the parts so they actively think about the structure of the information.

The link between self-control in motivating learning is thus clearly linked to feelings of self-efficacy and shows another dimension to feelings of competence. The component in 'treatments' to induce intrinsic motivation and conceptual learning are thus those that increase perceptions of control and active orientations to learning. This component appears to be a metacognitive training one in which students are directly trained in for example planning, continuous self-monitoring and self-evaluation (Thomas and Harri-Augstein, 1983; Benware and Deci, 1984; Wang and Lindvall, 1984).

Metacognition and self-regulated learning processes

This theory by Wang and Lindvall (1984) suggests that metacognitive skills contribute to the development of self-regulation and self-management skills as well as the sense of personal agency and self-monitoring (Baird and White, 1984). Wang and Lindvall (1984) found that these metacognitive skills contributed not only to improved acquisition but also to improved generalisation and transfer of knowledge and skills. Borkowski's (1996) process-oriented model of metacognition was developed from this perspective.

Strategy use and behaviour

Paris and Gross (1983) showed that motivational influences on strategy use included learners' values, beliefs and attitudes. These form the basis for meaningful goals and interests and energise strategic behaviour and the allocation of time and effort. Thus attributions, expectancies and values are used to explain the perseverance and effort put into learning tasks. It is therefore important that interventions should include not only cognitive strategies, but help for the learner to achieve a sense of self-control and how to make learning goals more personally relevant, acquire self-management skills and achieve a balance between views of success and failure. Boekaerts' (1999) model of adaptable learning is linked to this perspective.

In summary these theories of intrinsic motivation and the research that underpins them clearly indicate that if we are to improve the achievement of students both the affective and cognitive components of any training must be included. The theories all relate to the range of factors that induce cognitive dissonance and the ways in which it may be resolved. As can be observed, a considerable amount of theory and research emerged in the 1980s mainly in North America and it forms the platform for current research and practice in its new cycle.

Hard data on SRL?

There is little hard data that can be captured on SRL strategies, learners have to make them explicit by introspection, completing self-perception questionnaires, student surveys and interviews or the inputs and outcomes have to be observed and measured. This is because much of the processing is internalised and metacognitive. There is however evidence that SRL techniques can be learned and applied. For example, in the 108-hour BEd teacher education programme exemplified in Chapter 1, using problem-based and reflective study skills techniques in learner managed learning settings, the rates of 'firsts' in a 3-hour examination increased from 1–2% to 23.61%.

Directed Activities Related to Texts and Cognitive Process methods of teaching and learning encouraged the metacognition or thinking about thinking. This is known to increase intellectual abilities (Flavell, 1979; Shayer and Adey, 2002) and learning outcomes but again the internal processing is not observable. Shayer and Adey's approach showed that students could learn to become self-regulated learners in specific learning and teaching environments. Part of the programme was that after theory and practical work a whole session would be spent fortnightly in discussing and reflecting upon what had been learned and what were the metacognitive processes involved. Although applied in science where it raised or 'accelerated' learning outcomes they found it had also transferred to other subjects such as higher GCSE attainments in English and maths.

Pintrich (2000) provided a general framework for SRL derived from Brown et al. (1983). Its four stages were as follows:

1 **Forethought, planning and activation.** It includes identifying goals, accepting determined goals, planning time and space, developing perceptions about the tasks, and identifying the motivational effects.
2 **Monitoring.** This includes awareness of the effects of one's own motivation, one's cognition and consciousness of the situation, an awareness of one's time and the need for help, as well as the awareness of the task and the task-related issues.

3 **Control.** When the individual has chosen and implemented some learning strategies, further strategies are selected and applied. Behaviours are exhibited and observed along with an increase or decrease in effort while the procedures are re-evaluated and changes may be made in the assigned mission.

4 **Reaction and reflection.** This is the stage when individuals make cognitive judgments and evaluations. These can include showing affective reactions, persistence, giving up, choice making and evaluating content. It is the time when they re-evaluate the task and assess whether there is a difference between the target and the performance.

Pintrich's model was used by Cetin (2017) in an SRL study in Turkey. Teacher education candidates' self-regulated learning perceptions were examined by questionnaire to understand any differences between a group that used Pintrich's SRL model-based learning activities in a Life Science Teaching class and a group that did not use it in the class. It was found that educational activities related to Pintrich's model experienced by the teacher candidates had a positive effect on their SRL scores as measured by the Self-Regulated Learning Perception Scale (Turan, 2009) over those that did not experience such activities. This was shown by the significant increase of self-regulated learning perception scores.

SRL had increased the self-organising learning perceptions of the future classroom teachers. When the sub-factors were considered, 'Motivation and action to learning', 'planning and goal setting', and 'strategies for learning and assessment', there was no statistically significant difference between the pre- and post-test scores for these sub-factors only the sub-factor of 'lack of self-directedness' showed a significant difference in the pre-test. It showed that candidate class teachers did not have enough training in their elementary, middle school and high school education in a constructivist learning approach.

The results suggested that teacher-centred thinking continued to exist in classroom teacher candidates. The reasons for this were that the classroom teacher candidates might have been considering personal scores on marked items more than considering personal analysis of learning on any given topic. They may also have been continuing to think more about questions on examinations rather than concentrating on a sense of 'learning to learn'. They may prefer to acquire concrete knowledge and may not wish to concentrate on actively engaging in their learning environment, as they must in constructivist approaches. If this is the case, it makes the change from a teacher-centred approach to a student/learner-centred approach impossible for them and they may be unable to design future SRL lessons for their students.

What may be necessary to help students achieve learning change is to increase the length of the training in SRL experiences so that it is an intimate part of the whole programme. They need to be taught by the methods 'walk the talk' as well as giving them more practice in using SRL strategies in their lessons. Another factor to consider in the research is that details of the SRL tasks were not included and thus the quality of the experiences and the specific targets and processes could not be evaluated to show what might and might not instigate change after a history of didactics

Assessment for learning

Feedback and feed forward

In summary, the mix of motives that bring a student to apply to join an academic programme are typical of those seeking to gain any other academic award in a professional area. Once engaged with the programme these motives must be recognised and met if dropping out is to be avoided. There also need to be mechanisms formal and informal that enable student feedback to be given as this can contribute to feelings of autonomy and self-regulation. The feedback should be constructive and aim to improve the student learning experience and the design and content of the course. Feedback thus goes in both directions with feedback from the tutor on task and content as AfL – feed forward, and feedback from the student on the programme and learning progress.

Black and Wiliam (1998) in a meta-analysis of over 250 research studies over the previous decade found considerable evidence to show that effective feedback led to learning gains across all forms and fields of knowledge and skill and sectors of education, although the evidence came mainly from schools.

Students need to receive constructive formative, diagnostic and summative assessments from the tutor that support both learning and motivation. Examples of these different techniques in operation will be illustrated in the discussion of typical tasks in the later chapters. An important contribution is however the role of the student in AfL. Sadler (1989) identified three conditions necessary for students to benefit from feedback in academic tasks. He argued that the student must know:

- What good performance is, the student must have a concept of the goal or standard being aimed for.
- How current performance relates to good performance, the student must be able to compare current and good performance.
- How to act to close the gap between current and good performance.

From this analysis Sadler concluded students must already possess some of the same evaluative skills as their tutor. It also helps account for the common finding that students still make significant progress in their learning even when the external feedback they receive is quite impoverished. This is especially so in many large enrolment classes. In these, it is the end of semester/year essays or examinations that makes them work to master the content and the information about it they share with other students.

Sadler's analysis was found to be somewhat restricted when students' contributions to feedback in HE were investigated by Nicol and MacFarlane-Dick (2006).

They identified seven principles of good feedback practice. They reinterpreted research on formative assessment and feedback to show how these processes could help students take control of their own learning and support self-regulation. Their key argument was that students were already assessing their own work and generating their own feedback, and that HE should build on this ability. Students were to have a proactive rather than a reactive role in generating and using feedback capacity to self-regulate their own performance. Their synthesis led to the following seven principles of good feedback:

1　Helps clarify what good performance is in goals, criteria and expected standards.
2　Facilitates the development of self-assessment (reflection) in learning.
3　Delivers high-quality information to students about their learning.
4　Encourages tutor and peer dialogue around learning.
5　Encourages positive motivational beliefs and self-esteem.
6　Provides opportunities to close the gap between current and desired performance.
7　Provides information to tutors that can be used to help shape learning.

They concluded that HE programmes needed to incorporate these principles into the feedback systems including peer dialogue. For example, Nicol and MacFarlane-Dick (2006) discussed how students interacted with subject content, transforming and discussing it with others, in order to internalise meaning and make connections with what was already known. They suggested that terms like 'student centred learning' that had entered the lexicon of HE, were one reflection of this new way of thinking. The core assumptions were active engagement in learning and learner responsibility for the management of learning. They argued that despite this shift in conceptions of teaching and learning, a parallel shift in relation to formative assessment and feedback had been slower to emerge. In HE, formative assessment and feedback were still largely controlled by and seen as the responsibility of tutors and feedback was still generally conceptualised as a transmission process.

　Research has suggested that to remain effective, feedback to any evaluative assessment whether formative or summative must be provided as soon as possible after the event (Hammersley-Fletcher and Orsmond, 2005). A further feedback issue was identified in appraisal researches (Montgomery, 2002) and this was the problem that some appraisers, lecturers and senior managers found in giving positive constructive feedback. Some actually reported they felt it was 'too feminine' an approach and a few seemed to regard any praise as morally wrong. Different implicit 'theories' such as these were investigated in Canadian undergraduate teachers in training with similar results by Couture et al. (2003). Unfortunately, the evaluation and audit systems set up by agencies such as Ofsted are not usually based in constructivism.

　　Performativity, through its chain of targets and accountability, operates within a 'blame culture' where accountability becomes a means by which the institution can call to account its members. In many respects, performativity is reminiscent of Fordist work relations in as much as the worker is tightly surveilled, with attempts to render transparent the details of practice (Avis, 2005, 212).

The blame culture has been at work once again on a grand scale in the US. A 6-year project funded by the Bill and Melinda Gate's Foundation gave $575 million to improve student achievement especially of low-income minority groups and has failed. The school leaders involved agreed to recruit, reward and retain effective teachers and reject, and dismiss ineffective ones and so build a 'better' teaching force. Although conscientious efforts were made to implement the programme, the research evaluators found no significant increase in student test scores or graduation rates. It was only when successful schools were evaluated it was found that when teachers participated as partners and leaders of change, had opportunities for growth and principals were inclusive establishing school-wide structures to support student learning that schools achieved better results for their students (Moore-Johnson, 2019).

The situation in relation to staff appraisal in HE is even more complex. In Taiwan, there are separate research, teaching and professional intensive universities but in the UK staff may be expected to demonstrate expertise in relation to all three. In addition, they will also be leaders, coordinators and administrators whose management skills need to be appraised in relation to promotions, tenure and at interview for a new post. Although the managers may have agreed lists of university criteria for these, it is the teaching function that will remain 'fuzzy' and needs more research and CPD for those involved.

Assessment practices and their 'validity in the real world'

Hamilton and Stewart (2015, 334) offered a model of assessment processes from Business Studies at Kingston University that ranked the practices from the least to the most valid in real world terms, for example, from examination questions based on real world scenarios as the most common and the least effective through to competence-based assessment in the workplace as the most effective. The intermediate stages were as follows:

Case study analysis based on a real organisation.
Business report based on a genuine organisation but following academic writing conventions
Business presentation
Business simulations or role-play
Genuine real world documents, for example, marketing plan
Portfolios

Although this might be an authentic list for Business Studies, it does not always follow a similar path for others even though adapted. Nevertheless, Government agencies have become suffused with competency-based requirements not least in teacher education and HE despite the evidence that in a $3 million US project, it was found that giving training courses to student teachers on 10 established teaching competencies resulted in A-standard scores on all the competencies but the intending teachers still failed in the classroom (Tuxworth, 1982). Teaching a class of school pupils is a dynamic, interactive socially skilled process that is not easily reduced to a set of competencies. Nevertheless, the Teacher Education Agency, Ofsted and appraisal systems in FE/HE have followed that route.

It is easily possible to examine lecturer's research papers for their academic standard and value but a lecturer employed to teach must be seen teaching at interview and the performance should be evaluated by both staff and students who discuss and share the criteria they are using.

Systematic assessment for learning

Based on appraisal research in schools and HE (Montgomery, 2002, 2017b), it was decided to use a particular teaching strategy in a set of Distance Learning Masters' programmes, this was the continuous running record. It was a method of giving feedback emphasising the positive aspects of the written responses and adding in advice and raising questions. It was to be a **'textual coaching system'** and was designed to set up a 'learning conversation' (Harri-Augstein et al., 1985) in the learner's head inducing reflection on the topic. The intention was to help the learner's metacognitive efforts. This very close attention to the detail was an essential tool in developing a rapport between student and assessor as mentor. It was realised that some students would not read the notes at first but if the comments were couched in positive terms and were supportive then they would gradually be encouraged to do so. This form of tutorial coaching on both formative and summative DL tasks can be considered to be a distance mode of the Oxbridge tutorial system. It was a logical means for developing quality in thinking.

In the DL programmes (1991–2010) whatever the student was asked to write – formative or summative assignment, the assessor would not only give a summative mark in academic terms according to a shared criterion referenced scale, but would also write formative notes down the side and at the end as a running commentary. The commentary included praise and bits of advice and ideas on the professional and knowledge base and how to extend them.

> **Intrinsic motivation.** Both the DL materials and methods needed to induce intrinsic motivation by arousing interest, curiosity, a desire to find some answers, and personal involvement. They needed to offer suitable open-ended cognitive challenge, give opportunities for creativity and be fun to do to comply with student learning needs.
>
> **Extrinsic motivation.** The assessment options were – Formative, Diagnostic, and Summative and whatever form they took needed to be centred on tasks that would make the students want to do them.

Formative. There would be a series of eight or nine short formative tasks through the module related to the content of the programmes to underpin and support the learning. Each task response would be given constructive feedback to show how well it had been done and how it could have been improved. This was feedback and feed forward.

Diagnostic. The feed forward was also diagnostic in that it would show strengths and weaknesses. It would cover not only content and process, but also the general skills particularly in oral and writing competencies so the responses could be better expressed.

Summative. At the end of each course unit a summative assignment would be set and marked against a criterion referenced scale which was also shared with the students and that they had also practised using.

The MA programmes had been designed with these feedback objectives in mind before they were so succinctly defined by Nicol and MacFarlane-Dick (2006). In operation, evidence was collected that affirmed they were well-established and proving effective with the students. New tutors needed training and explanation of the purposes of the different types of feedback and then their efforts were monitored on a regular basis. This was possible because of the double marking of all the early assignments and then of a 15–20% sample of the assignments sent to the external examiners each semester for the examination boards. All the portfolios were available on the examination board days for the examiners to check.

Coaching and mentoring

It was essential for the learners to regard the tutor as mentor and develop a close relationship in academic terms. This was created by the supportive use of the running record, the Textual Coaching System that backed any oral feedback and could be discussed and reflected upon at leisure. It was not only a feedback system but also feed forward and an important contribution to personalising learning.

These principles and practices formed a particular pattern and pedagogy and significant improvements in the quality and nature of the thinking were found in both theory and practice assignments as the programmes progressed and evidenced deeper approaches to study. The standards of many individual achievements were high and evaluations of the external examiners and government inspectors confirmed this. In triangulated assessments the student's colleagues and senior staff were also able to accredit their progress.

Portfolios

All the assessed tasks for each module were to be bound into a portfolio form by each student and presented for final assessment and to the examination board. The final portfolio contained an evaluation of the course and examples of three tasks that had been particularly useful and successful professionally.

Optimal cognitive challenge, curiosity, interest and metacognition

Optimal challenge means that the programme contents and the tasks set must offer intellectual challenge that is within the powers of the student to achieve or who will be able to do so with appropriate supports and scaffolds. It needs to be within their Zone of Proximal Development (Vygotsky, 1978). This enables the student to feel competent and develop self-efficacy as the course progresses. Optimal challenge maintains these motivations.

In addition to the cognitive challenge, the content and tasks must arouse and maintain the student's interest and curiosity. This is an intellectual challenge for the course designer and tutors. As with the experiments in full and part time programmes the contents and tasks were designed on the basis of capability notions and some further details can be found in Chapter 5.

Conclusion

This chapter has considered EF skills, motivation and assessment. The EFs are the higher-order cognitive or mental skills involved in planning, monitoring and evaluating actions and learning outcomes. Motivations, although subdivided into intrinsic and extrinsic motivators were discussed in terms of their complex pattern of relationships with EFs.

In the final section of the chapter more detailed attention was given to feedback techniques and mechanisms shown to have proved effective in increasing and maintaining motivation and learning gain. The part played by feedback on learning and motivation was elaborated for both tutor and student forms as Assessment for Learning.

In the next chapter with the background to self-regulation, motivation, teaching and feedback established, consideration will be given to the problems and issues for motivation created by Distance Learning and how self-regulatory skills can still be promoted across the different disciplines.

Chapter 5

SRL problems and issues for distance and blended learning programmes

Introduction

Teacher development has a long history in the UK but little funded research until recently into effective methods of achieving it. In fact, lately it has been politicians who have determined who and what should be trained in the teacher education field where one would expect most of the expertise to be found. This has meant that freedom to innovate was lost and could only be found in the CPD field and Masters programmes. But even these programmes have been infiltrated by the 'policy makers'.

The situation in other countries is probably worse, with little or no history of freedom and innovation in teacher development. Pachane (2017) examined teacher education preparation at three key institutions, in the US, Brazil and Portugal and found that the Brazilian model was the most didactic, separating theory from practice in the traditional manner. The Portuguese model showed more attempts to integrate theory and practice, whereas the Harvard model was the most advanced in this respect but they did not investigate the UK practices where most advances have been made despite the heavy hand of the bureaucracy.

In higher education, there was no such tradition of training until recently when a PGCTLHE has been developed in the UK for new employees. This text does not automatically assume that employment to teach in higher education confers the title of 'teacher'. Instead, the role is designated as 'lecturer' or 'tutor' to distinguish them with apologies to those who are suitably qualified by training, research and/or experience. For decades the assumption has been 'a good man knows his subject' and was therefore qualified to teach (!).

Darling-Hammond (2013) pointed out that an important milestone for the changes in American teacher education programmes was the State Education Annual Report of 2002. She noted that the teacher certification system was 'broken' the report suggested there was a need to prepare teachers better in communication skills, mastery of content and to strengthen contact with schools, eliminating other bureaucratic obstacles. She found that the documents' proposals were used in some States to suppress the specific professional preparation of teachers, basically requiring the sufficiency test.

Darling-Hammond's study also analysed researches about the impact of the multiple types of preparation for teaching in the US. The results showed that the differentials of a good training course (138–139) were:

1 Clear vision of what is good teaching permeating the whole course and practical experience, creating a coherent set of learning experiences.
2 The existence of well-defined standards of performance and professional practice that are used to guide and evaluate course and practice.
3 A strong core curriculum, taught in the context of practice, based on knowledge of the development and learning of children and adolescents, understanding of the social and cultural context, curriculum, assessment and (didactic) pedagogy of content to be taught.
4 Supervised practical experiences of at least 30 weeks, and opportunities for the student to teach in each programme, experiences that are carefully selected to strengthen what is taught simultaneously in the course and intimately intertwined with it.
5 Use of case studies, research, performance evaluation and portfolios that relate learning to the problems of daily practice.
6 Specific strategies for confronting pre-established beliefs and assumptions of teachers in training about learning and learners, and learning about different experiences and people.
7 A strong relationship, shared knowledge and shared beliefs between school and university teachers, to work together on the transformation of teaching, school education and teacher training.

Although not all aspects of these requirements apply to training teachers for HE who will be assumed to have a good grasp on the subject curriculum the rest are useful criteria for their teacherly development if we substitute other professions and career options for schools.

As has been reported the training of lecturers for their roles in teaching in HE is a relatively recent innovation for new lecturers. It is however common for universities to recruit their untrained doctoral and postdoctoral students to carry out significant amounts of teaching, seminar and tutorial work. This has been one means of coping with increasing numbers of students and is a cheaper option than employing qualified staff on permanent or temporary contracts. Of course, it does help to supplement the income of these students.

A means of increasing institutional income has been to increase student numbers by the development of distance education programmes or open programmes that join the two as blended learning experiences. But distance learning sets up significant challenges for traditional modes of teaching and learning in HE, modes and methods that have been adopted over the centuries without question until recently. Distance education assumes that students are capable of independent study but as indicated in earlier chapters this is not necessarily the case. The problems are to find what can improve the student motivation to learn without the face-to-face support, without the tutorial group and seminar system.

The answer so far has been to design most distance and blended systems that attempt to model and then reproduce the face-to-face system at a distance. But it is possible that what may be discovered in broadening distance education approaches can provide for significant improvements in the full- and part-time system. Education in the UK is highly attractive to many from other countries and earns significant income for it as well as exporting it to satellite operations abroad.

Harrow School for boys is setting up a virtual sixth form for both boys and girls that will teach A-levels online to pupils living anywhere in the world (except the UK). It will charge £15,000 per year (the UK school fees for boys are £42,000 per year) and will initially focus on science and maths subjects, with Pearson's providing the technology platform. The new Harrow School Online will begin teaching from September 2020. Principal Heather Rhodes said the historic school was adapting to a 'rapidly changing world'. Students will have to pass an entrance examination to enter the online course

This is the latest attempt to use online technology to sell UK education overseas with the school's brand being used to attract pupils who want to be taught through the Internet. Sharon Hague of Pearson said the online platform had already been tested, and was being used by more than 75,000 pupils learning online in the US. It will be interesting to see the model of teaching and learning they will choose to adopt. The use of the term 'virtual' already suggests the likely outcome and may be important for younger students to wean them towards independent SRL.

Distance learning

The majority of institutions in higher education in the US offer some form of distance education and graduate and undergraduate enrolments increase in each year (Wallace, 2005). A wide range of terms is used to describe these courses such as: E learning, tele-learning, distance education, distance learning, virtual learning, individual learning and distributed learning.

These developments are to some extent the consequence of distances that have to be travelled to attend these institutions. In Australia where for example the North Western Territory is the size of Europe, distance education has for a long time been a means of providing for thinly distributed populations.

In the UK, distance education has been slower to develop but has roots in the 1960s when Wolsey Hall, Oxford was well known for its distance-learning courses. They were fully textual and assessed by essay questions marked by experts. The ability to read the set texts, abstract, summarise, paraphrase and put together a literate and lucid argument were the predominant skills required. To be awarded the Diploma, for example, it was necessary to have a first degree. A student without this might pass the course with A-grades but not be allowed to sit the examination and obtain the award. Nevertheless, it could be a worthwhile experience. Wolsey Hall now has a presence on the Internet and is still offering a wide range of courses.

In 1970, the Open University (OU) was established and its first graduation degree ceremony was held in 1973. It offered both undergraduate and postgraduate certificate and degree programmes by distance learning. It was centrally funded and offered lectures and demonstrations on television and radio, and extensive textual and support materials. The courses were assessed using computer marked short-answer papers, essays and projects, there were also timed papers under examination conditions. In addition, summer schools and residential programmes were initially built into the programmes of study. Most but not all distance learning variants in 1990s followed the OU model with textual materials and some residential weekends and summer schools. There were also examination centres and machine marking of some elements. The examinations took into account some universities that would not register any students for PhDs who had not taken examinations in their masters' programme. In Chapter 1, the reasons for the effectiveness of the OU courses was explained but not all the variants could follow the model at the tutorial and feedback level but might use some of the materials.

Residential weekends and summer schools precluded many women from attending because of their other commitments and they were also disadvantageous to poorer students who could not afford the fees much less the residentials. Students living abroad were also discouraged from taking part because of these regulations and so over time fully distance programme were established. Middlesex and one or two other universities also piloted fully distance programmes in their education and lifelong learning faculties.

Typical of the current distance programmes in the UK and US is that there is a lecture posted on line and students access it as and when they wish. A web-based discussion 'webinar' takes place at a later time and the students can read posted messages and make their contributions at any time or not at all and this may be monitored. They may also have scheduled virtual meetings with a tutor. There are also course websites that give the syllabus and its goals and objectives and tutors post their lecture notes and assignments. This saves a lot of trees.

The effectiveness research on distance programmes has mainly taken place in the US. The results have been equivocal with some showing no differences for classroom versus distance-based teaching while others have shown advantages in learning outcomes for one over the other. The reasons for this appear to lie in the inability to randomise the student subjects to the conditions and control other variables such as different teachers, different course materials and tasks and so on. It is thus that a series of meta-analyses have been relied upon to test the relative effectiveness. For example, Shachar and Neumann (2003) in 86 studies found student performance higher in distance programmes and student satisfaction higher in classroom-based courses. This sounds credible given the nature of courses giving learning gains shown in chapter one.

However, in a meta-analysis of 232 studies, Bernard et al. (2004) found no significant differences between the two in student achievement, satisfaction and retention but there was variability in effect sizes. This simply shows that some courses are far better and some are far worse than others and it is necessary to dig deeper into their educational strategies to learn from them. This will be the subject under consideration in chapter six.

At Johns Hopkins University, Wallace (2005) reported that much had been learned from failures since the first programmes were established in 1984. The standard procedure was that Distance Education 'instructors' were not only experts in the subject areas with advanced degrees and PhDs but they were also trained in the course pedagogy. This showed them how to establish a mentoring relationship with a specified group of students and they were assigned no more than 30 in their classes. Course time was also spent on community building amongst the group and beyond and there was advice and counselling available. The course goals and objectives and the requirements were made very clear. The content and pacing of the material were flexible but challenging and responsive to individual needs. As can be seen this procedure incorporates several of the criteria found to achieve higher learning gain.

Choosing the appropriate DL/DE format

There are a number of DL options available and these are:

- Full distance, textual and E-text – low tech. with electronic support
- Full distance, electronic – high tech. virtual
- Blended, some contact supported by on-line learning and tech. support
- Distance with regional satellite centres for contact sessions
- Distance with college residentials and summer schools

What choice is made depends upon answers to the following questions or issues. Should the contact programme and model be transcribed by inserting contact events? When supported electronically should it be transformed to virtual, induce student interaction with webinars, individualised with on-line learning strategies?

How should the assessments be organised – paced? What proportion of formative and summative assessments need to be designed? Should there be short answer multiple choice items, self-assessments, quizzes, machine marking, essay questions marked by the tutors or by computer concept analysis, examination rooms and timed essay tasks, problem based tasks, case studies and research projects?

What we learn in different transmission modes

Race (1992) discussed research results on the effectiveness of different modes of transmission in his inaugural professorial lecture on 'Developing competence'. They illustrate the amount that on average we learn from different formats and were as follows:

- Lecture 5%
- Books 10%
- Audio visual presentation 20%
- Dramatic lecture with A-V 30%
- Discussing lecture 50%

- Explaining to someone else 70%
- Teaching 90%
- Assessing 95%

From this listing, we can see why lectures need to be followed up by seminar discussions and plenaries. Unfortunately, some tutors often use these sessions to expand on the lecture to the smaller group or put in ideas and themes of their own so there are two lectures and much less discussion. Not all students participate in or attend the seminars or the lectures and can doze through the discussions.

It would appear that our favoured mode of transmission in HE is the least effective one and assessment and teaching are the strongest with explaining the key ideas perhaps to a group of peers or a partner or writing them down is a strong support to learning that will improve learning outcomes.

In face-to-face lectures and distance mode, a favoured form of transmission is the dramatic lecture with A-V. The following experience illustrates how ineffective this can be.

In a recent national high-profile lecture on promoting high ability, the speaker illustrated his main ideas with extracts from film. One key construct was to show how a particular activity developed a neural pathway that increased in strength with use. The illustration was to show the speaker arriving at and climbing in a mountainous region and the need to make a link across a gorge to another hilltop. There appeared to be no reason to do this! We observed the effort, the use of the climbing gear, the engaging of the first rope across, the building of a single rope path, the steady increase in size of the path, the footway was then reinforced and supports and rails were added. Finally, a complete suspension bridge from one top to the other was made and the team of people was shown walking across it with ease. The audience watched all this with rapt attention for over 5 minutes and the point was well made. However, when I arrived home and was thinking over the 45-minute talk, I was unable to remember anything else that the speaker had said that might be useful and in any case, I already knew the way in which neural paths were strengthened by repetition. I think we had been shown some stills of neural paths and dendrites. After this film clip, there was something about discoveries of new ideas and reference to his son's discovery of something and its successful publication in the journal Nature.

What this illustrates is a very expensive waste of time travelling to London, the conference fee and so on for nil return. There were no notes taken because no points were made that were constructive or new during the 'lecture'. The interesting factors were the power and impact of the visuals, the distinctive look of the speaker and his moustache, and his voice over as he dashed to and fro. In addition, there was the proud personal information about his son but no recall of what he discovered. A speaker colleague who always punctuated his lectures with jokes had a similar effect that we remembered the jokes but not the lecture content.

The visual medium is clearly very powerful; however, it may not be the message. It may even overpower any messages that we intend to transmit and prevent the engagement with the more important ideas. It may also ensure that we entirely miss the deep structure and the hidden messages and an underlying curriculum that may have an emotional content that is destructive to rational debate.

With Instagram and other platforms vast numbers of people are embellishing their lives and their daily activities uploading video and film of themselves. Given the nature and power of moving images, it is a pity that recommendations for image-based educational provision by the British Film Institute Working Group (1999) were not made widely available in schools and colleges and for lifelong learning.

There is however also a problem with the lecture in print being made available online. This was illustrated in long-term research reported by Sheila Harri-Augstein and colleagues at Brunel with both graduate and undergraduate students. They showed that many students engaged in Receptive rather than Reflective reading and so did not engage at a deep level with the text and its ideas. Their learning strategy was to do a read through jotting down notes. It helped them learn some facts but they did not gain the overall sense of the text, its deeper meaning and they could not summarise it. Others may learn to highlight the main points in text and others patch pieces into their essays but are they learning?

Harri-Augstein et al.'s (1985) research would suggest that 'Receptive' readers are likely to become 'Receptive' not 'Reflective' viewers and similar processes are involved. So, some find time to replay the lecture twice and apparently to no avail. To become more reflective the video could be stopped and sections found and replayed but it is a slow process to review sequential material in this way compared with the spatial accessibility of text. The same problem is seen with catalogues from publishers when using their websites to browse for books of interest rather than search a hard copy catalogue. However user-friendly these new systems appear to be they need serious modification if they are to be valuable for self-regulated learning.

An especially important question is whether virtual and video-enhanced programmes induce more reflective and critical thinking. Are they more capable of it? Or is the visuo-spatial format more fit for other purposes such as engineering, design and biology? Can downloading a lecture on film prove more effective than attending the lecture and being able to raise immediate questions? Research has shown that when students watched a video lecture twice in quick succession, they knew no more than when they watched it once and Setren (2019) showed that most students only watched part of the video in any case however highly motivated to succeed they were.

In appraisal, research teachers could see the problems of other teachers in the videos but would make similar errors themselves and not be able to correct them. Even effective teachers could not define how and why they were successful and needed a coaching system to reveal these things (Montgomery, 2017b).

The current form of distance learning tends to be predicated upon the full-time model. This assumes that what is engaged in with full-time students in face-to-face lectures and seminars can and should be transposed by electronic means into a distance mode without losing effectiveness. It initially increases the costs especially in the development period. These programmes may be directed from a central university hub with satellite tutorial centres at a distance. Other formats support this model with course materials in print and online as in the OU programmes.

The current full-time course models include many virtual features that are designed to make programmes more inclusive and flexible but there are inherent dangers that quickly become apparent and that may not be beneficial for long-term distance and SRL studies. For example in a recent contribution to an MA distance-learning programme the topic was Underachievement. The format was as follows: the tutor would provide a written lecture on the topic. This would be put up on the university website at a specified date, after about 10 days the student webinar was opened and students could post comments, questions and ideas and the tutor and other students could respond. The tutor's task was to check the postings and contribute, respond or guide as necessary. This clearly followed the traditional transmission format with the lecture followed by an attempt to discuss it in a seminar and expand and clarify points.

It was interesting to follow this up in more detail. The number of students on the programme was 57 who could respond. There were 15 people posting on the webinar and some posted several times and responded to each other rather than the text. In other words, the majority of students had not necessarily engaged with the text or the webinar and were perhaps saving the text for later study. Very little of what was posted was relevant or moved the understanding on. A lot of tutor and some students' time was spent in this pursuit and no obvious gain was observed in learning more than they might have done in attending a lecture or reading a book. The format did not permit formative activities.

Tutors engaged in such a watching brief often complain of the endless number of postings they have to read and respond to. They are also required to identify students and encourage more to participate and so on. E-mails have to be responded to within 48 hours and the work has expanded to fill more than the time available. This induces stress and reduces the time available for research. Then unhappily, the workforce can be supplemented by postgraduate students or there is a division of labour into researchers versus teachers. But unless teachers are engaged in research as CPD they cannot keep up to date and improve their practice.

In both full time and distance programmes text postings are not necessarily the means of transmission, instead there can be video lectures, audios/films and so on. Students can access these in their study bedrooms or remotely as and when they wish or can be present at the lectures. But what is achieved? All we have done is model the face-to-face format with some expensive technology. It does not mean that students have engaged at any deeper level with the material than they did before. There is just more flexibility in access and it enables them to take on full- or part-time employment while not interrupting their access to the course. Learning to touch type is also an asset on such programmes. With open access to journals, widely available patching and pasting can also become an important skill that can help bypass any 'brain engage' activity. But it does not increase learning gain or lead to deeper understanding (Mueller and Oppenheimer, 2014), it may also score highly on plagiarism.

Some key issues in curriculum design
in DL programmes

Eight issues seem particularly important in this area. The first already discussed is that there is a tendency for programme developers to try to replicate as far as possible all the features of good face-to-face or contact programmes and students given their past experiences continually ask for this.

The second issue centres upon teaching methodology. How far can students be taught at a distance? Should the emphasis be upon their learning rather than what the materials sent out contain and purport to 'teach? In essence, distance learning has been even more about 'telling rather than teaching' than tradition-ally taught programmes. How can we *teach* at a distance?

The third issue is about professional development. To what extent can medics, lawyers, teachers, performers and engineers, for example, be expected to learn new skills or enhance their professional capabilities by distance learning methods and materials? It is difficult enough to teach professional skills in any case in contact courses. Even the OU teacher education programme had to be discontinued because of its lack of effectiveness. At Masters level, the contact courses are often more about knowledge enhancement and the development of scholarship and research skills rather than dealing with professional capability. But should this always be the case in DL? In fact, there is a tacit assumption that with advanced knowledge about a field the individual will become a better practitioner. But is this true?

Once a DL course has been developed, there are also questions to be raised about its relevance and fitness for purpose. How responsive to new initiatives and change can such a programme be when materials have to be re-edited and remade in book or electronic form? Contact teaching can insert new material on the night and update continuously even though some tutors never revise or research their lectures once prepared.

Underlying all these issues is a fifth one – is there a special pedagogy for distance learning and linked to that is there one appropriate to the subject under study?

A sixth issue is the concern about the lack of group work. DL students fre-quently complain about this, they feel lonely. Some indeed cannot cope without the opportunity to talk and talk and leave the programmes almost immediately. Group work has been found to improve the quality of student's thinking but as a generality and compared with what, no group work? There appear to be no ran-domised control group studies of this amongst a range of 'treatments'.

It is possible to induce group work in DL by setting tasks that require it in interaction with friends and colleagues. It can also be developed when friends and colleagues are recruited to the programmes and form local study groups and collaborative networks. The partners and friends strategy has been particularly successful and satisfying for the learners. The promotion of teamwork in the workplace with colleagues can also be derived from the design of specific tasks. Workshops can be encouraged by sending practical materials to work on with colleagues.

The E-learning group work equivalent is to set up student 'chat rooms' but this does not always work well. Anxious students overuse and abuse them by trying to get the other students to help them do their work so they do not really have to think for themselves. Many students arrive on the course who are 'risk averse' and not used to thinking about a topic, questioning authority or thinking things through. They like to find the right answer somewhere and write it down. This is usually a product of their previous learning history, mindset or culture and difficult to change and it takes time for them to appreciate that everything does not have a correct answer or even any answer.

Seventh there is the issue of tutorials. In contact programmes, the development of mass higher education has increased student numbers without raising staffing levels and this has cut down tutorial opportunities. Unstructured and unsupervised group work and action learning sets have often replaced it. Students now seek to gain tutorial support by e-mailing and this puts tutors into overload. Lecturing to 200 students all of whom feel they have a right to E-mail with questions and requests and receive instant answers is not always built into the tutor's work programme. Tutors are frequently required to make their reply within 48 hours to comply with university procedures and total quality management guidelines thus quality in response cannot be assured. Electronic support has at least doubled the lecturer's administration and 'tutorial' time in addition to the longer preparation time that technology support requires.

DL has many advantages. Time does not have to be spent on repeating lectures and seminars once the initial preparation has been done. It can instead be spent on research updating, tutoring and answering those e-mail requests. The special DL tutorial that was developed in the suite of MAs already mentioned was to give students individual detailed written feedback on their formative and summative tasks as well as the E-mail responses to questions and telephone tutorials. Undergraduate students would need more support perhaps in the provision of regular virtual seminars or webinars through a programme of study. The final issue is the issue of retention and the management of dropout rates.

Retention

Dropout rates – reasons identified

The dropout rate from part-time and distance programmes is relatively high, in the order of 30% as a general rule if all is going reasonably well. It is a strong indicator of the general health of a course. There are however many factors that can provoke dropout that may or may not be course related. Zembylas (2008) showed that students in online environments experienced high anxiety at the beginning of modules, and stress and guilt about their difficulties balancing various roles and responsibilities. Female students experienced more varied and negative emotions compared with males (Conrad, 2002). Students in on-line degrees experienced negative emotional states that seemed to be more related to their studies and were not necessarily mental health issues (Pentaraki, 2017).

Although there may also be mental health issues that contribute to dropout rates, opportunities to direct students to professional help associated with the online courses could help keep them on the programmes. Clues to needs can be identified in the lengthy conversations with administrative staff in which personal needs are disclosed or the over-long E-mails explaining difficulties, feelings of failure and depression. Having a professional mental health consultant and a route for a student to obtain additional advice and support can save many from withdrawing.

Dropout rates – reasons identified – retention issues

One criterion for assessing the health of a course is the dropout rate or retention profile of the course in comparison with similar courses. As dropout is expensive for the institution and wasteful in terms of human resources, efforts are made to find the causes and remediate their effects.

In the US, Grandinetti (2015) reported that attrition was a major concern in schools of nursing and was most prevalent in baccalaureate nursing students as they first encountered their initial nursing and core science courses. The research findings in four nursing schools across the country revealed statistically significant evidence that those nursing students who scored moderately high on measures of motivation to learn, learner independence, intellectual curiosity and self-directed learning readiness for nursing education would be most likely to stay the course. It indicated that schools in the US and nurse education programmes were not promoting and developing self-regulated learners. The goal should be that once embarked upon a programme, there should be few student dropouts unless there was a major medical, family or financial problem. The option to return and resume their studies should also always be open to them.

In the UK, similar problems of retention are found across different programmes at the level of 30% with the lowest found in the Oxford tutorial system and the higher levels in distance and modular programmes. The rate also varies within colleges in different programmes.

The following are reasons for drop out identified over time in a suite of MA distance programmes:

Students' reasons. The reasons students gave when they withdrew from the programmes were: economic situation; social needs; family circumstances; medical issues; job situation; commitment; time poverty; intellectual capabilities; learning history; cultural factors; professional experience; previous training, relevance. The first five were the most common.

Institutional reasons for drop out. The Institution's bureaucracy and University procedures can cause drop out because:

- Registration procedures can be onerous and make accessibility difficult.
- Entry access is needed all year round but registry may only print the forms off per semester or even annually.

- Interviews may be traditional but not applicable to distance learning courses in which previous qualifications, employment and learning history are more relevant.
- Ease of access needed to the electronic systems and application forms.
- Student records systems that were student 'blind'.
- DL postgrads must not be sent threatening letters from admin. such as some undergraduates unfortunately were receiving on contact programmes where they could get immediate student union or tutor support.
- Intransigence of large systems designed for undergraduates should not be used and extended to masters programmes. Separate postgraduate and post experience programmes need separate and tailor-made admin systems.
- All administrative delays and blockages to be avoided.
- Course administrators must deliver the correct materials and to time.
- There are no vacations in DL; this creates staffing issues particularly in the long summer vacations.
- A coherent and systematic provision for Accreditation of Prior Learning is essential so that students do not have to repeat earlier work or have their Work-based learning ignored.
- Pricing. A standard price for all DL programmes is not reasonable. The price should reflect the genuine costs of the programme plus the institutional top-slice. This means that low-tech programmes should not be used to subsidise other much more costly high-tech. programmes.

Learning support – university/faculty level

- Students need quality in library and learning resources and ease of electronic accessibility. They need both electronic journals and hard copies services.
- They need high-quality administrator helpfulness and support. Sometimes this needs to be emotional support of the good listener.
- They need high-quality tutorial support, textual, E-mail etc. and voice mail.

Drop-out rates – course curriculum reasons

Lack of:

- Quality of the teaching and learning methods
- Quality of DL materials
- Relevance of the DL materials, too long between updates
- Quality of feedback and guidance
- Fairness of the procedures and assessments
- Relevance of the assessments
- Approachability of tutors
- Need for other student social contacts and talk time

In summary, the written and oral feedback from the suite of MA courses after each module and for the annual formal course reports and HMI inspections and vivas showed that they dropped out for personal reasons or because of the university's bureaucratic inconsistencies and treatments, not because they were unhappy with the actual course or its administration.

Muilenburg and Berge (2007) reported on their factor analytic study of student barriers to online learning ($N = 1,056$). Eight factors were identified:

Administrative issues
Social interaction
Academic skills
Technical skills
Learner motivation
Time and support for studies
Cost and access to the Internet
Technical problems

Independent variables that significantly affected student ratings of these barrier factors included: gender, age, ethnicity, type of learning institution, self-rating of online learning skills, effectiveness of learning online, online learning enjoyment, prejudicial treatment in traditional classes and the number of online courses already completed.

Student satisfaction evaluation questionnaires

These student satisfaction evaluations (SSEs) have become popular and league tables are published placing universities on the scale for a number of attributes including academic satisfaction and social aspects. In some institutions, students also rate their lecturers on a satisfaction scale and contracts and tenure can be affected by the results.

However, recent research shows that these SSEs are not as reliable or valid as was supposed. For example, some tutors can gain very high approval ratings because their courses and tests are the least challenging and require little effort from the student to succeed. What's not to like? More challenging courses in which high scores require significant amounts of student effort to achieve can be downgraded by many students (Stroebe, 2019).

An example design for distance learning

In the assessment and design of the tasks, a number of starting points had been learned from the undergraduate and postgraduate students in their course evaluations. They had always emphasised the value to them of the research project or dissertation. The MA programmes would have a dissertation to do at the end of the course and some practical small-scale projects would be needed throughout the programmes but there are limits. Projects would not get to the small areas of essential learning and reflection that the topics might need to evoke. Other assessment strategies had to be developed and they also had to be different from each other so that students did not become habituated.

The rationale underlying the assessment driven model

Traditional motivations to study were to obtain a 'ticket', gain further academic knowledge and skills, gain professional skills, research an area of interest, personal interest and stimulus, acclaim, job prospects and promotion. These might not prove strong enough for many to keep studying if the programme itself did not use strategies to maintain both extrinsic and intrinsic motivation especially when the work became difficult and there were competing job, family or health issues. Women were going to be the most likely recruits to the courses. Previous programmes had illustrated this. They also opted for part-time studies in comparison with men because they commonly had less personal disposable free time and income than most men candidates. This meant that the course inducements to study must be strong and remain so.

- But there would be no examination halls with cohorts of students writing essays under timed conditions to make them study. However, assessment had to become the most important dimension without being overwhelming and fear-inducing. Instead, it had to be positive and constructive.
- If critical and reflective thinking was to be induced, the assignments had to make this occur.
- Assessments would need to be **formative** so that students could learn from them. There would also need to be **diagnostic** and **summative** assessments to identify what they had learned as well as being used to give feedback.
- The programme module must be short enough so that feedback did not have to wait a year long. This had to be offset by giving enough time to send and receive materials and for the student to settle to the work and find 75–90 hours of independent study/learning time. This included studying the module text and reader, practice tasks in the classroom, research, negotiating with colleagues, reading and writing up time.
- The topics were initially divided into 12 times 10 credit modules for the Diploma and one 60 credit module for the dissertation. It was expected that students would complete 20 credits in each semester thus gaining regular feedback. Later the Certificate level modules were 6 × 10 credits, Diploma 3 × 20 credits and Dissertation 1 × 60 credits.
- In addition, the student must be caused to be **creative** as these sorts of activities had been shown to be highly motivating and satisfying.
- It was concluded that the DL course would be **assessment driven** with each student product marked in a detailed manner to try to set up a 'learning conversation'. This was designed to help them become more reflective practitioners and thus have a chance to develop independently of the programme. There would be eight or nine formative assessed tasks per module and one or two summative tasks.

- The marking would also have to be **positive and supportive** even where it was necessary to correct or remediate work. Experience had shown that negative comments and perfunctory remarks stopped the students reading further or thinking about what was written.
- Course work and essays over time had shown that the student might well be able to write a good essay or assignment but this offered no guarantee that any professional competency would result even if practical applications were discussed. Thus only two essays were planned in the whole programme. All the other assignments would have some form of capability or competency built into them.

Motivation and DL

The next and perhaps the most serious consideration for any programme is the one of motivation to learn. Intrinsic motivation or the will to learn needs to be strong to follow a programme of study of any kind but needs to be particularly strong to study alone at a distance. Even with all of the motivators combined, initial hard work for its own sake gradually declines as the novelty effect wears off. The full-time undergraduate students tended only to work or 'read for their degrees' if they had a particular interest in a topic. The feature that motivated them to acquire new knowledge and skill the most was an assessment, an extrinsic motivator.

In the contact programmes, it was the custom to set one or two research papers for a seminar group of 12–15 to read but not tell who would do the presentations as detailed previously. The problem was how to encapsulate this process in an individual learner at a distance to ensure the key papers had been read. Several solutions emerged and these are explained under Study Skills in the next chapter.

Crucial to any development is the issue of tutor time. Initially, it is to prepare the tasks and materials. In the MA programme examples, the design and preparation was carried out in the tutor's own independent time as no allowance could be budgeted for with £millions in budget deficit. But it did mean that copyright was retained and it was to be an experimental project. Some of the materials and booklets had already been trialled in other institutions and independent situations and were sold at conference and CPD workshops.

Marking would be the crucial contribution by the tutor(s) once the course was validated and up and running. This had to include the essential feedback. Feedback and assessment eventually would consume all the tutor time and systematic feedback can lose out but it is a problem that must be solved. The structure of this feedback system as AfL was discussed in Chapter 4 under extrinsic motivation and feedback and feed forward.

In this case, the tutor had a commitment to spend 1.5 hours per student per 10 credits. Therefore, the system design had to produce assessment tasks that could be marked in no longer than 1.5 hours. This meant that the popular learning logs, learning diaries and extended case studies could have no place unless the tactics were designed differently.

Because the MAs were to up-skill teaching professionals, three areas of capability had to be built into the course contents and assessments. These were:

Scholastic capabilities
Research capabilities
Professional capabilities

Some tasks would involve two or more linked capabilities.

The structure of the distance modules

Whether textual or electronic, it was important that the module had a stable format that a student could easily get to know. The predictability establishes confidence even if at a simple level. The textual format needed to be securely bound and attractive to look at and handle. After this, the title page looks like that in any other book with copyright details and date of publication. The next page contained important programme information and then paginated contents list, this was followed by the main pattern of the layout and recommended course texts notwithstanding that the module book is itself a text of the basic lecture information

After this, all the modules had the following format:

Introduction to the module. Giving and overview of the area and key definitions.
List of learning outcomes for the module.
Unit One – Theoretical and research background. To include relevant historical, legal, political, educational and psychological information and research findings as appropriate.
Research method section. Details of one particular research technique **appropriate** to the module contents (14 methods across the programme).
Unit Two. Professional applications and their research and practice backing.
References.
Appendices.
Task Boxes. Across each unit there were four or five formative task boxes and one summative one at the end of the each unit. Sometimes at the Diploma level, there would be one longer summative task rather than two. F, D and S refer to formative, diagnostic and summative task types.

The three capabilities in the design of assessments

Examples of some more of the formative style tasks can be found in the next chapter. The following mainly illustrate some of the summative tasks. The M codes refer to the Study Guide copies that can be found on the (Learning Difficulties Research Project) LDRP website www.ldrp.org.uk

1. Professional capabilities examples

Study Guide M3. Spelling and Handwriting – SEN and SpLD.

Undertake a Precision Teaching investigation with a pupil needing literacy help and write up the process and the findings as an experimental and evaluative report based on the structure given in the task box. (S)

Study Guide M5. Inclusive Teaching and Personalised learning. All the MAs.

Make an audio recording of a teaching session with a group of pupils and analyse it according to the structure and criteria set out in Flander's Interaction Analysis. Find the percentages of the different types of teacher and pupil questions. Reflect upon your analysis in relation to the theories of learning and teaching, (D) and (S).

Study Guide M13. Performance Management. All MAs.

1 Negotiate and undertake a peer appraisal of teaching performance using the '5-Star' observation and feedback model set out in this study guide. Evaluate the process and outcomes with your colleague/appraisee. Write an evaluative report of the project and include all supporting data and observational records. (S)
2 Give details of the school appraisal system and documentation and write a critical report comparing the two systems. (S)

2. Scholastic capabilities examples

Study Guide M2 SpLD: Reading and Reading Difficulties.

(a) **SEN and (b) SpLD Courses**. Select a test used in your school (or use the one in the appendix) and write a two-page report for your head teacher to determine if it is a 'good' test. (S)
(c) **GEd Course.** Read the article by Gross (2004) on early identification of giftedness and write a short report for your head teacher evaluating whether a chosen test for identifying high learning potential in the gifted and talented is a 'good test'. (S)

Study Guide M6 SpLD. Maths and Mathematical Difficulties. Undertake a critical review of the research paper on Dyscalculia in the appendix. (S)

3. Research capabilities examples

Study Guide M1. Introduction to SEN and Slower learners needs.

Undertake a case study of a potential slower learner with difficulties in Memory, Language and Thinking according to the case study method and criteria set out in the module task box in the Research Methods section. (S)

Study Guide M6. Assessment. Read the research article on 'Early Screening' and complete the flowchart on the Early Screening article to show main and subordinate points (F). Read the course notes on assessment and testing strategies and problems and calculate a simple Spearman's rho correlation' (F) with some data you have collected from pupils' work.

Study Guide M14. Research preparation. Read the short research article, the Friedman paper in the Reader. In it, there are 22 methodological errors. See how many you can find and write a list of all those you have identified with short explanations and reasons for your selection. Consult the list of 'The 39 Steps' guide to research problems to help you. (S)

Curriculum evaluation of the modules using Bloom's Taxonomy

Bloom's (1956) Taxonomy has been widely used in curriculum design and evaluation in HE.

1 **Knowledge.** It is defined as the remembering/recall of previously learned material from specific facts to complete theories. Knowledge represents the lowest level of learning outcomes in the cognitive domain.

2 **Comprehension.** The ability to grasp the meaning of material and represents the lowest level of understanding.

3 **Application.** The ability to use learned material in new and concrete situations it includes the application of rules, methods, concepts, principles, laws and theories.

4 **Analysis.** The ability to break down material into its component parts so that its organisational structure can be understood. This may include the identification of the parts, analysis of the relations between parts and recognition of the organisational principles involved.

5 **Synthesis.** The ability to put parts together to form a new whole. This may involve the production of a unique communication (theme or speech), a plan of operations (research proposal) or set of abstract relations (scheme for classifying information). Learning outcomes in this area stress creative behaviours with major emphasis on the formulation of new patterns, analogies or structures.

6 **Evaluation.** The ability to judge the value of material (statement, novel, poem, research report) for a given purpose. The judgments are based on definite criteria. These may be internal criteria (organisation) or external criteria (relevance for the purpose) and the student may determine the criteria or be given them. Learning outcomes in this area are highest in the cognitive hierarchy because they contain elements of all of the other categories, plus conscious value judgments based on clearly defined criteria.

Too often programmes only test applications levels and this is not enough intellectual challenge. Some designers regard Synthesis as the highest level of intellectual operation but this is arguable because evaluation incorporates elements of it. Sometime creative production is accidental or a by-product of something else and it is the evaluation of this that determines its value and enables it to be seen as the creative leap.

One imminent danger is bureaucratisation. For example, it is important to establish student self-efficacy at the outset of the programme and the early modules need to be shorter, for example, 10 credits (The Certificate level 60 credits UK, 20 credits EU). So that they can be completed in good time and receive feedback. To encourage independence not too much should be sent on line for interim marking and advice. Some students correct their originals and only put the new version in the module portfolio for assessment. Even half modules (Units) could be sent in for assessment if necessary at first. But was not allowed by the 'system'.

At the Diploma level 20 credit modules can be appropriate but this tends to be a rule made for undergraduate face-to-face programmes and an increase to 30 credit units was even enforced that was not appropriate for the student labour intensive Distance programmes. They were given a yearlong time for completion instead of a semester. This was too long for the maintenance of strong motivation at a distance when there are many other competing interests not least full-time jobs.

Conclusion

Distance and blended university programmes are on the increase worldwide and much has been learned about how to make them successful and compare favourably with contact programmes. However, from the research already cited in the earlier chapters, it would appear that there is an opportunity for increased learning gain if the traditional contact programmes became more flexible in their approaches. This would mean that techniques from DL that increased student independent learning and time on task were incorporated into the full time programmes.

This flexibility should not be devoted to more wizardry with technology but with the nuts and bolts of student motivation and learning and promoting their self-efficacy.

In a time of 'lockdown' worldwide due to Covid-19, the issues regarding distance learning discussed in this chapter have become highly significant. It is a time when highly creative developments from the widest range of sources can be expected and some important advances are likely to be made in the theory and practice of tertiary and secondary education.

Chapter 6

Strategies to promote learning gain in HE

Study skills

Introduction

When engaged in academic studies, learners need to be in control of the cognitive and contextual processes in constructing and confirming worthwhile learning outcomes. SRL is an approach where learners are motivated to assume this personal responsibility and control (Garrison, 1997). It is a proactive process in which individuals are expected to organise and manage their thoughts, emotions, behaviours and their environment to fulfil their academic objectives. But it has been established that not all students arrive in higher education (HE) with such well-developed skills and need help to learn and develop them. Others do have some of these skills and can make better use of their study time. But all of them can have difficulties with tasks that fall outside their areas of special interest that are seen as crucial by tutors for them to learn. Motivation to learn can then be inhibited by these tasks that do not appear to be relevant to the goals students have set themselves.

In addition, in the social life of the university most students will not give much attention to tasks set that are not going to be assessed in some way. There may also be part- or full-time employment or family needs that compete for their attention. It is therefore essential that all tasks set are assessed or give feedback in some form and are goal-directed and part of an explicit overall plan that enables successful completion of the course of studies.

In Chapter 1, three examples that were known to have promoted higher learning gain were discussed and strategies were:

- Tutor contact to discuss individual students' work to give feedback and feed forward
- Systematic structured feedback and feed forward by trained tutors
- A strategic problem-based motivational task approach with regular feedback often from the students

The effect of these techniques was radically to increase student time on task and direct attention to its crucial dimensions and promote deep and meaningful learning. The best or target ratio was 10 hours of student time on task to 1 hour of lecturer time.

This chapter is concerned with the study skills strategies that can be employed to increase student time on task during independent study.

- The strategies are usually a design or a plan for approaching a high-level goal and coordinate a set of tactics.
- Tactics are a form of schema represented as an action rule or process.
- Schemas are categories of things or events.

It was demonstrated in research since 1894 that teaching courses in reading and study skills had improved achievement (Kulik et al., 1983). These tended to be recipes and rules that showed enough success to be incorporated into courses of training. Since then there have been significant developments in cognitive psychology and the understanding of human learning moving it from rote training and behaviourist models to meaningful verbal learning.

What has become clear is that there are specific subject study skills that can be taught to and employed by students and there is also a set of generalised strategic approaches that can be used across subjects. It is this aspect that needs more attention. It is also important that students are made aware of the fact that there is a range of options available to them and that they are not left to stumble across a strategy and then employ it without explicit knowledge of the technique and its suitability or otherwise in a particular situation.

The function of the strategies is to provide a mental model or metacognitive routine or 'learning conversation' to guide the student's actions in planning and solving or resolving a particular problem task. It then provides an evaluation format and monitoring strategy. This can all take place with inner speech and so it is only accessible through introspection and perception questionnaires.

Cognitive process strategies

These were a set of teaching for learning activities that constructivist teachers engaged in and 10 cognitive process strategies (CPS) were identified and adapted for use in undergraduate and post graduate programmes and for CPD. They were essentially developmental 'brain engage' strategies. Metacognition in which we think about our thinking was intimately involved that Flavell (1979) found was a key to improving intelligence. It is thus an important 'tool' for reflective teaching and learning in constructivism. Strategies that were designed to set up 'learning conversations' in the students' heads were a part of this process so that their metacognitions could be more precise, made explicit and more easily shared. The 10 strategies make a cognitive curriculum that could underpin any of the subjects in a discipline. Depending on the subject matter, some of the CPs would be more appropriate than others and at different times and stages.

The cognitive process strategy curriculum

- **Developmental positive cognitive intervention.** This was achieved in the running commentary and the positive constructive advisory notes on the formative and summative tasks and in answers to E-mail and telephone questions. It was the feedback and feed forward system in the MA distance programmes. In the contact programmes, it was used in lecture interactions, seminars, workshop feedback and tutorials and on essay marking.
- **Challenging questioning.** To provoke thought and reasoning, it involves more open questions. This was achieved in the setting of problem-based tasks and abstract reasoning questioning.
- **Cognitive process study and research skills.** These were introduced and practised especially in the formative tasks.
- **Teaching thinking skills.** A full range of lower and higher order thinking skills and protocols were explained and then practised at different levels such as in analysis, synthesis and evaluation in Bloom's (1956) hierarchy (see Chapter 5).
- **Reflective teaching and learning.** Both formative and summative tasks required the students to reflect upon their own learning as well as that of others and the information and research to which they were introduced.
- **Real-world and problem-based learning.** Investigative and open tasks were designed to promote and develop problem solving skills and protocols as intrinsic to the subject content not 'bolt-on' provision.
- **Developing creativity.** All the modules offered opportunities for open learning and creative responses such as in designing and making, developing, synthesising and exploration.
- **Games and simulations.** Tasks were set that used appropriate learning games, simulations and role play in the subject context and their evaluations.
- **Experiential learning.** Learning experiences were negotiated and then followed the learning cycle to reflective evaluation.
- **Self-regulated learning strategies.** Goal setting, planning, monitoring and evaluation were implicit and made explicit in the tasks.

Collaborative learning and team building. Some tasks were designed to engage others as team members. Explaining and sharing tasks and ideas have also been shown to lead to higher cognitive outcomes and help in team building related to employability skills.

In the model in Figure 2.1, the other central objective was to communicate thoughts succinctly. This means that student talk and its development is an essential part of any educative process. State schools however are continually falling short in this dimension according to successive Ofsted reports and Chief Inspectors and this continues in HE. Disadvantaged groups with excellence gaps and especially those from most State schools have problems in this respect. The assumption in HE must be that 'talking into learning' is an essential component of student studies and provision must be made for this and strategies employed to make it happen to gain the highest learning gains. It may even mean introducing Rap as part of the communication development and assessment in the least likely subjects.

The talking curriculum

- TPS. Think – Pair – Share
- Explainer time
- Hot seating
- Small group work
- Group problem solving
- Collaborative learning
- Reciprocal teaching
- Peer tutoring
- Role-play and drama
- Debates
- Presentations and 'teach-ins'
- Poster presentations and discussions
- Exhibitions and demonstrations
- Organised meetings
- Action learning sets
- 30-second theatres in problem resolution (Gibbs, 1988)
- Seminars
- Micro-teaching
- Think back (Lockhead, 2001)
- Rap and Slam poetry
- Songs

Each one of the CPS formed a practical agenda for the design of particular curriculum and assessment tasks. The first category-Developmental Positive Cognitive intervention has been discussed under feedback in Chapter 4. The next two categories are discussed in more detail below and the rest are developed as examples in Chapter 7.

A. Challenging questioning

Problem-posing questions

Challenging questions are widely used in HE to get students to think about a topic or an issue and some tutors are especially skilled in this area. Three questions might be raised during or at the outset of a lecture or at the end of it with a choice of one or two for students to discuss or write responses. In the presence of 200 students in a lecture hall, a written response is not feasible and so the tasks are often left to their reflective insights or the seminar discussion. In DL, the student responses need to be collected and assessed. The choice has to be made between a short formative task or a long summative task and carefully defined and designed question tasks.

How, Why, What if? In essence all are typical of the way more challenging open questions begin rather than fact checking ones such as What, When, Who and Where.

Questioning text

The type of questions will vary but to reflect on text there are several possibilities that students need to be made aware of:

What is the author trying to say?
What is the point that the data makes – does it match up to the claims?
Does the text really explain what it sets out to?
What do I still need to know?
Do I understand all the words and concepts?
Does it make sense to me? Why not?
What other explanation is there?
What is fact and what is an opinion?

Questions to uncover assumptions

What actions, beliefs or conclusion are being recommended? What are the reasons for them? Has anything been taken for granted and if so why? Are they correct or incorrect?

Questions to evoke causal reasoning

How is A like B? Things known about B that might also be like A.

What are the reasons for the similarities?

Questions that require causal reasoning are particularly important and an example might be:

Study the text and decide who if anyone was responsible for the action
Develop an argument for each one in turn. Select the best case and draw a causal chain.
Are there any analogies between the (play) and real life today?
What other plays or novels use this story theme?
Hitler: A Study in Tyranny by Alan Bullock.
What reasons does the author give for the crisis in 1934?
To what extent do you think that Rhoem was a genuine threat to Hitler's leadership?
Attempt to predict what might have happened if Hitler had not moved against Rhoem.

Generalisation

What generality has been suggested?
What sample is needed to support this?
Is the sample large enough?
Is the sample really representative of the whole group?
Is the generality well supported by the sample?
If not then what additional information is needed?

B. Cognitive study and research skills

Students' own motivation also plays a part in their potential for success, as does their personal theory of intelligence and ability. This is especially so if they attribute failure to stable unchangeable factors they can do nothing about (Dweck, 2011). Their motivation to learn is then low because they feel it is useless to try.

In the early study skills research, these learners came to be considered as skill-less and the tutor just needed to train them in the appropriate skill to improve their achievements. In modern times, the term 'strategy' is more commonly used and this indicates that alternative modes of learning are being made available to choose as and when appropriate to a problem.

> Learning strategies can be defined as behaviour of a learner that are intended to influence how the learner processes information. Examples include under-lining of key ideas in a passage, outlining of ideas in a lecture or trying to put some newly learned information into one's own words.
>
> Mayer (1992, 11)

In fact, we have moved on from the study skills rules approach indicated by Mayer to expanding the final part of the quote that focuses upon meaningfulness, constructing meaning and metacognitive reflection. Thus although the skills approaches have produced learning gains of 17–20% the newer strategic approaches can produce learning gain of around 70%.

Study skills are usually applied in the revision period before examinations and during note making but they can promote more learning gain if they are moved forward into the prior learning period and during learning itself. An example already given was 'flipped learning'. Revision and integrating the knowledge from the course into some final meaningful whole can take place in a shorter time and be more effective if student-thinking time on task can be increased. Initially, they will need more and structured support to enable them to engage with the task and have success in completing it. This will improve self-efficacy and self-confidence as they approach more challenging tasks.

Although a lecture in whatever format may be expertly structured as in Reception Learning, it is surprising how different students' understanding and interpretations can be. In any case they will usually only remember 5% of it

(Race, 1992) unless they have a photographic memory and then they may have still have problems in sorting out the main ideas, schemes and themes. Others, especially from traditional courses have been passive learners and remain so in 'robot' mode unable to apply what they have been told even when they have been given example applications.

The following seven examples of study skills are typically used.

1. The hook and eye technique

This consists of drawing a ring round key concepts or themes in a text and linking them with lines to their next point of emergence. It makes a mess of the paper but helps focus the mind.

2. Underlining and highlighting

These techniques are widely used when reading a text in preparation for note-taking to identify important ideas. They allow immediate access to these key issues in later note taking or re-reading.

Both these techniques should only be used when the text is owned. Highlighting text is regarded as an important SRL strategy but although students may know about it, they may not choose to use it. It is often cited as an important component in training studies in SRL research but it is ugly to look at and spoils books so some will not use it on this account. However, it is only one minor technique in a broad range of more interesting learning strategies that are available. Having busily underlined half the text as some do, job done, a student may still completely forget what was in it.

3. Mind maps

This was a technique widely promoted by Tony Buzan (1977) and adopted for use particularly with dyslexics and slow writers as they found note-taking so difficult. They were encouraged to draw a series of balloon outlines and attach key words and concepts to them to show relationships and main ideas. This has been extended as concept mapping below.

4. SQ3R

SQ3R stands for Survey, Question, Read, Recite, Review and there are other variants such as PQ3R (Problem, etc.). Research has shown (Bond and Tinker, 1967; Fischer, 2014) that half the students taught to use it are unmotivated to do so and do not achieve the learning gains. The reason appears to be that it is useful to try but can become extremely tedious if it is the only technique available. The more creative learner is especially unmotivated because of the rote memorising aspects especially in the Recite phase.

SQ3R is essentially a post hoc revision activity and the CPS strategies to be discussed are arranged to take place before and during as well as after new material is introduced. They are designed to promote reflective and deeper understanding during the learning process even though the learner may be solitary.

5. Skimming and scanning

Skimming tends to be the very rapid running the eyes down the text, an index or a directory to note or find anything that might need closer attention, a surface strategy.

In scanning a text, reading key words, summary, headings the first sentence, subheadings and conclusion Anderson (1980) found that there were other activities going on. He found that nearly all his students were trying to answer three additional 'how' questions. These were:

- How much do I already know about this topic and text? If anything is already known it can act as an 'advance organiser' to make later acquisition more effective. Or it may be somewhat familiar and the student decides to save time and stop reading/watching and do something more interesting.
- How interested am I in it?
- How difficult or time-consuming will it be for me to learn what I need to know from it?

If by scanning they could not answer all these questions, they went on to read sections in more detail or the surveying would break down and they turned to another book or another activity.

6. Patching and snapping

The student looks for key words in web articles or texts, and patches them onto the laptop pages for later consideration and use. Maybe a student just puts them all together with some connecting sentences and hands in the essay. Plagiarism.

In a lecture, the happy snappers capture the Power Point slides on their iPhones or other devices to save writing them down and missing bits. This is for later study and they also may word-process what they can of what is being said in the lecture. Research by Mueller and Oppenheimer (2014) suggested that this too is a bad strategy in their article, *'The pen is mightier than the keyboard. Advantages of longhand over laptop note taking'*. The reason was that handwritten notes cause the student to concentrate hard to summarise where possible what is being told and the manual writing process connects with meaningfulness in the word lexicon (James and Engelhardt, 2012). If after the lecture and within 24 hours, the student runs through the content and adds additional notes this can be a more effective method for increasing learning gain.

7. Reading comprehension training

These training sessions involve the following skill-set – Preview headings, recite subheadings, ask questions for subheadings, read to find important details, reread subheadings and recite important details, rehearse. This is another post hoc memory training set of rote activities that are not particularly interesting. The following techniques are examples of more 'engage brain' or cognitive study skills.

Reading to learn project

Using a Reading Event Recorder the researchers from Brunel University identified four different types of reading strategy (Harri-Augstein et al., 1985). They found that first-year students on several degree programmes who were ineffective readers engaged in several rapid read-throughs of text. They were later unable to summarise what they had read or satisfactorily complete a short answer factual recall test on it. Successful readers engaged in reading through the text but rolling forwards and backwards in order to check up on points and the most successful also paused for thinking and reflection time as well as to organise their notes.

Partially effective readers engaged in slow runs through the text stopping to make notes as they did so. These students were only successful on the objective test and not the summary. It is typical of the strategy that many students use to collect information for an essay. They do not do a survey read to get an overview but just do a note-taking run expecting by this means to understand what is written. The result is that the essay too often looks like a neatly written/word processed version of the original note-taking exercise and is not usually organised to answer the question.

Directed activities related to texts – DARTs

In 1980, the UK Schools Council published a handbook detailing the methods teachers and trainers had used in a Study Skills project to try to improve independent learning in schools. Concern had arisen because of the lack of such skills in secondary school pupils and university students. The activities were referred to as DARTs. The central issue was that students were not aware that different types of text needed different strategies for reading for understanding. They tended to use one type of reading strategy for all purposes. This was Receptive reading, the type that is suitable for reading a novel or a newspaper. One quick reading of the text gathers up the sense of it.

What was observed was that a slower and more deliberate searching of text read was often necessary for complex subjects and textbooks where the text is concept dense. This was called Reflective reading. The difficulty found was how to slow down the readers' reading to absorb the deeper meanings. The most common and traditional strategy the students discovered for themselves was to read a little, make some notes then read some more and make some more notes. Pausing for thinking time also appeared to enhance understanding.

The problem was that students did not always want to spend extra time on note-taking and reflecting that understanding complex text required and quickly reverted to receptive reading. Often they could not see the necessity for working over text to search for deeper meaning. DARTs were thus designed to slow down the reading and induce reflection so that students could see the purpose of it and gain greater enjoyment from reading without having to make endless pages of notes.

Students engaged in reading the research literature for projects and dissertations are confronted by similar problems and need to adopt reflective reading strategies. They need to pause during reading to think, search text backwards and forwards during reading and re-read sections. They often ignore these strategies for the note-taking and spend more time on that than thinking about what they read as they read. The result is a set of final 'fractured utterances' cobbled together to make a report gleaned from their notes. If they stick closely to their notes then they do not recall how much is in the original author's words and can fall into unintentional plagiarism.

This problem has arisen in a new form in the technological era. Because of the lack of study skills development across subjects, students think that they are doing research when they patch in chunks of text from websites.

Based on the information elicited from the analysis of the essay tasks in the Oxford Tutorial system, there are three main areas that need to be covered in the study skills strategies. These go beyond the simple underlining, skimming and scanning and SQ3R strategies, for example,

Clarifying and organising. As in questioning, concept mapping, diagramming, categorising and classification.
Reading for meaning. As in sequencing, concept completion, main ideas, flow-charting, reflection, recognising intent, bias, falsehoods and propaganda and summarising.
Writing to inform. Scaffolding, Zone of Proximal Development (ZPD), graphic organisers, protocols, analogising and modelling.

In addition to the above three areas each subject in the arts, humanities or sciences will have unique skills sets that need to be taught or upgraded. But thinking and communication are involved in all subjects and activities, they are the general capabilities.

Talking approaches can help build skills in composition and organisational abilities and this is the value of tutorials, seminars and debates. They can be supported by the technique of scaffolding. Direct teaching of **'scaffolds'** can be especially helpful because those from disadvantaged linguistic backgrounds will have had fewer opportunities to learn them to assist their learning and understanding. But scaffolds can help them close the Excellence gap.

> Scaffolding thinking consists of supporting student application of a cognitive operation by structuring the execution of that operation with verbal and/or visual prompts, they benefit immensely from having their initial attempts to practice a procedure scaffolded until they have internalised the procedure and can execute it on their own.
>
> (Beyer, 1997, 171)

The model sometimes used in HE is Vygotsky's (1978) ZPD in which scaffolds are provided by the mentor to extend the student knowledge. Vygotsky first pointed out the role of inner speech in the development of cognition from the earliest of years and scaffolds can be used to develop this.

Cognitive process study skills

These can apply to textual, visual, auditory and performance material.

1 Concept mapping
2 Concept completion activities
3 Locating the main points and subordinate ones
4 Flow-charting
5 Prediction activities
6 Sequencing and scaffolds
7 Drafting and editing
8 Organising - tabulating, classifying, ordering
9 Comparing and contrasting
10 Summarising
11 Recognising intent, bias and propaganda
12 Drawing inferences and abstractions

A university student engaged in research might need to use all of these strategies in preparing a dissertation or independent study. Some students may not have experienced many of them and others need to be taught them rather than hoping they will develop them incidentally. It is important to incorporate these study skills into all subject areas rather than try to teach them as a separate skills course (Meek and Thomson, 1987). Bolt-on provision has been shown to be ineffective and non-transferable as in the Blagg et al. (1993) 'Bo-peep theory' of transfer.

They investigated Study Skills training in Work-based Learning and Further Education programmes and identified three models of transfer as follows:

- The 'Bo-peep' model: Transfer will take care of itself. Their researches showed that this was not the case, learners too often failed to deploy or adapt their intellectual resources in unfamiliar circumstances.
- The Lost Sheep model: Transfer rarely occurred so most new problems were likely to need additional training.
- The Good Shepherd model: Transfer did occur when it was shepherded, nurtured and mediated.

They found that the particular types of learning and teaching that fostered transfer were those that were taught in context and were problem based. It is evident that in self-regulated learning, the Good Shepherd model is the model to aim for. Unfortunately, most of the research that investigates study-skills training is based upon training courses that are 'bolt on' provision and assume the 'Bo-peep' and 'Lost sheep' models of transfer.

The DARTs activities were summarised by Lunzer and Gerchow (1984) as falling into two main types:

1 **Analytical study of text**
    Analysis: Underlining, segmenting, labelling, grouping and ranking
    Alternative representation: Listing, tabulating, diagrammatic representation
    Extrapolation: Student-generated questioning, imaginative extension
2 **Reconstruction of text**
    Deletion
    Sequencing
    Prediction

Diagrammatic representation was expanded to include the following activities: hierarchical table or family tree diagram, flow diagram, interacting diagram, labelled and simplified diagram, free diagram and diagram completion.

Priming, front-loaded learning or 'flipped' learning

This is useful in a first study module to set the scene and establish student confidence and was exemplified in Chapter 1.

1. Concept mapping

Instruction: 'Draw a concept map of your knowledge and understanding about subject XXX'. A key construct was selected that students would have some prior knowledge of to bring to the programme. The concept map would bring this past knowledge into focus and prime the memory to receive and integrate any new information. Example constructs used were SEN (special educational needs), UAch (underachievement, HLP (High Learning Potential), Creativity, Appraisal etc. A key construct in any discipline can be chosen.

The tactics were as follows:

A1. Below is an example of a concept map on the subject of RUN. You may already use concept maps in making study notes.

A2. On the next page is a key construct in this subject area. Draw your own concept map of this topic. It should summarise what you know and think about the topic. (A whole page is given for this with the construct in a ring in the centre.)

B1. The student listens to the lecture on the topic, reads the lecture notes or watches the video.

C1. Several days later, the student is asked to draw a second concept map of the subject incorporating any new knowledge and thoughts.

D1. Then 'Write down 10 differences between the first and second concept maps and give your reflections on what you were thinking about each one'. Metacognition. (Formative and Diagnostic)

E1. 'Assess the level of your two concept maps using Bigg's SOLO taxonomy (below) and give your reasons'. (F and D)

E2. 'Compare the SOLO system to the assessment system used by the university as detailed in the Student Handbook on the website'. (F)

The concept map drawn before the lecture or readings represents the 'flipped learning' technique that helps front-load learning. The tutor when marking the differences can evaluate the development and quality of the thinking at surface and deep levels and suggest further areas for analysis and reflection. The grade given was based upon the university assessment criteria (A 20-point system also cross-referenced with the 12-point grade scale which the students were more likely to be used to), so the student begins to become familiar with criterion-referenced systems.

The tutor needs only look at the two maps to check whether the evaluations are correct but has the 10 differences and the SOLO level as shown in Table 6.1 and rationale to mark for the grade.

Table 6.1 SOLO taxonomy (Biggs and Collis, 1983)

Taxonomy level	Description
Pre-structural	There is no evidence of any knowledge of the processes or content
Uni-structural	One relevant aspect is understood and focused upon
Multi-structural	Several relevant and independent aspects are given but are not integrated into an overall structure
Relational	Relevant aspects are integrated into an overall structure. Main issues and ideas are incorporated into this.
Extended abstract	The integrated knowledge is generalised to a new domain.

2. Concept completion

An example of a concept completion activity might be to read, for example, the poem by Stephen Spender and try to reconstruct the author's original intent.

> **Ultima Ratio Regum** (first verse only here)
>
> The guns spell money's ultimate reason
>
> In letters of _____ on the Spring hillside.
>
> But the boy lying _____ under the olive trees
>
> Was too young and too _____
>
> To have been notable to their important eye.
>
> He was a better target for a _____ .

The last concept is more difficult to reconstruct and causes students who do not know the poem to think very carefully about the whole structure, meaning and the context. When there is 'the reveal' a reflective piece of writing can be obtained and they can be set to research the actual context and write further 'articles' as a Sun reporter and/or a Sunday Times leader etc.

A similar concept completion exercise can be used with any short but critical piece of text. (The technique is different from Reading Test 'cloze' procedures when every fifth or seventh word is deleted.)

3. Locating the main point

Students can be asked to identify the main point or main idea of an author or a lecture they have just heard or viewed. Pictures and adverts can also be examined and ideas about them analysed using this procedure. Identifying main and subordinate ideas can lead on to producing flow charts and chronologies or time lines whatever method of recording and representing might be appropriate.

For example in this poem by Sir Walter Raleigh students might be asked to identify its main point and the type of structure he uses then decide on a similar structure and write some lines of their own using the technique.

> What is our life? a play of passion;
> Our mirth, the music of division;
> Our mother's wombs the tiring houses be
> Where we are dressed for this short comedy
> Heaven the judicious sharp spectator,
> That sits and marks still doth act amiss
> Our graves that hide us from the searing sun
> Are the drawn curtains when the play is done.
> Thus march we playing to our latest rest;
> Only we die in earnest - that's no jest.

When students had deduced it was a metaphor they were given the following simile:

'Life is like an apple'

Two Dundee head teachers on CPD wrote their response:

> Life is like an apple.
> From seed to core
> And nothing more,
> Naught but rot in store.

Other main point exercises can be used in science, arts and humanities showing how in simple reports, newspapers and illustrations, the main point is frequently in the first sentence. The question then can be: *Identify the main point of this extract:* _____ *and then decide which of the following writing patterns is exemplified in it.*

a   illustration – example
b   definition
c   comparison – contrast
d   sequence of events
e   cause and effect
f   description
g   a mixture – state which

They can then be asked to try to write a paragraph about a relevant subject topic using three different patterns, for example, topics might include Volcanoes, lectures, deforestation, the Long Parliament, gills, global warming, the Holocaust, neurons, etc. It then becomes easy for them to look for and recognise writing patterns that authors use and employ them in their own writing.

4. Flow charting

Laurie Thomas and Sheila Harri-Augstein (1975) undertook a long-term research project on Reading to Learn using materials such as the Darwin example below. They charted the eye movements of undergraduates reading complex text extracts with the results already described above.

4A. READING FOR THE MAIN POINT

The task was to summarise and to complete a Flow Diagram of the Logical Structure of the Paragraph. The student is asked to reflect afterwards on the eye scanning strategies used to do the task and note down how long this all took.

An example of the training material used by Thomas and Harri-Augstein: Darwin's 'Origin of Species' (adapted from)

1   Again, it may be asked, how is it that varieties which I have called incipient species, become ultimately converted into good and distinct species, which

in most cases obviously differ from each other far more than do the varieties of the same species.

2   How do those groups of species constitute what are called distinct genera? And which differ from each other more than do the same genus, arise?

3   All these results, as we shall more fully see in the next chapter follow from the struggle for life.

4   Owing to this struggle, variations, however slight, and from whatever cause proceeding, if they be in any degree profitable to the individuals or a species, or in their infinitely complex relations to organic beings and to their physical conditions of life, will tend to the preservation of such individuals, and will generally be inherited by the offspring.

5   The offspring also, will thus have a better chance of surviving, for, of the many individuals of any species which are periodically born, but a small number can survive.

6   I have called this principle by which each slight variation, if useful, is preserved, by the term Natural Selection, in order to mark its relation to man's power of selection.

7   But the expression often used by Mr Herbert Spencer of the Survival of the Fittest is more accurate, and is sometimes equally convenient.

8   We have seen that man by selection can certainly produce great results, and can adapt organic beings to his own uses, through the accumulation of slight but useful variations, given to him by the hand of Nature.

9   But Natural Selection, as we shall hereafter see, is as immeasurably superior to man's feeble efforts, as the works of nature are to the works of Art.

Their original task was modified by giving students during a lecture on Study Skills an actual 'Darwin' flow chart to fill in with the purpose of helping them find main points and promote talk about it between pairs.

Put the main point sentence number in the double-lined box shown in Figure 6.1.

4B. RESEARCH PAPERS

After a training session such as the above on main ideas and flow charting, students were set to read a research paper such as Leach (1983) on early screening techniques after they had been given a lecture (or DL lecture notes) on Assessment and Testing. They were then given an empty flow chart (see Figure 6.2) to complete after they had read the paper. The contact course students were encouraged to work in pairs or groups of three.

4C. STUDENT DESIGNS

Once the students became familiar with the technique, the next stage was to set other papers for them to read and then to design their own flow charts for others to complete. This ensures that several versions can be examined for the

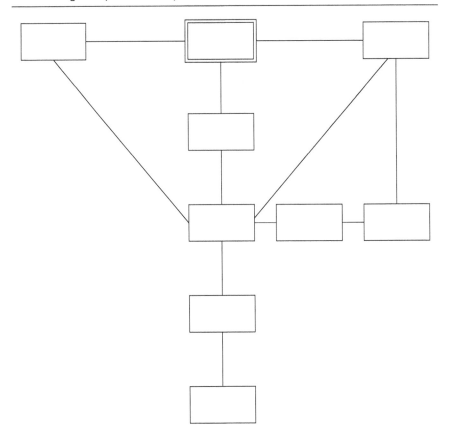

Figure 6.1 Origin of species flow chart.

best design and fit with the paper and that there is a constant supply available for other students to work on. It also cuts down the tutor time in designing them. Significant chapters in books or even whole novels can also be used for flow charting. They can also be set tasks that involve them flowcharting an essay or article that they have personally written to discover how it can be improved.

5. Prediction activities

Basically the question is 'What might happen?' 'What will happen if ...?' or 'What happens next?' just before the denouement. It can be a predictive task that is context defined as in time or place. It can ask 'What did they do next?' or 'What would you have done?' 'What should they have done?' and so on. It can lead on to hypothesising and then testing in all manner of fields.

A set of tactics might be:

- What might happen?
- What clues will show whether it will happen?

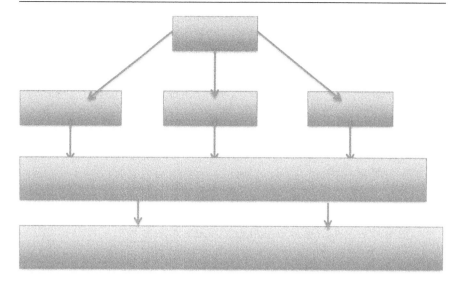

Figure 6.2 Flow chart for the Leach paper.

'Try to put only single words in the small boxes'.

- What real clues are there?
- Do these clues show that it will happen?
- Conclusion.

6. Sequencing and scaffolds

Sequencing involves ordering material to illustrate a theme or present an argument. A training item would be to take a section of text containing an argument, an everyday artistic or scientific sequence or a historical sequence, and putting it in random order for the students to correct.

Scaffolds are a form of sequential guidance that can be particularly helpful to share with the students. Making them aware of the sequence of an argument, a chapter, book or a research paper can help inform their own communications to make them clearer. It also helps them recognise the structure of an author's work whether it is text, film or communication of any kind. Three general examples follow but each subject area will have its own sequences that need to be made explicit.

6A. THE SEQUENCE OF A RESEARCH ARTICLE IN SOCIAL SCIENCES

Title, Abstract, Key words, Introduction/background, Method, Results, Conclusions/Discussion, References

Other disciplines will have their own relevant structures and formats and students can learn to check this with a few journals.

6B. THE SEQUENCE AND STRUCTURE OF AN ESSAY

This is frequently defined by the question asked. In answering an examination type question in education, the technique was:

Tactic 1. Put a ring round each of the different parts or concepts contained in the question – unusually three to five.

Tactic 2. Write a title containing the key elements to be answered.

Tactic 3. Critically discuss the concepts in the question.

Tactic 4. Explain at least two theoretical views or approaches to the concepts or question.

Tactic 5. Present and discuss three to four pieces of empirical research that illustrate the theories and problems identified.

Tactic 6. Explain their practical implications in classrooms or do this with the discussion of the research findings in five.

Tactic 7. Write a summarising statement at the end.

Tactic 8. Proofread what you have written.

6C. THE SEQUENCE OF A RESEARCH PROGRAMME

The diagram in Figure 6.3 illustrates the whole research process from initial observations through to developing a hypothesis and on to testing it and developing a theory. It describes a research programme. Most research projects are based in one or other of the two types of theory – developing or testing. In theory testing, for example, the hypothesis is usually developed from reading other people's research and observations and finding an omission or raising a further question, very typical of much student research. Social Anthropology and Sociology are to a larger extent based in the developing theory area. Historical research based on original sources would also rest in this area as might critical reviews of literary texts and an author's profile of works. The performance of a play or dance could also be based in both areas of theory. Composing new work could also be regarded

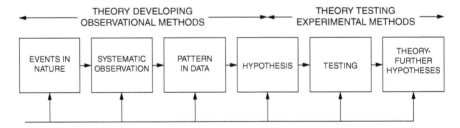

Figure 6.3 The research process (figure based on ideas suggested by Entwistle and Nisbet, 1972).

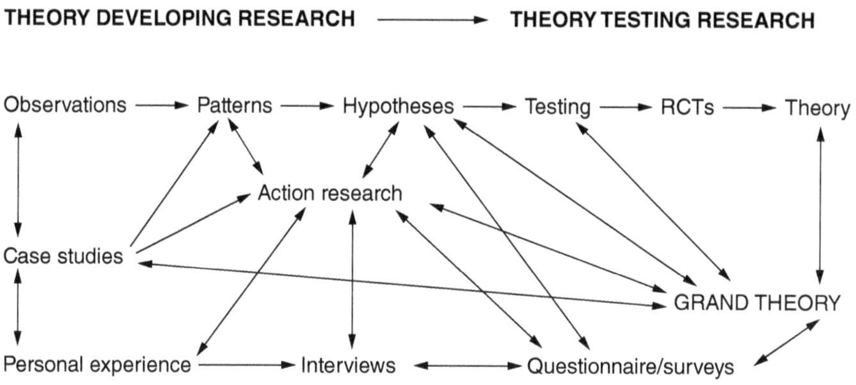

THEORY DEVELOPING RESEARCH ⟶ **THEORY TESTING RESEARCH**

Observations ⟶ Patterns ⟶ Hypotheses ⟶ Testing ⟶ RCTs ⟶ Theory

Action research

Case studies

GRAND THEORY

Personal experience ⟶ Interviews ⟵ Questionnaire/surveys

Figure 6.4 An extension of the Entwistle and Nisbet research process.

as theory developing research with more emphasis on the unique resources and experience of the composer.

Creativity training and development will be given further consideration in Chapter 7. To a large extent, it can be considered to begin in personal experience in Figure 6.4 and lead to a form of Action Research.

Psychology students in the past were told that they must write up their dissertation research as a hypothesis – test investigation and were failed or 'referred' to amend it if they did not do so. There are however a variety of research procedures that can be engaged with in a range of subjects.

In Figure 6.4, the diagram shows the potential ranges of research and how they fit within the Entwistle model in Figure 6.3.

Another area of contention in research design is the admissibility or not in some quarters of qualitative research as opposed to quantitative methods whereas most research needs to be a mixture of both in due proportion in any sphere involving human behaviour.

Narrative into theory (Berthoff, 1987). There is a subtext underlying most of the research methods in Figures 6.3 and 6.4 that Berthoff defined as Narrative into theory. This is a process in which we write our experience and observations and as we write ideas, it shapes them from the narrative into theory and this is a legitimate theory developing process.

6D. THE WRITING OF A DISSERTATION

The standard advice that used to be given to students was 'Tell them what you are going to do and why – do it – then tell them what you have done and found out'. This was also used as a structure for the different chapters. If students have not had previous experience of independent project work this can be helpful as a general strategy.

One of the most difficult things for students is to find a way to start and they can finish up delaying starting until it is almost too late for them to do their best work. They initially may have problems in 'question finding' and then when they have started they often do not have sufficient experience of the essential need to draft and edit their work. This problem is exacerbated by the Word Processor. We see our work in print and run a spelling and grammar check but then do not read and edit it as the first draft of many because it looks so good.

Strategy to help get started on a dissertation.

1 Write down the area(s) of potential interest/study in as few words as possible.
2 Jot down ideas that arise from thinking around the key words, maybe draw a concept map.
3 Leave a couple of days to keep thinking about the topics, perhaps find out what others are doing.
4 Collect a few books and papers on the topics. Check library and online resources.
5 Skim a few of them and check for any previous notes.
6 Narrow down the topic areas chosen to two or three, preferably one and write a series of problems or questions that might need answering.
7 Select the one question or problem that you have the most likely chance of being able to investigate.

Take a pause of a day or two. Then start again.

1 Define the research question as narrowly as possible.
2 Select one hour of the day for, for example, reading research and study the text/materials and make some notes.
3 Do this at a regular time and place for six more days.

Take a pause for a day or two and start again, reflection time.

1 Write 500 words about the topic. Do not use any of the notes you have made yet.
2 Next day re-read and edit the 500 words and write 500 more.
3 Continue with more reading research.
4 Start to add extra ideas and information from any collected notes to the 1000 or so words.
5 Re-read and edit the draft so far and check that it is a response to the question raised.
6 Write notes to identify further things that need to be investigated and practical activities and research that might be relevant. Define the research question as narrowly as possible.

7 Continue and adapt the process with regular note-taking, drafting and editing.

Take some advice.

1 Write the research question as a title for the dissertation with a brief abstract to show how it will be investigated.
2 Check with the tutor that it is in a suitable format and meets the exam requirements and is ethically sound.
3 Start writing the report.

6E. THEMATIC ANALYSIS

TA has its origins in the 1970s (Merton, 1975) although in practical terms many studies have used the same or similar techniques under the general heading of Qualitative Analysis. Clarke and Braun (2013) teach TA to their students and identified six phases in the process of carrying out research using a TA scaffold as follows:

1 **Familiarisation with the data.** This is what all research involves – immersing oneself in the data and the literature surrounding it.
2 **Coding.** Generating pithy labels for the important features. This involves data reduction and analysis.
3 **Searching for themes.** Searching the data for coherent meaningful patterns, coding the codes to identify similarities in the data-research constructs.
4 **Reviewing themes.** Ensuring the themes work in relation to both coded extracts and the full data set.
5 **Defining and naming themes.** A detailed analysis of each theme is written and the story it tells. It identifies the essence of each and finds a pithy name for it.
6 **Writing up.** This involves the weaving together the analytic narrative and vivid data extracts to tell a coherent and persuasive story about the data and contextualising it in relation to existing literature. As can be seen it is a pithy version of the tactics set out in 6d above.

6F. GROUNDED RESEARCH

This follows the theory developing process outlined by Entwistle and described by Strauss and Corbin (1990) as grounded research. In developing the 5-Star plan the procedure was as follows:

• **Recording and counting.** Hundreds of lessons, lesson extracts, lesson events and lesson notes were recorded. A range of recording techniques and strategies were trialled.

- **Patterning.** Observing and noting certain recurring patterns in the data and cues or indicants. In feedback sessions and reflections on lessons, patterns were noted and often cross-referenced to theory and other research.
- **Coding.** Key patterns were named and re-sorted or categorised and classified during and after repeated observations.
- **Clustering.** Grouping and categorising activities, settings and interactions during data review and reflection are undertaken.
- **Factoring.** Cluster groups were reduced to a small number of factors with explanatory power and which might be renamed, to feedback to students. For example the CBG, 3Ms and PCI etc. of the sampling frame.
- **New relationships.** These were then sought between factors. For example, the concept of the Tactical Lesson Plan was evolved from the data to help teachers structure the learning opportunities of the pupils and the pace of the lessons.

This process models the statistical procedure of **Factor Analysis** when all the numerical data is fed in and patterns and clusters are evoked. It is also applied with (Artificial Intelligence) AI packages that undertake conceptual analyses of text.

6G. GRAPHIC ORGANISERS

6g.i. In essay planning or decision-making the graphic organiser (Swartz and Parks, 1994) can provide a helpful scaffold to develop the fullest responses. In a question about the best method of producing energy to prevent further global warming the following type of organiser can be used.

OPTIONS	RELEVANT CONSEQUENCES			
	Ease of production	*Availability*	*Cost*	*Consequences*
Coal				
Wind				
Nuclear				
Petro-chems				
Tidal flow				
Solar				
Anaerobics				
Wood				
River dams				
Burn rubbish				
Shale gas				
Natural gas				

6g. ii. Graphic organisers in Drama and Dance – making a video
The developments are set on a time line as a series of boxes containing the following prompts (Taylor, 1991, 103 – *Lesson Structures*).

Stimulus: Discussion of what the video is to be about
Group work: Improvisation of content
Group work: Scripting
Group work: Rehearsal
Presentation
Rough shoot
Screening appraisal
Final shoot

6g. iii. Story boarding, a related technique
Writers and playwrights may similarly use scaffolds as they follow different genres.

6g. iv. Movements and themes in musical compositions
Composers also use performance scaffolds and follow various compositional traditions.

6g. v. Interview protocols
Interviewers have protocols for getting the best results from their interviewees. Some are semi-structured and others are fully structured protocols. An important consideration in interviewing is not just the questions but 'active listening' and paraphrasing at just the right moments to reinforce.

Many students have for so long in schools been passive learners that they hear but do not remember or action what they have learned. Active listening exercises can be useful to prime them for listening and learning across disciplines. It is also useful as a soft skill in employment.

7. Drafting and editing

7A. ESSAY MARKING

The strategy frequently used is to give two complete example course essays: one very good and one very poor and ask the students to mark them according to the course assessment criteria and provide supportive written feedback to the writer. Students in contact programmes can benefit from pairing and sharing their analyses. In the early stages, this gives confidence and feelings of support and self-efficacy to students. It gives them explicit understanding of the course-assessment criteria.

7B. EDITING TEXT

The piece of text in Appendix 1 gives an example of a training exercise that can be useful early in a programme to help student's drafting and editing of their own essays.

There are a number of problems with the draft:

1 The structure appears to be an account in chronological order at first but then the dates are not in sequential order. So what structure is being used?
2 The structure is perhaps one of issues as stated in the first paragraph but they seem to be lost as the account progresses and other issues assume importance.
3 We can see it is notes as almost every paragraph begins in the same way with the researcher's names and dates or 'A study by – ', 'The study by – ', etc.

    The Task is to rewrite the introductory sentences to paragraphs 2, 3, 4 and 5 so that the text no longer reads as notes and each paragraph begins in a different way.
4 Cue the students to the dates issue and what many reviewers will do.

7C. ESSAY REVIEW CHECKLIST

Ashman and Crème (1993, 20–21) devised the following guidance points for their students.

Have I answered the question that was set?
Have I divided up the question into separate smaller questions and answered them?
Have I covered all the main aspect?
Have I covered them in enough depth?
Is the content relevant?
Is the content accurate?
Have I arranged the material logically?
Does the essay move smoothly from one section and one paragraph to the next?
Is each main point supported by examples and argument?
Have I acknowledged all sources and references?
Have I distinguished clearly between my own ideas and those of others?
Is the essay the right length according to the word limit and its own purpose?
Have I written clearly and simply?
Have I read it aloud to sort out clumsy and muddled phrasing? (Maybe use inner speech?)
Are the grammar, punctuation and spelling acceptable? (Grammar check)
Is the essay neatly and legibly written? (Word processed?)
Have I presented a convincing case that I could justify in a discussion?

8. Organising – tabulating, classifying, ordering

Putting results into columns and tables is a common activity in many courses and familiar to all students. The items in the columns are then put in an order of, for example, magnitude or importance and so on. For example, find 3 or 5 or 10 main points from a lecture, chapter, article, performance and place in rank order of importance – easy to mark and helps diagnose difficulties.

Classification involves organising subjects and materials into like-minded characteristics, or orientated groups and then giving them a category title or pithy label. Most will be familiar with this type of system in the classification of plants and animals. Life is often spent in categories – modern, classical, popular, genre, class and so on but students may need to have these made explicit in the subject area in order to study their effects.

9. Comparing and contrasting

a. These are popular tasks and underlie many exam questions. Graphic organisers can be used to support them especially where students are not well organised or practised in such tasks. For example:

Task: Compare and contrast the two characters (methods; outcomes) in a particular text.

Tabulate:	How they are the same?	How are they different?
i.		
ii.		
iii.		
n.		

Using this strategy makes it easier to compose the essay and include all the relevant facts.

10. Summarising an example summative assignment

At the end of a unit of study instead of asking for an essay on the topic under study the summative task can be to write 3 or 4 × 500-word summaries to explain to a group of non-specialist colleagues the nature of the following: for example, Dyslexia; Asperger Syndrome; High Learning Potential; Disadvantage

This task exemplifies writing for different audiences and prevents copying out streams of notes from the lectures or patching in sections from articles, and really requires students to think about the core of the topics.

Summarising is a powerful tool and is a useful employment skill to practice as is writing for different audiences in different registers because the writer needs to put him or herself in the shoes of the reader or listener and think what they need to learn from the text that will help them understand a topic and be useful to them. It is a type of 'learning conversation' with the reader such as they might hold verbally in a seminar or in the refectory.

Other summarising techniques are as follows:

Bullet points. Identify 3, 5 or 10 key points.

Mini-sagas. A 50-word summary of a whole book, chapter, article or play. The saga must be written in exactly 50 words no more no less

Postcards. Fifty words to be written on a postcard about a place under study as it is now or in the past or future. The style can be in the manner of a particular author or historical period.

Tweets. Writing a summary view in 280 characters

Bio pics. One hundred and fifty words to be written about a famous author, scientist, performer etc. A second copy to be written in a newspaper or magazine style or from a negative critical stance.

Biogs. The students write their own biographies to the present time in 250 words to be placed on their portfolios as in a first book/work. They should also write a further 50 or so words to predict their subsequent career, which they need not share. Cartoons and sketches will be appropriate in some subject areas.

Key words. Five key words chosen to define the content of a reading, research article or review.

Blogs and Twitter. Keep a sample profile of these about a module.

Raps or Slam poetry. Can sum up a short course.

Diagramming. A diagram or visual model such as Figure 6.3 summarises in visual form a large amount of textual or verbal data. It can be a useful strategy to ask students after a set of readings or a lecture to draw a diagram of the structure of the contents. Students can benefit from sharing these with peers and with the tutor for feedback.

Précis. This is the formal term for a summary and can be a very hard task to do well to include all the main ideas in a succinct format. The smaller types above can be useful training activities.

11. Recognising intent, bias and propaganda

An illustrative training item can be useful to show and discuss before a more challenging one is found in the subject area. A simple example is shown on the next page. Newspapers and theatre or book reviews are the usual sources and now we have Fake news and Podcasts to work on. The task is to write T, F, O, B (True, False, Opinion or Bias) in a ring round or by the side of the appropriate phrase.

12. Drawing inferences and abstractions

Inference is the process of drawing a conclusion or reaching a conclusion on the basis of previously made or accepted judgments. For example, the pituitary gland

---

'London could drown this winter' (T,F,O,B?)

It would happen because over the centuries Britain has been slowly tilting.

London is sinking because of all the weight of people and buildings in the South East and the tide in the Thames is rising because of global warming. The biggest threat is a combination of heavy rain in the head waters of the Thames and fast drainage into the river from all the towns downstream. Severe weather conditions in the Atlantic and the North Sea. Low air pressure combined with the tides backed up by a northerly gale. This will cause an enormous surge of water down the East Coast of Britain and up into the capital's river meeting the overflow from down river.

More than a million Londoners living in low lying areas and flood plains each side of the Thames from Richmond to Havering could find their homes, roads, shops, factories, hospitals and schools under water.

Faced with such an appalling risk the GLC built a permanent defence – the Thames Barrier at Woolwich. It is the biggest moveable flood barrier ever built. It has been dubbed one of the 'wonders of the world'.

---

in the brain is responsible for growth. This person has a pituitary gland problem. His growth will be likely to be affected.

On the other hand someone else might erroneously conclude that – this person is small and therefore she has a pituitary gland problem.

Speakers and writers for clarity often state their main proposition in their first sentence and then assemble a series of arguments or points to support it. Where this structure is not used the reader or listener has to abstract the main proposition from the talk or text.

Design an assessment tool

The students can be given access to three key research papers to study (or other appropriate materials). Their task is to design a short answer examination paper worth, for example, 70 marks. This is long enough to provide some strong enough challenge and for the student to have to engage in reflective rather than receptive reading. Some of the questions should demand more than just factual recall.

The structure of the paper could be as follows:

1 Twenty true or false questions with boxes to put in T or F
2 Ten multiple-choice questions with four options in each to select from, with tick boxes for the correct answers
3 Twenty to thirty sentence-completion items to make up the other 40 points
4 The student should hand in an example correctly completed test paper as well as a blank one. This enables the tutor to identify areas of error and misconception as well as gather in some useful test items for a test bank.

Misrepresentation

Perhaps every tutor in HE at some point should design an exercise within the course to illustrate for students the misuse and abuse of logic and the regular misrepresentation and use of emotive language. A general example might be 'firm, stubborn, pig-headed (Thouless, 1967, 2011) 'He is firm. She is stubborn and they are pig-headed. This demonstrates not only the use of increasingly emotive language but also an underlying stereotypic attitude of the speaker or writer to women and to out groups.

Thouless gives 38 dishonest tricks that are used in argument and shows methods that can be used to overcome them (pp. 171–6).

Conclusion

The main point of this chapter has been to present different ways in which student time on task can be attracted, maintained and increased. The reason for this is because increasing student time on task has been found to promote learning gain and academic achievement especially when it is given to organising, understanding and constructing personal meaning within the subject knowledge area.

The main forms of the intervention in this chapter are termed Cognitive Study Skills and were constructed to 'engage brain' before and during active learning rather than the post hoc rote memorising revision techniques that are normally used. The examples describe strategic approaches to study and the tactics that can be employed that will achieve the goals and purposes set and also be enjoyable so that motivation and self-efficacy are increased. The examples have been developed and tested in contact and distance postgraduate and undergraduate programmes and were shown to increase learning gain. They were especially necessary for those students with excellence gaps.

The overall purpose was to promote the metacognitive and reflective capacities of students to engage in inner speech or learning conversations so that they would become more skilful self-organised and self-regulated learners.

In higher education, the topic of Self-Regulated Learning, Distance Education and Blended Learning has become an important area of research and development. It is very much related to futures scenarios and managing the increasing numbers of students entering Higher Education. As numbers of students have risen needs have widened and new strategies for teaching them have needed to be developed.

Chapter 7

Strategies to promote learning gain in HE

Problem-based learning

Introduction

Jerome Bruner (1966) described the activities that he thought were essential to make teaching and learning realistic and constructive for students. He termed it Discovery Learning and it was an inquiry training that enabled students to gain a fundamental understanding of the underlying principles of the subject they were studying. In this process, they also learned the concepts and relationships. When they worked in these ways, he found that they grew in intellectual potency, were intrinsically motivated, had mastery of principles that enabled them to apply their learning and showed gains in memory as a result of the organisation of their knowledge. It did not mean that they were required to 'reinvent the wheel' on each educational opportunity as was often believed to be the case.

Taba (1962) identified four steps in discovery learning that can also be used as a teaching-learning protocol:

- The problem creates bafflement.
- The learner(s) explore the problem.
- The learners are prompted to generalise and use prior knowledge to understand a new problem or pattern.
- There is a need for opportunities to apply the principles learned to new situations.

In the modern period the terms have changed to Real-world problem solving (RPS) (Gallagher, 1997) in which 'fuzzy' problems are the initial presentation of the task and Problem-based learning (PBL) when the problem may be simulations, games or inventions and somewhat more defined. These are also typical of many research issues and learning to handle them is an important skill. Initially, many students are fearful of such uncertainties especially if they have come from a traditional didactic schooling. However, there are strategies, tactics and scaffolds they can learn to employ that will help them succeed and become more self-sufficient and close the excellence gap.

These strategies were defined as Cognitive Process Strategies (CPS) and three categories of CPS have already been discussed in detail. The examples were

Developmental Positive Cognitive Intervention through formative, diagnostic and summative feedback (in Chapter 4), Challenging Questioning, and Cognitive Study and Research Skills (in Chapter 6). In this chapter, the rest of the range of strategies will be discussed and examples given from successful higher education (HE) programmes that achieved higher learning gains by using them.

The list of remaining strategies is:

- **C. Teaching thinking skills**
- **D. Reflective teaching and learning**
- **E. Developing creativity**
- **F. Real world and Problem-based learning**
- **G. Games, simulations and role-play**
- **H. Experiential learning**
- **I. Self-regulated learning**

C. Teaching thinking skills strategies

McGuinness identified several 'core concepts' with regard to thinking skills and learning. Although she was reviewing the situation in schools for the DfE the constructs apply equally to learning and teaching in HE. Students in HE are also learners who need to construct meaning for themselves and be systematic in their approach and adopt a critical attitude and communicate effectively. Thus how tutors can intervene to support this is an important area of study if higher learning gain is to be achieved.

> Although it may seem self-evident, focusing on thinking skills in the classroom is important because it supports active cognitive processing which makes for better learning. Thus, pupils are equipped to search out meaning and impose structure; to deal systemically, yet flexibly, with novel problems and situations; to adopt a critical attitude to information and argument, and to communicate effectively. Standards can only be raised when attention is directed not only on what is to be learned but on how students learn and how teachers intervene to achieve this.
>
> (McGuinness, 1999, 5)

The key conclusions of her report were: a framework for developing thinking skills was needed that included:

- The need to make thinking skills explicit in a curriculum.
- Teaching thinking through a form of coaching.
- Taking a metacognitive perspective.
- Collaborative learning (including computer-mediated learning).
- Creating dispositions and habits of good thinking.
- Generalising the framework beyond a narrow focus on skills to include thinking curricula, thinking classrooms and thinking schools.

She identified three models for delivering thinking skills:

1 Enhancing general thinking skills through structured programmes that were additional to the normal curriculum, for example, Instrumental Enrichment (Feuerstein, 1980), Somerset Thinking Skills Course (Blagg et al., 1993) and CoRT Thinking Programme (de Bono, 1983).

   But these are 'bolt on' provisions and can lack transferability except in the hands of experts. It requires extra effort and skill to make these experiences into the 'Good shepherd' transfer model.

2 Targeting subject-specific learning such as science, mathematics, geography, for example, CASE (Cognitive Acceleration through Science Education) (Shayer and Adey, 2002), and later through Technology Education (CATE). These involved reflective periods each fortnight for thinking about the thinking engaged in, metacognition.

   In HE, it is often assumed that students will go on after the lectures and tutorials to reflect not only upon what they have learned, but also the processes that were involved. Strategies that have been used to promote this are learning logs and diaries.

3 Infusing thinking skills across the curriculum by systematically identifying opportunities within the normal curriculum for thinking skills development (Swartz and Parks, 1994) and ACTS – Activating Children's Thinking Skills, McGuinness, 1999). The processes they used have been to give discreet practice on strategy training and then organise ways in which they might be repeated in an applied subject specific context.

The more successful thinking skills approaches tended to have a strong theoretical underpinning, well designed and contextualised materials, explicit pedagogy and good teacher support. But much of the research on the efficacy of teaching thinking had been conducted under optimal learning conditions. Problems with scaling up and transferring the effects to everyday classrooms were identified. In particular, it was noted that the more successful were characterised by explicit models of teacher development and teacher support. This would also apply to lecturer and tutor training and support as was designed into the successful Oxbridge and OU systems. It also became an essential part of the contact and distance programmes already described. Tutors wanted to provide the correct answers and they had to be prevented from thinking for the students. Each week before the workshops and seminars, they had to be briefed and then debriefed afterwards to keep them on track and stop them from handing out their own notes to students and doing fill-in mini-lectures. In the distance programmes, they needed to be trained in the feedback systems and this had to be carefully monitored.

What McGuinness did not identify in her survey was thinking skills and problem-solving activities that were **intrinsic** to the subjects under study, making them an inclusive way of life in student classrooms. These are the methods found to be the most effective as a way of teaching in all subjects by structuring the processes of learning before and during study and ensuring the model of transfer was that of the 'Good shepherd'.

> Thinking skills' programmes enjoy a periodic popularity and seem to provide an antidote for teachers to the instrumentalism of prescribed curricula as they address more general aims of education.
>
> (Leat, 1999)

However, along with most other curriculum innovations thinking skills have usually failed to make a lasting impact or become established within education systems as pointed out by Leat. There are a number of reasons for this and one can be the lack of transfer observed in some of the methods especially the 'bolt – on' type so that little is achieved in terms of higher learning outcomes and learning gains.

A second reason is because in some methods the initial training time required takes time out of the content programme the tutor has available and telling the information in the lecture format can be regarded as the quickest and the best vehicle for transfer. But we know that the lecture is the least successful method for the students but it keeps the lecturer busy and satisfied. Lecturers often find it difficult to change roles and become facilitator even follower is some situations. It is this adaptability that needs to be developed through further training and lecturer CPD.

Thinking skills approaches that work generally offer a range of tactics that can be used to address and solve problems by being intrinsic to the study programme. The TASC approach is one of these and there are many others with similar protocols such as in designing and making and investigative learning and problem solving. The 'TASC wheel' summarises these strategies and students of all ages learn to follow the procedure in the order written on it. Both children and adults have been able to use it successfully and it guides thinking and action in a systematic way that supports self-regulation, planning and monitoring.

TASC stands for Thinking Actively in a Social Context – Wallace (2009)

The TASC problem-solving approach was first developed with and named by underachieving learners in KwaZulu Natal 1984–1998 and then when Wallace returned to the United Kingdom was introduced here. Now it is available and used in 10,000 schools and colleges worldwide. It quickly gained wide acceptance and the ways of working were found to be open and motivating for the whole range of learners and promoted thinking skills and creativity. It was also found that TASC fostered independence and self-regulation of learners. Teachers and tutors became providers of the resources and facilitators. The disorganised underachievers could use the protocol to organise their attack on problems and keep themselves on task through the learning conversations they could follow step-by-step in their own heads.

The protocol:

- First **Gather and Organise** what you already know about the subject, topic, problem, situation. Then decide how and where you can find out more information – do the research.

- Clearly **Identify** what the problem actually is by stating it simply as 'What am I trying to do?' (Goal[s]) and 'What is preventing me from doing it?'(Obstacle[s]). Then decide on the criteria for success and work towards that (Possible Solution[s]).
- **Generate ideas** – (together with others) think of many possible ways of solving the problem without stopping any flow of thoughts by pre-judging the value of them, for example, brainstorming or 'synectics'.
- **Decide** on the best ideas and outline a possible course(s) of action: plan the stages systematically: outline stages of the task clearly and if in a team identify who is responsible for the carrying out of each stage of planning.
- **Implement** the ideas by putting the decision(s) into action, monitoring progress and adjusting plans as is necessary.
- **Evaluate** progress and successes throughout the project, judged against the agreed goals, obstacles and solutions discussed at the Identify stage. If necessary, backtrack and reformulate ideas and plans previously agreed upon.
- **Communicate** and share ideas throughout the whole project, but also take time to share and celebrate the outcomes and successes. Share successes with the wider community and discuss the stages and processes of overcoming obstacles and achieving goals.
- **Reflect and Learn from Experience** – discuss/record the success of strategies that were used, evaluate the quality of the group interaction and reflect on how the successful strategies can be transferred to other situations. Discuss changes that need to be made in any future project to make the whole action more effective and sustainable.

The titles of the steps give not only a system to follow to a resolution but also a language to use in one's head or explicitly to plan, monitor and evaluate one's actions. These are the substance of metacognitive processing and SRL.

Not surprisingly a task strategy wheel has been promoted in the *Power of Process* McGraw-Hill (2019). A psychology student example:

1 Before reading: (a) Consider the methodology. (b) Read the abstract.
2 During reading: (a) Identify the type of research. (b) Identify the dependent and independent variables.
3 After reading: (a) Summarise the findings. (b) Formulate an overall opinion.

As a former psychology student, it seems an unattractive process and difficult to consider the methodology without having read anything. Read the title and the abstract then consider? Reading more depends upon the purpose.

The advice process goes on as follows:

1 Recall what you have just read. (Think over?)
2 Outline or map the article. (Identify the three to five main ideas.) (Methodology?)

3   Summarise the findings. (Significant results?)
4   Evaluate the quality of the results. (Think on?)
5   Decide if the conclusions are warranted.
6   Form an overall opinion.
7   Design a follow-up. (Think of?)
8   Conduct a risk-benefit analysis. (Why? Depends?)
9   Evaluate the effectance.

Steps 1–3 seem reasonable to commit to paper the rest might be metacognitively processed and as long as the full reference details are taken it can be found again if needed. The purpose for steps 1–9 (Author's comments in the brackets) need to be defined as it depends on the reason why the student is reading the paper – final examinations, course test, dissertation, critical review postgraduate research?

D. Reflective teaching and learning

The reflective teacher is one who is able to develop teaching and learning for critical thinking. Developing reflective thinking and the metacognitions of learners is the key objective. Pollard (1997) identified the aim of reflective teaching as a move from routine action to reflective action. While routine action is the type of practice that is relatively static, reflective action embraces the idea that teacher/lecturer competence and professional development is a career long process guided by self-appraisal and empirical evidence. Through making the unconscious explicit, we are in a better position to decide whether what is believed in fits the purpose of what we are trying to achieve.

Pollard (1997, 11–18) described reflective teaching as having six key characteristics:

- An active concern with aims and consequences and technical efficiency. Which means being engaged in all aspects of university life and constructive criticism.
- It follows a spiral process of evaluation and development as in Action Research.
- The lecturer needs competence in research methods that enable the evaluation of evidence and its application to policy and practice.
- An open mindedness and supportive responsible approach.
- An evidence-based approach in judgment and knowledge about educational processes and student needs.
- Self-appraisal supported by research based in knowledge of development and trends in education.

In summary, through reflective teaching, lecturers professing to teach are being asked to examine their personal values and aims carefully. Reflective teaching is flexible and learner orientated so that learners also can become reflective and learn in ways best for them. Their contribution and collaboration is important in the intimate relationship between teaching and learning.

Four processes that are engaged in during some HE courses to promote reflective learning are learning logs and learning diaries, critical incident analysis and case studies. The problem is that there is room for reflective learning in all aspects of teaching and learning if tutors both model and implement it. Opportunities can be provided for reflection on progress in learning in every programme and these need to be made explicit and given time. This will show students how important they are for creating meaning and understanding and learning gain. Too many still arrive at university believing that memorising is their key to success.

I. Diaries

These were introduced into some programmes to provide data for a dialogue with a tutor, usually on a termly basis. The diary could include notes from lectures and questions and comments with reflections and ideas to follow up. As can be imagined the tutor, even with a small tutorial group could become inundated with pages and pages of text to wade through. The most conscientious students would do their diaries daily and in full. Others might be less conscientious but still pile in data. It became an unmanageable task for tutors as many students had not learned to be selective or reflective and would include everything relevant or not.

In essence, the diary is written each day after the learning session to record the experiences and the reactions to them. This needs to be done each evening and can be taken further and analyse and draw conclusions. Word counts and time limits might be suggested to make the task and the review manageable.

2. Learning logs

Some students had participated in programmes involving Records of Achievement' in which they had produced a portfolio of their achievements not just at school but in the wider community and in personal interests other than school subjects. This type of strategy was introduced into HE in the form of learning logs. Students were encouraged to write notes during their learning experiences and reflect on their achievements usually on a weekly basis. They were encouraged to raise questions about the topic that they needed to investigate. The idea was to hand these logs in at intervals so that tutors could determine progress and discuss the log with each student. It was a more closely defined task than the Diaries and intended to make the tutor time on task manageable.

Log books are also used to record during what is going on, usually in laboratory experiments and in art and design work to capture ideas, plans and make sketches for later analysis. They are more like jottings but can also be used to discuss points and issues with the tutor.

3. Critical incident analysis

In this technique, there is a time line established along which outline notes are made and each week one 'learning incident' is identified that the student describes in more detail and reflects on what occurred, why and what the implications might be. This can then be discussed with the tutor or might be handed in for written comment. It does make the tutor's task easier and can give insights into the student's progress and further learning needs. It can also offer opportunities for a reflective tutor to improve the teaching and learning experience.

4. Case studies

Case studies are widely used in HE but perhaps the following example has cross curricular significance it is based upon a paper by Sternberg (2013, 17) on ethical behaviour and each discipline will have its own examples, as will individual students. Enacting ethical behaviour is much harder than would appear because it involves multiple, and largely sequential steps.

To behave ethically, the individual has to:

1 Recognise that there is an event to which to react: for example, a friend downloads and pays for an essay to present for assessment.
2 Define the event as having an ethical dimension.
3 Decide that the ethical dimension is of sufficient significance to merit an ethics-guided response.
4 Take responsibility for generating an ethical solution to the problem. It has to feel personally relevant or maybe it is 'none of my business'.
5 Figure out what abstract ethical rule(s) might apply to the problem. Is this one plagiarism or criminal deceit?
6 Decide how the abstract ethical rules actually apply to the problem so as to suggest a concrete solution.
7 Prepare for possible repercussions of having acted in what one considers an ethical manner.
8 Act.

Effective teaching of ethical reasoning involves presenting case studies, but it is important that students also generate their own case studies from their experience and then apply the steps of the model to the problems. They need to think creatively as they use the model of ethical reasoning about ways of defining and redefining ethical dilemmas that enable them to get through the various steps. The model provides a scaffold for reflection and action.

Reflective learning Action Sets

Small groups of students, 3s and 4s join together for a short discussion period during a seminar session or in independent study time, for example, to determine a Twitter message (280 characters) that summarises the main idea or theme of the article, text or presentation.

In a problem-based session, the Action Sets can be used to select or invent a protocol for dealing with the issue and thus make their reflective processes explicit – the 'learning conversation'.

E. Developing creativity

Creativity is the ability to produce work that is novel (e.g. original, unexpected), high in quality, and appropriate (e.g. useful, meets task constraints) Sternberg et al. (2005). Researchers consider the creative process as a dynamic movement between divergent-exploratory thinking and convergent-integrative synthesis in domain-specific talents (Besancon et al., 2013). Those who invent new products or processes in a particular field need both divergent and convergent thinking skills to harness and transform innovative concepts into a workable and useful solution. While some great inventors such as Leonardo da Vinci contributed broadly across disciplines, many inventors create within a domain-specific talent.

Young learners are said to be more creative than older students and this is likely to be because they have not been over-trained in the education system to be convergent thinkers. It is probable that in many HE programmes there is more room for some creativity training than may currently be considered. Over time, a number of strategies have been recommended. One of the important features of creativity is that it needs personal time and space to develop and these are not readily available in any overfilled curriculum such as in the sciences and medicine with their extensive laboratory work.

Wallas (1926/2014) famously defined the creative process as

Preparation, Incubation, Illumination, and *Verification.*

Although each step of the model can take a different amount of time, and is often recursive, other researchers have verified Wallas' basic process steps through the years. This is usually true whether the person engages in adaptive creativity *(solving a problem)* or expressive creativity *(developing an artistic product).* Later this view of the creative process was modified by describing it as 1% inspiration and 99% perspiration.

The following 10 statements can be used to think how much tutorials, independent study and workshops encourage creativity:

- Framing questions that have no one right answer.
- Space for activities that are curious, authentic, extended in length, sometimes collaborative and reflective.
- Opportunities for playfulness and experimentation.
- Opportunity for generative thought with ideas greeted openly.
- Opportunity for critical reflection in a supportive environment.

- Respect for difference and the creativity of others.
- Creative processes are visible and valued.
- Students are actively engaged as co-designers.
- Space is left for the unexpected.

The assessment methods are varied to promote and take account of creative responses. Adapted from Lucas et al. (2013).

The psychological components of creativity

The initial impulse in modern times came from the work of Guilford (1950) and derived from his distinction between 'convergent' and 'divergent' thinking. Early theorising adopted a simple approach (intelligence = convergent thinking, creativity = divergent thinking), but this has since been expanded, for instance Torrance and Hall (1980) concluded that creative thinking involved:

- Uniting disparate ideas by putting them into a common context.
- Being able to imagine, at least as a theoretical possibility, almost anything.
- Enriching one's own thinking through the application of fantasy.
- Adding spice to one's thinking through the use of humour.

Necka (1986) emphasised the following six aspects in the process of creativity: Forming associations; recognising similarities; constructing metaphors; carrying out transformations; selectively directing the focus of attention and seeing the abstract aspects of the concrete. Necka (1992) stated that the intellectual operations involved in creative thinking belonged to six groups, each of which can be trained. These were:

- Thinking in the abstract
- Making associations
- Deductive reasoning
- Inductive reasoning
- Metaphorical thinking
- Transformations

These are all underpinned by motivation, which is often the most difficult to induce. By training in these separate areas, he and his team claimed to be able to enhance creative thinking of groups.

Necka's model of creativity goes beyond thinking to encompass motives and skills, but thinking was still of great importance in his approach. The aspects he emphasised included:

- Forming associations
- Recognising similarities

- Constructing metaphors
- Carrying out transformations
- Selectively directing the focus of attention
- Seeing the abstract aspects of the concrete

Simonton (1988) advanced what he called the 'chance-configuration' model of genius and this approach was applied to creativity. He concluded that creativity involved the production of a large number of associations, more or less randomly or blindly, and the chance occurrence of 'configurations' – happy combinations that represented just what was needed to solve the problem. The creative person is especially good not only at producing associations, but also at recognising that a configuration has occurred, and grasping that it offers a solution. Weisberg (1986) examined self-reports and case studies of famous creators and combined this information with data obtained in experimental studies. He concluded that creativity arose not from random combinations, but from 'chains' of ideas connected associatively in a long series of strictly logical small steps, for which knowledge of the field is vital.

Historical studies such as that of Cox's (1926) retrospective studies of geniuses such as of Newton, Copernicus, Galileo, Keppler and Darwin showed clearly that in addition to high intelligence these people were marked by tenacity and perseverance. Biermann (1985) concluded, on the basis of a study of creative mathematicians of the 17th to 19th centuries, that fascination with the subject matter and consequent extreme motivation was one of the major features of his subjects and the obsessive nature of the work of many gifted individuals. Goertzel et al. (1978) also showed the importance of motivation in their case studies of historical figures.

Studies of creative mathematicians, scientists, architects, painters and writers found that they seemed to possess special personality characteristics which set them apart from less creative colleagues: these were flexibility, sensitivity, tolerance of ambiguity, sense of responsibility, empathy, independence, positive self-image. Experts in creativity studies distinguish between creative potential and productive creativity. In both, chance plays a role because if, for example, there is no clay to work on it can be impossible to show a talent or begin an early career in sculpture. The same is true for a talent in playing a particular musical instrument or working in a particular medium.

There are other considerations about creative development that are not so clear. For example, creativity in science may require an openness of mind and a willingness to master a large amount of material before the questions at the frontiers of that knowledge can be framed and lead to new and creative insights. But the ability to raise those relevant questions is a talent in itself. What facilitates this kind of talent seems to be multifactorial. It seems to depend upon not only an openness of outlook that will consider alternatives to previously adhered to beliefs but also the ability to consider the negative instances and their value in problem solving.

For example a mathematician tells us that she has in mind a simple rule. The rule is exemplified by the numbers – '2-4-6'. The task is to define the rule by posing more instances. The mathematician will only tell us –'Yes'. That is an example of her rule or 'No it is not'. How many instances do we take to find the rule? (4 or 5?). One postgraduate mathematician posed rules for 45 minutes and still did not have the answer.

Another aspect that was found to be relevant to creative thinking was in the concept of Divergent Thinking in which many solutions and examples are proposed as in, 'How many uses can you think of for a brick?' as opposed to Convergent Thinking in which we narrow down on to one solution. The problem with divergent thinking, also termed Synectics and 'Brainstorming' is that the divergent answers need to be gathered, organised and used or applied in some way. This is more difficult and may even lead nowhere. A schizophrenic may be able to propose many extraordinary uses for a brick but not necessarily in a structured or purposeful way. It has become evident that convergent or divergent thinking may lead to creative or no creative outcome so neither may be relevant to the creative process (Dietrich, 2019).

Performance approaches – exhibitions, concerts, posters and 'Halls of Fame'

It is easy to see how the performance arts can encourage creativity and are often called the 'creative arts'. The students work in studios and workshops or orchestras, groups, duos, trios, choirs and bands. They practice and at intervals perform. They are given feedback as they practice, may attend master classes and coaching workshops and they give performances and exhibitions and gain feedback. They may also at times be video recorded and can be coached and they learn to reflect on their skills and give themselves feedback. The same can be true for students in sports areas.

There are fewer such opportunities for creative development in the so-called 'academic' fields. Students may have the opportunity to attend inspirational lectures or workshops but the problems of these have already been pointed out. There are however many opportunities to develop creativity and creative outputs and outlets such as the following:

Posters. It has become traditional for delegates to conferences to be invited to present a poster illustration of their current work summarised in poster format. At breakout sessions and in set periods, the poster designer(s) stand by the poster and offer to give explanations and answer the questions of the circulating delegates. Towards the end of the conference delegates often vote for 'the best' poster. Smaller versions of these presentational events can be introduced into many programmes. These can be a set topic to research and then present the findings in poster format.

A4 posters can be handed in for formative assessment, larger A5 formats can be exhibited for student evaluations when the criteria they are using can be elicited and formalised by the group as in Bloom's (1956) taxonomy.

Similar demonstrations and performances are now possible in Virtual Learning Environments (VLE) and through video- and web-based designs.

Pamphlets. In earlier centuries, the pamphleteers were well known and it is still a common means of communication today for political parties, agencies, individuals and companies wishing to sell goods and services. A pamphlet in a discipline can be designed to persuade the reader of a point of view, give information that would encourage further reading, illustrate different species, techniques or historical events and compare and contrast events, objects, people, research, methods and situations and so on.

Newspapers, magazines, broadcasts, reviews, comedies. These are familiar everyday experiences and student creativity in these areas can be encouraged within the forms and fields of knowledge. Most will already have Facebook, Instagram and blog experience that can be put to more constructive and positive use.

Exhibitions. The posters and pamphlets can be organised as exhibitions down a corridor or in a hall. They may be put on display to inform and interest visiting students from schools and dignitaries on official visits. They can be the outcomes of workshop and seminar studies when everyone has a chance to participate.

Halls of Fame. In every discipline, there will be models of excellence and people who have achieved significance in their field in the present period or in the past. Students in pairs can be encouraged to research the background story of their chosen character (real or imaginary) and find a photograph, sketch or image and then their task is to provide a written summary rationale for their chosen character to be included in the Hall of Fame. The portraits and summaries can be displayed and the duos give a brief presentation to justify to their 'audience' why their person should be included in the Hall of Fame. It can provide broader opportunities for gender and BAME equality and awareness raising.

Encouraging pairs work can increase motivation for increasing student time on task and give support to those who are shy at speaking in a public forum. It emphasises the importance of the communication of knowledge in a range of forms.

Peer Mentoring. It is well known that students entering their first year at university may also be leaving home, family, friends, familiar places and routines. The new learning environment may be far more challenging intellectually than any they have experienced before. It is by comparison with school lacking any structure to organise their day and they can opt in or out as often as they choose. This can place many of the less robust in a very vulnerable position, socially, mentally and intellectually. Living independently for the first time can also be additionally challenging when this includes shopping, cleaning, washing clothes and paying the rent.

A group of second year students suitably briefed can be assigned to the first year intake for the first 6 weeks of the programme. Having a designated peer to support them and guide them through the initial difficulties in settling in can be very helpful. However, for the mentor there are also gains in experience in supporting younger and less experienced colleagues that might be useful in in the employment field and can become part of a portfolio of skills. After the initial 6 weeks, the participants can agree whether or not to continue the relationship or change to a different mentor or stop. Mental health issues will be more easily identified and in some cases will be avoided by some consistent peer support.

Supplemental instruction. This was introduced from the United States and involved successful second-year students mentoring first year students who were having difficulties understanding aspects in the introductory stages of learning in the discipline.

Strategic approaches to creativity

1. Synectics or brainstorming

1 First, state the purpose.
2 Second, generate the possibilities.
3 Third, reclassify the possibilities into types.
4 Fourth, review the possibilities to pick out unusual ones and feed them into (2). Use (3) to generate more possibilities.

These types of approach raise many issues. In any brainstorm or group problem-solving activity, it may well only be the contribution of one creative person that is ultimately of any value. Training may simply make the group effective in waiting for and eliciting that creative response whatever is the source from which it arises. In the system favoured by Necka, it could be argued that training on all the parts that make up a proposed system may never result in a truly creative response that was not possible before the training was given. In addition, it has often been found in skills training that the whole is more than the sum of the parts. Again efficiency in problem solving may be all that is facilitated. Both methods, holist and partist are likely to lead to 'feel good' factors.

Necka included in his definition aspects such as deductive reasoning abilities that are possibly necessary factors in some creative activities but are not sufficient conditions for creativity, not the creative process itself. Notions of metaphorical thinking, playfulness with imagery, analogies, inductions and transformations seem closer to creative processes.

There is also that unexplained phenomenon of sudden insight and knowing the answer to a problem in one creative but invisible leap (Koestler, 1967). Often the only route to this is to immerse the mind in study of the subject and then to sit quietly and think about it, letting the mind rove round the area and raise questions about it. Even then, a resolution may only come in a dream as Kekule's benzene ring did, in a flash of blinding light, or as we step into a lift.

2. SCAMPER

Osborn provided the SCAMPER checklist for developing creative ideas as follows:

- **Substitute.** Change elements in the problem – who else? What else?
- **Combine.** Bring together with other ideas, purposes.
- **Adapt.** What else is like this? Create metaphors.
- **Modify.** Magnify, minify, multiply – what to add, alter, change.
- **Put.** To other uses new ways to use, other uses if modified.
- **Eliminate.** Remove irrelevancies, parts, wholes.
- **Reorganise.** Try different patterns, layouts, schemes.

Brainstorming and drawing the concept maps enables students to bring to the forefront of the mind the previous knowledge and experience, and inspect it to try to establish connecting links. Having heightened awareness in this way there is a better chance that the information in the new learning will be integrated into the past structures.

3. Lateral thinking

Edward de Bono (1970, 1974) placed great emphasis on Lateral Thinking and offered many examples of our tendencies to be stuck in a particular frame or mode of thinking when we needed to 'think outside the box'.

An example of this would be Scheerer's (1963) nine-dot insight problem

```
*    *    *

*    *    *

*    *    *
```

The task is for the problem solver to join all the dots with four straight lines without lifting the pen from the paper. de Bono claimed to be able to train people to become more lateral thinkers but this did not prove that they became more creative. Creativity for him was an element within lateral thinking. He distinguished between Vertical Thinking, which is rather like convergent thinking, drilling down into a subject with an emphasis on logic. Lateral Thinking he considered under the following but not exclusive four headings:

- Recognition of dominant, polarising ideas
- Search for different ways of looking at things
- Reversal of the rigid control of vertical thinking
- The use of chance

4. Infusion for Creative Thinking

Swartz and Parks (1994) divided Creative Thinking into two main strategies:

1 Alternative Possibilities
2 Composition

First they described the process of generating different possibilities and then of creating metaphors (288–336). In generating possibilities, they suggested a number of strategies beginning with:

1 Decide what you want to describe about something.
2 Describe the key characteristics of it.
3 Think what other objects, etc., share these characteristics.
4 Select which of these key characteristics might make a good metaphor.
5 Think what the details of metaphor fit the characteristics you are describing.
6 Consider whether there are differences that make the metaphor misleading.
7 Is the metaphor a good fit? Why?

They then created a series of boxes (Graphic Organisers) to fill in to go through the above steps from topic to metaphor with a series of detailed examples. But there was no hard evidence that a creative product emerged from the process.

5. Creative problem-solving model

Leroux and McMillan (1993, 53) offered the following creative problem-solving model. It was originally developed in business and industry training.

Fact finding	Gather all possible information on the question or 'MESS' that has been raised.
Problem finding	• Look at the information to identify the core of the Problem. They must rephrase the question to an open-ended way. For example, 'How can we earn the money to pay for ...'
Idea finding	• Brainstorm all possible ideas to make money. The rules include: no criticism, acceptance of all ideas, quantity of nine ideas is desirable and combination of ideas is encouraged.
Solution finding	• Ideas are evaluated against criteria that students establish such as time involved in earning money, organisation of the project, feasibility and so on.
Acceptance finding	• Students have to present the plan in a way that will convince the boss to agree.

6. Teaching for creativity

In his work with students Sternberg (2000) identified a useful protocol to help them deal with creative issues as follows:

1 **Redefine the problem.** Help students see an aspect of the world in a different way from which it is usually seen.
2 **Analyse one's ideas.** Help students critique strengths and weaknesses of their ideas.
3 **Sell one's ideas.** Teach students the importance of selling their ideas to others.
4 **Knowledge is a double-edged sword.** Help students realise that theories apply only to a limited range of behaviour.
5 **Decision.** Help students realise that new ideas are not immediately accepted.
6 **Take sensible risks.** Help students realise that creativity involves some degree of risk.
7 **Willingness to grow.** Encourage students to grow by challenging their own beliefs.
8 **Believe in yourself.** Show students that if they believe they can do something, they often can.
9 **Tolerance of ambiguity.** Help students recognise and appreciate that ambiguity is inherent in much thinking in the academic disciplines.
10 **Find what you love to do and do it.** Show students how any field of endeavour can accommodate a wide variety of outside interests.

TEACHERS WHO FOSTERED CREATIVITY

Soriano de Alencar (1995) found that teachers at all levels who fostered creativity showed some common characteristics:

- They encouraged students to be independent learners and independent thinkers.
- They encouraged them to formulate their own ideas and motivated them to think and reason. They cultivated interest in new knowledge and discussion and asked challenging questions. They also presented challenging tasks and simulated analysis of different aspects of a problem.
- They respected students' ideas and were enthusiastic. They accepted them as equals and rewarded creative behaviour.

7. Productive creativity

Productive creativity is important for society and brings acclaim. It is the production or discovery of something useful and new and perhaps something beautiful in terms of art, design and architecture. A recent example has been the discovery of Graphene and more recently the exploration of its uses.

ZEITGEIST

However, not all new and potentially productive works are recognised as such in their time and there is a tendency for fashions in thought or traditional ways and methods of thinking and acting to put up barriers to innovations of many kinds. Goethe called this the 'zeitgeist' or Spirit of the Age. The scientific community, for example, may not be ready for the innovation and cannot tolerate or accept any new ambiguity.

Commerce may be similarly weighted against new developments because of the investment made in something else that has been more costly. Even education is not exempt from this. For example, dyslexia can be overcome in most cases by the end of the Reception year but no one seems to want to pursue this because of the investment of their beliefs in something else and the vast industry that backs this in terms of careers in diagnosis, research programmes and commercial remedial products (Montgomery, 2019).

For example, many famous scientific and artistic products considered outstanding today were originally ignored, such as Bach's musical compositions (Ferguson, 1935) and Mendel's work on genetics (Hartwell et al., 2004). Likewise, science and art have a long history of eventually discarding works and ideas that at one point in time were considered exceptional. Many discoveries are also made independently by two, three or even more scientists at around the same time (Simonton, 1984). These 'multiple discoveries' show the importance of having access to the appropriate knowledge.

One of the most direct applications of this idea was illustrated by Qin and Simon (1990) in their research on scientific discovery. They recreated several aspects of the historical conditions in which Kepler discovered one of his laws. They then presented the situation to students, who were unaware of that discovery but had all the necessary knowledge (akin to Kepler) and examined how they were able to discover the law. In this instance, Qin and Simon found no evidence that Kepler possessed abilities beyond those of many college students in his researches.

IQ AND CREATIVE ACHIEVEMENT

It is fondly believed that the higher the IQ, the greater the potential achievement but this is not true. Torrance (1963) determined that a threshold IQ of only 120 was needed for any creative productivity and Ericsson et al. (1993) showed that the mean IQ of students in HE was around 121 IQ points and that IQs as high as 127 were frequently higher than that of their lecturers.

Gagné's research (2004) showed that:

- There were very few profoundly gifted individuals perhaps 3 in a million with IQs of 180+.
- Extremely gifted were those with IQs of 165+ and they were 1 in 100,000.

- Exceptionally gifted were those with IQs of 155+ and they were found in 1 in 10,000.
- Highly able individuals were those with IQs of 145+ and were found in 1 in 1000.
- Moderately able were 130 IQ and above and were found in 1 in 100 individuals.
- Mildly able were those with IQs 115 and above and there were 1 in 10 of them.

The longitudinal research of Terman (1925–1954) in the United States showed that among those with the highest IQs (the mean was 154, N=1,500) perhaps one might be remembered in 100 years time and a handful might become nationally known figures. In the United Kingdom, Freeman's (2001) longitudinal research showed that those with the highest of IQs did not become the highest achievers. Similar results are emerging from the Fullerton Study (McCoach et al., 2017).

DYSLEXIA

Dyslexia is the most common form of learning difficulty and there are 10% in the population in the United Kingdom with the condition, 4% of them are in the severe category (British Dyslexia Association, 2020). There are significant numbers of dyslexics in HE and although they have usually learned to read by this stage their dyslexia is seen in their problems with spelling especially new and technical vocabulary and in essay writing. Some may also have poor and illegible handwriting. If their IQ is tested, the scores are impacted by the dyslexia and to obtain a fair assessment of potential 10 points can be added to any overall score (Silverman, 2004).

As has already been discussed the highest achievers share a set of personal characteristics and motivations that given mild ability and/or talent, they can achieve unlimited heights although being born into advantaged and cultured backgrounds can facilitate recognition and success if the zeitgeist is right. For dyslexics to gain a place in HE can be as a result of such persistence and motivation and the greater range of freedoms at university should enable them to shine. There is also now a better understanding of their needs and text readers and voice activation technology support for the severe cases can be engaged to help them and replace the scribes of the past.

INNOVATIVE INITIATIVES

It is surprising how often and for many years a person famous for some creative product or process has spent the time working away at it unnoticed. Families of creatives are also often involved in constructing a facilitative environment and providing the modelling, the skills and the tools for later productivity. This makes it more likely that their offspring will be free to engage in more creative pursuits and be recognised in the company of peers.

In the outlines above personality characteristics were also found to be important and self-efficacy and persistence against the odds are two of them and a certain obsessiveness has been mentioned. This means that creativity is not confined to certain groups or subjects and more creative productivity could be facilitated if universities and tutors were more open to it and held positive attitudes.

CONJUNCTIONAL

This type of innovation or creative product arises from a convergent thinking process in which after considerable study of the context and background the researcher narrows down to some key concept or constructs. An example of this would be Renzulli's (1976) 'Three-ring Concept' of giftedness that he summarised as in the diagram of the Model of modern teaching Figure 2.1 in Chapter 2.

EXTENSIONAL

This type of innovation involves the same sort of preparation as above but incorporates the use of analogies and metaphors often from other fields. For example in early years reading research on visual methods, studies in perception and tank recognition revealed a pattern recognition teaching technique that increased the speed of access to literacy of all the children involved compared with controls (Montgomery, 1977).

DYSJUNCTIONAL

This also follows the same process of preparation and a thorough grounding in the subject but some chance factor or event evokes the 'Aha' insight. An example of this was Kekule's benzene ring. He could not solve the problem of its molecular structure until one night in a dream he saw the molecules all get up and dance round in a ring (Koestler, 1967).

F. Real-world and problem-based learning

> PBL is characterised by an enquiry process where problems – mostly from real and complex situations – are formulated and drive the whole learning process. Learning through PBL promotes critical thinking, self-learning skills, lifelong learning, self-achievement, self-regulation, self-efficacy, communication skills, and interpersonal skills for students.
>
> Guerra and Kolmos (2011, 4)

As already discussed in Chapter 4, human nature is such that if you present a person with an open-ended situation in which the answer to a problem is not given it sets up cognitive dissonance and the mind automatically tries to solve the problem and make closure unless it is ill. Although not everything can be converted into a problem, there is considerable scope for doing so.

Engineering. Elena Rodrigues-Falcon (2015, 250) at the University of Sheffield described the 'Kieron Challenge' PBL project with engineering students. The problem was to make life easier for 7-year old Kieron who had cerebral palsy, and his family and carers. It involved some of the students meeting the family and finding their needs and difficulties.

Seventy students then generated ideas and some of these gained sponsorship from local companies to produce prototypes. In the following year another group of students worked on a project to support patients at the Sheffield Children's Hospital, others worked with a local hospice and yet others for children at a special school. The interactions with the patients and participants generated high levels of commitment among the students and enhanced their satisfaction with the course and its professional outcomes.

Design and technology courses also regularly identify real problems such as this for students to resolve.

In Business Education, studies not only do the students experience casework analysis of institutions but also engage in Work-Based Learning placements. During these placements, they identify problems and work on their resolution with other students or they may be given problems to work on while they are in work and may share their findings with colleagues in the workplace. Internships such as this are an important part of many different professional courses.

The sciences have extensive examples of historical and current problem solving, and problems to be solved or resolved. Immersing oneself in the subject area is the first step but then problem finding can be the most difficult part of the process. Historical examples can often be a way in as can reading lists of short stories, plays and novels.

Novelists have undertaken problem based writing. For example, Sacheveral Sitwell wrote a revised interpretation of the Cinderella story and in 'Fatherland' Robert Harris wrote what happened when Hitler won the war. Crime novels are often very much about problem solving and investigative cases.

Problem-Based Teaching of Literature. Markušić et al. (2019) described the situation in which the students go through five stages, namely: the problem situation, problem definition; problem-solving methods; independent research work; analysis, correction and supplementation of research results; and new tasks for independent work. They gave the example in the interpretation of Henrik Ibsen's play A Doll's House (1879), the problem situation is created by setting a disputable thesis: *Nora is materialist, she pretends to be happy with her family, makes her children feel safe but not loved, and continuously takes on the role of a victim in order to free herself from the burden of family life. (p. 21)*

The students are divided into groups and each group receives problem-based tasks, such as the following (Naplačić, 2012, 50–51):

- Describe the image of the Helmer family in relation to society and in relation to itself – the positive and the negative sides.

- Determine the similarities and differences in the motherhood of Anna Karenina, Emma Bovary and Nora.
- In addition to duties of a husband and father, what else makes Torvald similar to Charles Bovary and Alexei Karenin?
- Is Ibsen's drama a kind of myth on the beauty and ideal nature of family life? Explain in terms of the following dimensions: Nora → a daughter, Nora → a wife, Nora → a mother, Nora → an emancipated woman.

Is a woman who abandons her children in pursuit of self-actualisation a sinner or a sufferer?After the discussion groups, the students engage in independent research to work on the solutions or they may go on to use the text for the screening of film or radio adaptations.

Alternatively, it may be transformed into another type of literary work. Role-play can be included and named groups work on the problem as, for example, marriage counsellors, financial advisers psychoanalysts, family friends, the society and the Helmers' children.

In a further session, the students were presented with the postulates of contemporary feminism and then issues are posed such as:

- Why do feminists consider Nora to be their paragon?
- Does emancipation focus exclusively on women and their needs?
- A woman's absence from home creates a void that is difficult or impossible to fulfil!
- Feminism does not accept the claim that a woman is subject to man!
- Feminism attempts to eliminate the differences between men and women!
- Are contemporary women happier than their mothers and grandmothers were?
- Has feminism changed the quality of male-female relationships and the quality of a woman's life in general?

Apart from giving their own views, students give examples from the text associated with the issues.

G. Games, simulations and role-play

An outline of simulation-based initiatives and role play was given in Chapter 1 in relation to different types of professionally based programmes such as in medicine, nursing and teaching. In addition to these examples, role-plays are intrinsic to Dance and Drama but can be broadened to include other subjects as in critic's forums and peer review panels in languages, arts and the social sciences. In the sports arena, the roles of coach, judge and referee can be included.

Games. The design of Games and simulations is intrinsic to technological and design fields but can be extended to mathematics, the sciences and historical and geographical areas, in fact any subject area if a little ingenuity is expended. It may just begin with a problem put to students such as – 'The task is to design a game or an experience to help members of the public get a better understanding of X or Y. The target audience might equally be set to be primary or secondary pupils or a group of student peers or experts as appropriate. The task can be set for collaborative groups, pairs or individuals and can end with presentations and exhibitions that enable the best game to be identified plus the criteria for doing so.

The skills that are enabled in this kind of open task include the public communication of ideas and the subject, social and collaborative skills in team-building, all skills needed by employers. The games can be board games or electronic. When this was made part of a teacher education programme – the students had to design and make a 'Whole book game' suitable for the age range they were intending to work with and include packs of study skills question cards. It generated very strong interest and several games were so well designed they were suitable for commercial publication. A main assembly hall was only just large enough to show all the exhibits and students were on hand to explain and demonstrate their game to visitors, tutors and peers. In a follow-up debriefing the criteria for assessment of the best games were evolved, as in Bloom's (1956) taxonomy.

Role-play. Consideration needs to be given to the wider range of fields and forms of knowledge in which learning is usually desk based and passive to make them more participative and engaging.

An example of this was provided by Beverley Milton Edwards (2015, 283–285) in the School of Politics and International Studies at Queen's University, Belfast. The course was on Conflict Resolution in Middle Eastern Politics using blended learning in a web-based project. The aims of the module were to:

> Provide students with an understanding of the political culture, history, institutions and current dynamics of the region; the opportunity for independent initiative through role – play, computer – based learning; written presentations and conflict resolution and negotiation skills. (p. 283)

The student cohort was divided into teams and they could subdivide into working parties. The 'Israeli' team, for example, lodged over 40 communications on the dedicated message board, approached the other teams, pre-negotiated, analysed intelligence, organised their portfolio and prepared press statements and position papers. On the day of the role-play, they successfully negotiated with the other teams and adhered to the rules of the game.

The students' feedback on the experience were as follows:

> I learnt … how compromise is difficult to reach … about constraints … very helpful weblinks … public speaking skills … debating skills … difficulties of real-life disputes … negotiating skills … calmness under pressure … research skills … diplomacy. (p. 285)

Professional courses of training and Simulation-Based Education

Mooting in Law Schools was popular in the 1980s and has come back again as a vehicle for developing performance skills of the barrister and as an assessment tool for the faculty. Jo Anne Boylan-Kemp (2015, 319) at Nottingham Law School describes one such project. The format involved four students, two for the appellant and two for the respondent. One student in each pair is the lead and the other is the junior. Two grounds for the appeal are given and in advance of the moot the students have to research the law relating to them in order to develop a persuasive argument grounded in legal authority. The students then present their submissions to the moot judge who is a Law school academic or a legal practitioner.

Mooting is incorporated across the degree programme and the results have attested to its value. Most students achieved higher marks in mooting than any other assessment in the same subject achieving 2.1 and first-class marks in the moots. It is considered very valuable for their career prospects as well as enhancing their research skills.

It can also be seen to include the critical feature of increasing students' independent study time on task as in the role-paly example above. The presentational forum requires the students to evaluate, assess and then 'teach' the content they have learned to resolve the problem integrating the knowledge with the taught components. This inevitably leads to deep learning and accounts for the improved results over years when mooting was not practised, although transfer to other components needs to be analysed.

Teacher education has always acknowledged the need for its students to have real experience of teaching pupils as part of the programmes. It may offer this in sequential or concurrent training. In sequential training, the student follows a subject degree programme and then enters a teacher education programme that is mainly practice-based. This is typical of PGCE courses. In concurrent training typical of BEd courses, the subject and practice elements follow in an annual cycle throughout the programme. In addition to the extended practice periods or internships, the students may engage in micro-teaching in small groups. One student takes the video, one teaches and one observes and gives feedback. The process is repeated and roles are rotated. Debriefing takes place in the plenary. The important element is to prepare them to give feedback in a positive and constructive format and gives them some skills practice in presentation.

Medical education has long been custom and practice in medical education that students practice some of the basic skills on manikins giving them injections and rectal examinations before any 'hands on' with real patients. They dissect cadavers to follow blood vessels and nerves and stitch them up and also practice operating on pigs' organs and tissues. To improve communication skills they undertake role-plays with volunteers and are given video and personal feedback. Other examples might be simulated ward rounds, letter writing and role-play interviews with difficult patients. All of this falls under the umbrella of Simulation-based Education (SBE) and English medical training is well advanced in its practical work in this area as well as with real patients in comparison with Germany, for example, where the training is still essentially theoretical (Reitinger, 2015).

The reason for these developments was because the traditional methods of healthcare training in the United Kingdom of 'unstructured clinical supervision' was found to be ineffective and so there was a move to a competency-based or outcomes-based model of teaching and learning (Cleland, 2017). SBE has also increased over recent years in health care because of safeguarding issues regarding patient protection and this has limited the access of inexperienced students to them. Despite the fact that it is psychologists who are very often involved in the SBE developments in medicine and that the outcomes-based approach has also been adopted in applied psychology Cleland finds little evidence of similar SBE progress (p. 40).

H. Experiential learning

Experiential learning involves learning by doing or ACTION LEARNING (Revans, 1976). As has already been pointed out many students remain passive in the learning process but their learning could be more effective and deep if they were at least at times direct participants. Experiential learning in Politics courses usually takes the form of work placements or in-class simulations. In Education and Medicine, it can take the form of internships and placements.

Kolb's (1984) experiential learning cycle was widely adopted in management and business education programmes. Since then it has become more widely known and incorporated in a number of other programmes. In Chapter 1, the learning cycle linking Concrete experience to Reflective observation to Abstract conceptualisation to Active experimentation was illustrated and examples of its success in improving student learning outcomes were described. The topic was a project on sustainable development (Zanaty and Kitama, 2015). It was argued that it was a critical learning process in improving students' self-regulation.

Although learners may often learn without direct experience by observing and modelling others, and some learners can be particularly adept at this; it does not mean that direct experience is not useful. The experience does however have to be cognitively challenging and interesting, otherwise it is no more than other mundane activities. It also needs input from a 'critical friend' or reflective discussion on what was learned and how it was learned in order to tap into the metacognitive processes.

Some experiential learning examples can involve museum, concert and theatre visits, local studies, visits to companies and laboratories, visits to events and sites of interest and so on. Other techniques can involve drawing and painting from life, the building site, the historic site, the store front, the beach, the weeds in the pavement, a flower head, a shed and so on. Detailed study such as this can be a powerful influence on creative writing for different audiences. Participation in social events and with others in projects provide direct experiences that can lead to more interesting writing. Placing the experiences in historical or ecological contexts can broaden the perspectives.

The studies showed however that unless the learner reflected upon the learning during and after the event it was not so effective and meaningful and it would not result in 'deep' learning. But there are some problems with the Kolb model. The prime one is that learning cannot really be in a cycle because cycles bring us back to the same point from which we departed. In learning, the process is additive or cumulative and we are in a different cognitive place at the end of it in terms of knowledge structures and hierarchies of concepts.

The spiral model below (Figure 7.1) indicates that learners can progress from Surface to DL by a variety of experiential learning methods mediated by the tutor or other feedback. It is encouraged by reflective talk and metacognition. In DL the reflective talk is replaced by the establishment of learning conversations set up in the student's head derived from the feedback especially the 'running record' or commentary and various scaffolds.

In the first cycle in Figure 7.1, mediation by the tutor or collaborators establishes the facts and processes, what was seen, done and observed. In the second cycle, the talk moves to reflective talk and the abstract conceptualisation and deeper meaning and relationships. In DL, the student needs to learn to use inner speech or learning conversations in both cycles and then use the running record to mediate both cycles when the feedback arrives.

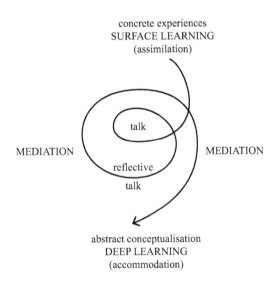

Figure 7.1 Cognitive process learning spiral.

I. Self-regulated learning

Self-regulated learners plan, goal set, monitor and evaluate all aspects of their lives. These self-organising skills can be facilitated and developed by an education that employs the cognitive process strategies exemplified above in all curriculum subjects. SRL competency also leads to higher learning gain and career progression.

Conclusion

SRL was the concluding strategy in the CPS list and this book has been devoted to exploring ways of developing it. The findings show that it is important to do this across the age and ability ranges in order to improve the ways in which people and society operate and advance. Intrinsic motivation is the key to becoming self-regulated and four elements are found to be essential to this – autonomy, competence, relatedness (connecting to others) and relevance (Ferlazzo and Sypnieski, 2019).

Ramdass and Zimmerman (2011) defined SRL as a proactive process in which individuals were expected to organise and manage their thoughts, emotions, behaviours, and their environment to fulfil their academic objectives.

> SRL is thus an active, constructive process in which learners set their own goals and then seek to monitor, regulate, and control their cognition, motivation, and behaviour, in accordance with their goals and the contextual features of the environment.
>
> (Pintrich, 2000, 453)

The building block of SRL is the development of 'inner speech' or metacognition. The key mechanism for developing metacognitive functioning was the 'learning conversation' we hold with ourselves and the language used is based upon the strategies and scaffolds we learn or develop. The means of promoting metacognition was found in the cognitive strategy processes described across these chapters.

The type of curriculum we offer in HE should enable the development and use of higher order thinking abilities and provide the possibility of exploring continually new knowledge and new information. Students should be encouraged to select and use primary sources of information and engage with complex and in-depth study of important ideas, problems and subjects. They need to learn to integrate knowledge between and within subject areas, and increasingly engage in autonomous learning activities. Higher learning gain can move students from competence to expertise to eminence.

Postscript

Looking to the future, distance learning at all levels of education is likely to be extended as full or blended programmes and it is important that Higher Education (HE) leads the way. The 'way' it has been argued is not the replication of face-to-face methods in virtual and blended modes but for it to become more strategic and learner centred with a genuine ratio approaching 10 hours student study time to one of tutor time.

Significant advances have been achieved across the sector but teaching still has a low status in many institutions and policy-makers minds. Research, because of the revenue and prestige it can generate has the higher status. But high-quality teaching and learning can also lead to more productive outcomes in research too.

In 2020, two issues are prominent in HE. The first is the need to improve access for disadvantaged groups to increase social mobility. Estimates showed that it would take the Russell Group 100 years more at the present rate to achieve the target of even 10%. Successful institutions have set the attainment grades at three B's instead of three A's to take account of the difficult contexts from which some of the students come. Others have increased 'outreach' provision to schools and offer bursaries, Foundation and Access courses when students are on campus. The contribution of schools to raising the achievement and aspiration of their pupils is crucial to this end and will follow when their own education in the universities provides the right models and strategies.

The second issue is the need to increase higher learning gain of students in HE. The evidence shows that this is achieved by increasing student independent study time on subject study tasks. Unfortunately, this cannot be achieved easily when most of the students especially the disadvantaged have to work as well as study in order to pay their fees and maintenance. This has several implications. Student fees and grants could be funded by a 1 % increase in taxation for all of us who gained our awards in the period when tuition was free/funded by the State. This could be part of the notion of a £10,000 wallet for the Lifelong Learning of all individuals. It would improve life skills and employability, and lift achievement more widely contributing to the gross national income in a competitive future. The second implication is that education and training of all HE lecturers is essential and there need to be annual programmes of in-house CPD updating.

The notion of metacognition, 'learning conversation' or inner speech has been the underlying theme in the design and development of the study programmes discussed and were shown to be the means of empowering and improving learning. The scaffolds and strategies involved in study skills and problem-based learning activities provided a structure for engaging in the reflective processes. It is these processes that enable the improved management and control of planning, monitoring and management of learning, the essential executive function skills of self-regulation.

There are however some caveats. It is possible for us to imagine we are the 'Queen of the May' or see fairies at the bottom of the garden and could confuse this with evidence from the senses upon which to reflect. Thought processes are somewhat flexible in this respect. After an incident, the observer may innocently tell the police at interview a number of incorrect 'observations' and perceptions. Self-reflection therefore needs to be grounded in evidence and truth, and its use needs to be disciplined not engaged in as a sport, a subterfuge or abused.

Over 100 years ago, introspection was still a main method of enquiry until it was overtaken by practical and experimental methods. The result was that to answer the question of how many teeth a horse had instead of thinking and introspecting on the number the investigator actually went and counted them. 'Horses for courses'. As in all things, balance is needed.

The Covid-19 pandemic resulting in a 'lockdown' worldwide has meant that much of education has had to migrate to the internet. This has placed us in an enviable position. Now is the time for creative thought and innovation in teaching and learning developments. The danger is that the innovations may simply be the reproduction of the old face-to-face 19th-century didactic methods transformed to be used in a different medium. We can do better than this. We can make transformational educational change for life in a new working and leisure environment, real 21st-century stuff!

Appendix 1

Reference chapter 6 redrafting and editing

Are boys or girls disadvantaged by particular early learning contexts?

Significant researches about this topic began in the 1970s and laid the foundations for the debate that has continued on an off since. For example, Maccoby and Jacklin (1974) stated that sex differences have been demonstrated in four areas of behaviour: girls have greater verbal ability than boys but boys excel in visuo-spatial ability, mathematical ability and are more aggressive (pp. 351–352). By the time these factors become measurable, differences certainly exist, but the origin of these differences is unclear. Harding (1979) examined C.S.E. and O level results in maths and science at 16 and found evidence that we too often equate achievement with ability or aptitude when it may instead be contextually related arising from teacher and peer expectations and stereotypes.

Birns (1976) in an extensive review of research found that most sex differences in behaviour related to personality and cognitive development were not apparent at birth or during early infancy but did become apparent during the pre-school period.

A study by Condry et al. (1974) in which 200 college students rated the video-taped behaviour of a 9-month-old infant shown that when the infant seen crying in an ambiguous situation was perceived as a 'boy' then the 'boy' was seen as angry, when perceived as a 'girl' then 'she' was seen as afraid. Both men and women students rated the 'boy' as more active and potent than the 'girl' with men finding greater variations between the sexes. The study confirmed the view that sex differences in the neonatal period are 'in the eye of the beholder'.

The study of Goldberg and Lewis (1967) in which they compared 32 male and 32 female infants at the ages of 9 and 13 months showed that at 6 months mothers of girls touched, talked to and handled their children more than did mothers of boys. At 13 months, they found the girls were more dependent, showed less exploratory behaviour and their play reflected a more quiet style. Boys were independent, showed more exploratory behaviour, played with toys requiring gross motor activity, were more vigorous and tended to 'run and bang' in their play (p. 33).

Pederson and Bell (1970), however found that pre-school girls were not more dependent, more prone to cry or less persistent than boys but in this same study females were found to be more sedentary and to have longer attention spans and persistence. Boys engaged in more gross motor activities and showed greater manipulation of toys.

It is assumed by many that males are more aggressive than females and yet Maccoby et al. revealed no sex differences except in activity level in some studies after one year. It is often this activity level that is assumed to be closely related to aggression and it is certainly true that by the age of three boys are more aggressive and disruptive than girls in nursery school (Serbin et al., 1973).

Ethological studies of rough-and-tumble play by Blurton-Jones showed that London nursery school girls engaged in significantly less rough and tumble play than boys, whereas Bushman girls and boys of the same age engaged in similar amounts of such play (Konner, 1973), suggesting a strong cultural influence on London children's play behaviour in the pre-school period.

Seavey et al. (1976) dressed an infant in yellow and adults were asked to play with the '3-month-old baby'. They found that the adults reacted differently to the same infant with a different gender label and in the 'no gender' condition, men were more anxious than women. In a study by Smith and Jones (1978), infants were dressed in cross-gender clothes. It was found that the perceived 'boys' were verbally encouraged to be more physically active and engage in large-scale physical play. Moss (1974) stressed the importance of consistent differences in parent behaviours with both parents encouraging social behaviour in girls. He suggested that girls are taught to laugh and smile and also be content when they are ignored. Boys in infancy are given more attention and are more aroused and stimulated by parents.

TASK: Rewrite the introductory sentence of each paragraph so that each reads differently and not like notes as now.

Supplementary tasks:

1 Write a reference list for the sources cited in the text using either APA or BPS formats.
2 Find references for the research topics and themes that give 21st century findings that confirm or reject the early findings.
3 Select one of the authors cited in the text such as Maccoby or Harding and produce a research profile.
4 Read TWO articles cited in the text. Check that the findings are correctly explained and write a 500-word analysis of your findings.
5 Tabulate the research identified in the text (a) by chronological order and (b) by theme and critically discuss which is more applicable to public understanding.
6 Discuss the construct that 'Only recent research is relevant to today'.

Bibliography

Allen, M., Bourhis, J., Burrell, N., and Mabry, E. 2002 'Comparing student satisfaction with distance education to traditional classrooms in HE: a meta-analysis'. *American Journal of Distance Education*, 16(2), 83–97.

Anderson, J. R. 1980 *Cognitive Psychology and Its Implications*. San Francisco: Freeman.

Ashman, S. and Crème, P. 1993 *How to Write Essays Pamphlet*. London: Polytechnic of North London.

Astin, A. W. 1993 *What Matters in College: Four Critical Years*. San Francisco, CA: Jossey-Bass.

Ausubel, D. P. 1968 *Educational Psychology. A Cognitive View*. New York: Holt Rinehart and Winston.

Avis, J. 1996 The enemy within: quality and managerialism in education. In J. Avis and J. Bloomer (eds.), *Knowledge and Nationhood: Education, Politics and Work* (Vol. 1), 105–120. London: Cassell.

Avis, J. 2005 'Beyond performativity: reflections on activist professionalism and the labour process in Further Education'. *Journal of Education Policy*, 20(2), 209–222.

Bailey, R. 2003 'The difference that makes the difference: understanding excellence' Keynote lecture at the NACE Conference York, June.

Bain, J. D. 1993 'Towards a framework for more effective teaching in higher education: some experiences based on a new Graduate Certificate in Higher Education'. Invited presentation, Swinburne University of Technology, August.

Baird, J. R. and White, R. T. 1984 Improving learning through enhanced metacognition: a classroom study. *Paper presented at the American Educational Research Association*, New Orleans LA, April.

Bakken, J. P. 2017 *Classrooms, Assessment Practices for Teachers and Student Improvement Strategies* (Vol. 1). New York: Nova Science Publishers.

Bandura, A. 1986 'The explanatory and predictive scope of self-efficacy theory'. *Journal of Social and Clinical Psychology*, 4, 359–373.

Barkley, R. A. (ed.) 1998 *Attention Deficit Hyperactivity Disorder: A Handbook for Diagnosis and Treatment*, 2nd edition. Hurstpierpoint: IPS Publications.

Barnard, H. C. 1963 *A History of English Education from 1760*. London: University of London Press.

Barr, R. B. and Tagg, J. 1995 'A new paradigm for undergraduate education'. *Change*, 27(6), 13–25.

Bartlett, Sir F. C. 1932 *Remembering. A Study in Experimental and Social Psychology*. New York: Cambridge University Press.

Beeth, M. E. and Hewson, P. W. 1999 Learning goals in an exemplary science teacher's Practice. Cognitive and social factors – teaching for conceptual change. *Science Education*. Wiley On-line Library

Bender, S. L. and Privitera, G. F. 2016 'The influence of feedback of diagnosis and executive function skills on the rates of false positive and false negative outcomes for ADHD'. *Emotional and Behavioural Difficulties*, 21(2), 181–199.

Benware, C. and Deci, E. L. 1984 'Quality of learning with an active versus passive motivational set'. *American Educational Research Journal*, 21, 755–765.

Berk, L. and Winsler, A. 1995 *Scaffolding Children's Learning: Vygotsky and Early Childhood Learning*. Washington, DC: National Association for Education of Young Children.

Bernard, R. M., Abrami, P. L., Lou, Y., Borokhovski, E., Wade, A., Wozney, L., Wallet, P. A., Fiset, M. and Huang, L. 2004 'How does distance education compare with classroom instruction? A meta-analysis of the empirical literature'. *Review of Educational research*, 74(3), 379–439.

Berthoff, A. 1987 The teacher as researcher. In D. Goswami and P. Stillman (eds.), *Reclaiming the Classroom. Teacher Research as an Agency for Change*, 23–38. Portsmouth, NH: Boynton-Cook-Heinemann.

Besançon, M., Lubart, T., and Barbot, B. 2013 'Creative giftedness and educational opportunities'. *Educational and Child Psychology*, 30(2).

Beyer, B. K. 1997 *Improving Student Thinking: A Comprehensive Approach*. London: Allyn and Bacon.

Biermann, A. W. 1985 'Automatic programming. A tutorial on formal methodologies'. *Journal of Symbolic Computation*, 1(2), 119–142.

Biggs, J. B. and Collis, K. F. 1983 *Evaluating the Quality of Learning: The SOLO Taxonomy*. New York: Academic Press.

Biggs, J. E. (ed.) 1991 *Teaching for Learning. The Viewpoint from Cognitive Psychology*. Hawthorne: Australian Council for Educational Research.

Black, P. and Wiliam, D. 1998 'Assessment and classroom learning'. *Assessment in Education*, 5(1), 7–74.

Blackmore, J. 2005 'A critical evaluation of peer review via teaching observation within higher education'. *International Journal of Educational Management*, 19(3), 218–232.

Blagg, N. R., Ballinger, M. P., and Lewis, R. E. 1993 *Development of Transferable Skills in Learners: Research Series*. Sheffield: The UK Government Employment Department.

Blake, N., Smith, R., and Standish, P. 1998 *The Universities We Need: HE After Dearing*. London: Routledge.

Blaschke, L. M. 2012 'Heutagogy and life-long learning: a review of heutagogical practice and self-determined learning'. *The International Review of Research in Open and Distributed Learning*, 13(1), 56–71.

Bloom, B. S. (ed.) 1956 *Taxonomy of Educational Objectives* (Vol. 1). London: Longman.

Bloom, B. S. 1985 Generalizations about talent development. In B. S. Bloom (ed.), *Developing Talent in Young People*, 507–549. New York: Ballantine Books.

Boekaerts, M. 1999 'Self-regulated learning: where we are today'. *International Journal of Educational Research*, 31, 445–457.

Bond, G.J. and Tinker, M.A. 1967 *Reading Difficulties*, 2nd edition. New York: Appleton Century Crofts.

Booth, K. 2015 Case study 19.1: Behind the headlines in international politics. In H. Fry, S. Ketteridge and S. Marshall (eds.), *A Handbook for Teaching and Learning in Higher Education*, 4th edition, 280–282. London: Routledge.

Borkowski, J. G. 1996 'Metacognition: theory or chapter heading?' *Learning and Individual Differences*, 8, 391–402.

Boud, D. 1986 *Studies in Self-Assessment HERDSA Green Guide No. 5*, Birmingham Polytechnic SCED (Standing Conference on Educational Development) Educational Development Unit, Birmingham Polytechnic, Birmingham, UK.

Boud, D. 1995 *Enhancing Learning Through Self-assessment*. London: Kogan Page.

Boud, D. 2000 'Sustainable assessment: rethinking assessment for the learning society'. *Studies in Continuing Education*, 22(2), 151–167.

Boud, D., Keogh, R., and Walker, (eds.) 1985 *Reflection: Turning Experience into Learning*. London: Kogan Page.

Bourdieu, P. 1991 *Language and Symbolic Power*. Cambridge: Polity Press.

Bourne, T. and Flowers, S. 1997 'Teaching and learning in higher education. A glimpse of the future'. *Reflections in Higher Education*, 9, 77–102.

Boylan-Kemp, J-A. 2015 Case study 21.2 'Embedding mooting skills into the legal curriculum' 318-319 In H. Fry., S. Ketteridge, and S. Marshall, (eds.) 2015 *A Handbook for Teaching and Learning in Higher Education*, 4th edition. London: Routledge.

Bransford, T. D., Brown, A. L., and Cocking, R. R. (eds.) 2001 *How People Learn: Brain, Mind, Experience and School*. Washington, DC: National Academy Press.

Bratislava, 2016 European Council Symposium on Promoting Giftedness and Talent, April.

British Dyslexia Association 2020 www.bda-dyslexia.org.uk (Accessed 21/2/2020).

British Film Institute (BFI) 1999 *Making Movies Matters: Report of the Film Education Working Group*. London: BFI.

Brookes, J. and Brookes, M. 1993 *In Search of Understanding: The Case for Constructivist Classrooms*. Alexandria, VA: Association for the Supervision and Curriculum Development.

Brown, A. L., Brandsford, J. D., Ferrara, R. A., and Campione, J. C. 1983 Learning, remembering and understanding. In J. H. Flavell and E. Markham (eds.), *Carmichael's Manual of Child Psychology* (Vol. 1). New York: Wiley.

Bruner, J. 1966 *Towards a Theory of Instruction*. New York: W.W. Norton.

Burgess, R. G. 1990 A problem in search of a method or a method in search of a problem? A critique of teacher appraisal. In H. Simons and J. Elliott (eds.), *Rethinking Appraisal and Assessment*, 24–35. Milton Keynes: Open University.

Butler, D. L. and Winne, P. H. 1995 'Feedback and self-regulated learning: a theoretical synthesis'. *Review of Educational Research*, 65(3), 245–81.

Buzan, T. 1977 *Make the Most of Your Mind*. London: Pan Books.

CATE. 1983 *CATENOTE 1* London: DES Council for the Accreditation of Teacher Education.

Cetin, B. 2017 'The influence of Pintrich's self-regulated learning model on elementary teacher candidates in a life science course'. *Journal of Education and Training Studies*, 5(8), 30–36.

Charness, N., Krampe, R. T., and Mayr, U. 1996 The role of practice and coaching in entrepreneurial skill domains: an international comparison of life-span chess skill acquisition. In K. A. Ericsson (ed.), *The Road to Excellence: The Acquisition of Expert Performance in the Arts and Sciences, Sports, and Games*, 51–80. Mahwah, NJ: Erlbaum.

Charness, N., Tuffiash, M., Krampe, R., Reingold, E., and Vasyukova, E. 2005 'The role of deliberate practice in chess expertise'. *Applied Cognitive Psychology*, 19, 151–165.

Chen, X. D. 2011 'The meta-teaching research'. *Journal of Shaanxi Normal University (Philosophy and Social Science Edition)*, 1, 150–155.

Clark, T. and Roberts, J. L. 2018 'What are excellence gaps and how can we close them? An interview with Jonathon Plucker and Scott Peters'. *Gifted and Talented International*, 33(1–2), 64–70.

Clarke, V. and Braun, V. 2013 Teaching thematic analysis. In A. L. Michalos (ed.), *Encyclopaedia of Quality Life Research*. New York: Springer.

Claxton, G. 2007 *Building Learning Power*. Bristol: TLO Ltd.

Cleary, T. J. 2018 *Self-regulated Learning Guide. Teaching Students to Think in the Language of Strategies*. London: Routledge

Cleland, J. 2017 'Simulation-based education'. *The Psychologist*, September, 37–40.

Cleland, J. and Durning, S. J. (eds.) 2015 *Researching Medical Education*. London: Wiley-Blackwell.

Coffield, E., Moseley, D., Eccleston, K., and Hall, E. 2003 'A systematic review of learning styles and pedagogy'. *Proceedings of the 8th Annual European Learning Styles Conference Bridging Theory and Practice*, University of Hull, June 30–July 2.

Connolly, V., & Dockrell, J. and Barnett, A. 2005 'The slow handwriting of undergraduate students constrains the overall performance in exam essays'. *Educational Psychology*, 25, 99–109.

Conrad, D. L. 2002 'Engagement, excitement, anxiety and fear: learner's experience of starting online course'. *American Journal of Distance Education*, 16(4), 205–226.

Cooper, P.(ed.). 1999 *Understanding and Supporting Children with Emotional and Behavioural Difficulties*. London: Jessica Kingsley.

Corrardi, H. 2015 Case study 15.3: Classroom inversion and just in time teaching for biochemistry students. In H. Fry, S. Ketteridge and S. Marshall (eds.), *A Handbook for Teaching and Learning in Higher Education*, 4th edition, 222–223. London: Routledge.

Couture, C., Royer, E., Dupuis, F. A., and Potkin, P. 2003 'Comparison of Quebec and British teachers' beliefs about training and experience with ADHD'. *Emotional and Behavioural Difficulties*, 8(4), 286–302.

Cox, C. M. 1926 *Genetic Studies of Genius* (Vol. 2). Stanford: Stanford University Press.

Cruickshank, D. R., Bush, A., and Myers, B. 1979 'Clear teaching. What is it?' *British Journal for Teacher Education*, 5(1), 27–33.

Cullen, S. M., Cullen, M.A., Dytham, S., and Hayden, N. 2018 *Research to Understand Successful Approaches to Supporting the Most Academically Able Disadvantaged Pupils*. London: DfE.

Dansereau, D. F. 1988 Cooperative learning strategies. In C. F. Weinstein, E. T. Goetz, and P. A. Alexander (eds.), *Learning and Study Strategies: Issues in Assessment, Instruction and Evaluation*, 103–120. San Diego, CA: Academic Press.

Darling-Hammond, L. 1985 'Valuing teachers. The making of a professional'. *Teacher's College Record*, 87, 205–218.

Darling-Hammond, L. 2013 Teacher preparation and development in the United States. In L. Darling-Hammond and A. Lieberman (eds.), *Teacher Education around the World: Changing Policies and Practices*. New York: Routledge.

de Bono, E. 1970 *Lateral Thinking*. London: Ward Lock.

de Bono, E. 1974 *CoRT Thinking Notes*. Blandford Dorset: Direct Education Services Ltd.

de Bono, E. 1983 *Cognitive Research Trust (CoRT) Thinking Programme*. Oxford: Pergamon.

De Corte, E. 1995 Learning and high ability: a perspective from research in instructional psychology. In M. W. Katzko and F. J. Monks (eds.), *Nurturing Talent: Individual Needs and Social Ability Proceedings of the 4th ECHA Conference*. Assen, The Netherlands: Van Gorcum..

De Corte, E. 2013 'Giftedness considered from the perspective of research in learning and instruction'. *High Ability Studies*, 24(1), 3–19.

Dearing, R. 1997 *The Dearing Report. The National Committee of Inquiry into Higher Education*. http://beileeds.ac.uk/Partners/NCIHE/

Deci, E. L., Eghrari, H., Patrick, B. C., and Leone, D. R. 1994 'Facilitating internalization: the self-determination theory perspective'. *Journal of Personality*, 62, 119–142.

Deci, E. L. and Ryan, R. M. 1985 *Intrinsic Motivation and Self-determination in Human Behavior*. New York: Plenum.

Department for Employment 2001 *Further Education*. London: DfE.

Dewey, J. 1938 *Experience and Education*. Kappa Delta, NY: Collier Books reprint (1967).

DfEE 1998 *High Status, High Standards Requirements for Courses of Initial Teacher Training Circ No. 4/98*. London: DfEE.

DfEE 2000 *Performance Management in Schools: Model Performance Management Policy*. London: DfES.

Dietrich, A. 2019 'The Rocky Horror pixel show'. *The Psychologist*, March, 29–35.

Doll, J. and Mayr, U. 1987 'Intelligenz und schachleistung – eine untersuchung an schachexperten. [Intelligence and achievement in chess – a study of chess masters]'. *Psychologische Beiträge*, 29, 270–289.

Duffy, L. J., Baluch, B., and Ericsson, K. A. 2004 'Dart performance as a function of facets of practice amongst professional and amateur men and women players'. *International Journal of Sports Psychology*, 35, 232–245.

Dweck, C. 1999 *Self-Theories: Their Role in Motivation, Personality and Development*. Philadelphia, PA: Psychology Press.

Dweck, C. 2011 *'Mindsets and Academic Achievement' Keynote Address*. WCGTC Biennial Conference, Vancouver.

Edgington, U. 2015 Performativity and accountability in the UK education system: a case for humanness. *Pedagogy, Culture and Society*, 1–6.

Edgington, U. 2015 *Constructing Creative Non-Fiction: Telling Teachers' Stories About Being Observed*. Sage Research Methods.

Edosomwan, S. O. 2016 'Childhood learning versus adulthood learning, the theory of pedagogy and andragogy'. *US China Education Review* A, 6(2), 115–123.

Education Policy Institute, 2019 'The achievement gap at 16 years', London: EPI Report, July 30.

Elliott, J. and Labett, B. 1974 *Teaching Research and Teacher Education*. Norwich: University of East Anglia CARE mimeo.

Entwistle, N. J. and Nisbet, J. 1972 *Educational Research in Action*. London: University of London Press.

ERA. 1988 *Education Reform Act*. Westminster: HMSO.

Ericsson, K. A. 2003 'Exceptional memorizers: made, not born'. *Trends in Cognitive Sciences*, 7, 233–235.

Ericsson, K. A., Krampe, R. T., and Tesch-Römer, C. 1993 'The role of deliberate practice in the acquisition of expert performance'. *Psychological Review*, 100, 363–406.

Ericsson, K. A. 2015 *Expert versus Novice Performance: A Historical Review Keynote Presentation at IRATDE Conference*, Antalya, Turkey, August.

Feldman, A. 1997 'Varieties of wisdom in the practice of teachers'. *Teachers and Teacher Education*, 13(7), 757–773.

Ferguson, D. N. 1935 *A History of Musical Thought*. New York: F. S. Crofts & Co.

Ferlazzo, L and Hull-Sypnieski, K. 2019 'Ways to nurture intrinsic motivation'. *Education Week*, 1, 1.

Festinger, L. 1957 *A Theory of Cognitive Dissonance*. Stanford, CA: Stanford University Press.

Feuerstein, R. 1980 *Instrumental Enrichment*. Baltimore, MD: University Park Press.

Feuerstein, R. 1995 *Mediated Learning Experience*. London: Regents College Conference.

Fiedler, E. D. 2015 You don't outgrow it. Giftedness across the lifespan. In C. S. Neville, M. M. Piechowski, and S. S. Tolan (eds.), *Off the Charts. Asynchrony and the Gifted Child*, 183–210. New York: Royal Fireworks Press.

Fischer, C. 2014 'SRL with students of different abilities', *ECHA Conference Keynote*, Ljubljana, Slovenia.

Fisher, A. 1988 *Critical Thinking. Proceedings of the First British Conference on Informal Logic and Critical Thinking*. Norwich: University of East Anglia.

Fisher, A. 1991 Critical thinking. In M. J. Coles and W. D. Robinson (eds.), *Teaching Thinking. A Survey of Programmes in Education*, 49–58. Bristol: Classical Press.

Fisher, A. 2006 *Critical Thinking for Students. An Introduction*. Cambridge: Cambridge University Press.

Flavell, J. H. 1979 'Metacognition and cognitive monitoring'. *American Psychologist*, 34, 906–911.

Freeman, J. 2000 Teaching for talent: lessons from the research. In C. F. M. van Lieshout and P. G. Heymans (eds.), *Developing Talent Across the Life Span*, 231–248. Hove, Sussex: Psychology Press.

Freeman, J. 2001 *Gifted Children Grown Up*. London: David Fulton.

Freeman, J. 2010 *Gifted Grown Up*. London: Metric.

Fry, H., Ketteridge, S., and Marshall, S. (eds.) 2015 *A Handbook for Teaching and Learning in Higher Education*, 4th edition. London: Routledge.

Gagné, F. 2004 'Transforming gifts into talents: the DMGT as a developmental theory'. *High Ability Studies*, 15(2), 119–47.

Gagné, R. 1973 *The Essentials of Learning*. London: Holt, Rinehart and Winston.

Gallagher, J. J. 1991 'Personal patterns of underachievement'. *Journal for the Education of the Gifted*, 14, 221–33.

Gallagher, J. J. 1997 'PBL. Where did it come from? What does it do and where is it going?' *Journal for the Education of the Gifted*, 21(1), 3–18.

Galton, M. and Simon, B. 1980 *Progress and Performance in the Primary Classroom (The ORACLE Project)*. London: Routledge.

Gardner, H. 1983 *Frames of Mind: The Theory of Multiple Intelligences*. New York: Basic Books.

Gardner, H. 1993 *Frames of Mind*. New York: Basic Books.

Garrison, D. R. 1997 'Self-directed learning: toward a comprehensive model.' *Adult Education Quarterly*, 48, 18–33.

Gerber, A., Cavallo, M. J., and Marek, E. H. 2001 'Passkey to learning in science education in elementary schools'. *Teaching Elementary Science Education*, 7(1), 1–15.

Gibbs, G. 1988 *Learning by Doing: A Guide to Teaching and Learning Methods*. London: Further Education Unit.

Gibbs, G. 1990 *Improving the Quality of Student Learning: A Summary Poster*. Oxford: Oxford Centre for Staff Development.

Gibbs, G. (ed.). 1994 *Improving Student Learning: Theory & Research*. Oxford: Oxford Centre for Staff Developmen

Gibbs, G. (ed.). 1995 *Improving Student Learning Through Assessmente and Evaluation*. Oxford: Oxford Centre for Staff Development.

Gibbs, G. 2006 How assessment frames student learning. In C. Boyan and K. Clegg (eds.), *Innovative Assessment in Higher Education*, 23–36. Abingdon: Routledge.

Gibbs, G. 2015 Maximising student learning gain. In H. Fry, S. Ketteridge, and S. Marshall (eds.), *A Handbook for Teaching and Learning in Higher Education*, 4th edition, 193–208. London: Routledge.

Gibbs, G. and Simpson, H. 2005 'Conditions under which assessment supports students' learning'. *Learning & Teaching in Higher Education*, 1, 2004–5.

Goertzel, M. G., Goertzel, V., and Goertzel, G. 1978 The personal characteristics and environmental circumstances of successful women musicians. *The Goertzel Studies*. New York: Chapman and Hall.

Gould, J. & Ashton Smith, J. 2011 Good Autism Practice www.autism.org.uk accessed 3/3/2014

Grandinetti, M. 2015 'Predictors of self-directed learning readiness of nursing students'. *US-China Education Review*, 5(7), 443–456.

Graves, N. 1993 *Learner Managed Learning*. Leeds: Higher Education for Capability/World Education Fellowship.

Gregory, K. and Clarke, M. 2003 'High stakes assessment in England and Singapore'. *Theory and Practice*, 42, 66–78.

Grolnick, W. S., Deci, E. L., and Ryan, R. M. 1997 Internalization within the family: the self-determination perspective. In J. E.Grussec and L. Kuczynski (eds.), *Parenting and Children's Internalization of Values: A Handbook of Contemporary Theory*, 135–161. New York: Wiley.

Guerra, A. and Kolmos, A. 2011 Comparing problem-based learning models: suggestions for their implementation. In J. W. Davies, E. de Graaf, and A. Kolmos (eds.), *PBL Across the Disciplines: Research into Best Practice*, 3–16. Aalborg: Aalborg University Press.

Guilford, J. P. 1950 'Creativity'. *American Psychologist*, 4, 444–454.

Hague, D. 1991 *Beyond Universities: A New Republic of the Intellect*. London: Institute of Economic Affairs.

Hamilton, S. and Stewart, T. 2015 'Business and management' 326–344 in H. Fry., S. Ketteridge and S. Marshall, (eds.) 2015 *A Handbook for Teaching and Learning in Higher Education*, 4th edition. London: Routledge.

Hammersley-Fletcher, L. and Orsmond, P. 2005 'Reflecting on reflective practice within peer observation'. *Studies in Higher Education*, 30(2), 213–224.

Hansford, B. C. and Hattie, J. A. 1982 'The relationship between self and achievement performance measures'. *Review of Educational Research*, 52, 123–142.

Harri-Augstein, S., Thomas, L. F., and Smith, M. 1985 *Self Organised Learning*. London: Routledge and Kegan Paul.

Hartwell, L. H., Hood, L., Goldber, M. L., Reynolds, A. E., Silver, L. M., and Veres, R. C. 2004 *Genetics: From Genes to Genomes*, 2nd edition. Boston, MA: McGraw Hill.

Hase, S. and Kenyon, C. 2000 *From Andragogy to Heutagogy*. In Ultibase articles. http://utibase.rmit .edu.au Articles/dec00/hase2.htm (Accessed 03/04/2020).

Hattie, J. and Marsh, H. W. 1996 'The relationship between research and teaching: a meta-analysis'. *Review of Educational Research*, 66(4), 507–542.

Heng, M. A. and Tam, K. Y. B. 2006 Reclaiming soul in gifted education: the academic caste system in Asian schools. In B. Wallace and G. Eriksson (eds.), *Diversity in Gifted Education: International Perspectives on Global Issues*, 178–186. London: Routledge.

Hirst, P. 1975 *Visiting Professorial Lecture*. Kingston upon Thames: Kingston Polytechnic.

Holland, J. L. 1997 Philosophy of education. *Making Vocational Choices: A Theory of Vocational Personalities and Work Environments*, 3rd edition. Odessa, FL: Psychological Assessment Resources.

Honey, P. and Mumford, A. 1986 *A Manual of Learning Styles*. Maidenhead: P. Honey.

Hull, C. L. 1943 *Principles of Behavior*. New York: Appleton-Century-Crofts.

James, K. and Engelhardt, L. 2012 'The effects of handwriting experience on functional brain development'. *Neuroscience and Education*, 1(1), 32–42.

Jin-ran, D., Ying J., and Wu Kai-Iun. 2016 'A study on high school chemistry teachers' meta-teaching ability'.*China Education Review*, 6(2), 132–137.

Kalyuga, S., Ayres, P., Chandler, P., and Sweller, J. 2003 'The expertise reversal effect'. *Educational Psychologist*, 38(1), 23–31.

Kelly, G. A. 1955 *Personal Construct Theory* (Vols. 1 and 2). New York: Norton.

Kemmis, S. and Henry, C. 1983 *The Action Research Planner*. Deakin, Australia: Deakin University Press.

Kennedy, D. 1987 Draft of letter to College Principals. From Paul 1990.

Knapper, C. 1995 'Approaches to study and lifelong learning: some Canadian initiatives'. I G. Gibbs (ed), *Improving Student Learning Through Assessment and Evauation* Oxford: Oxford Centre for staff Development, 11–23.

Knowles, M. 1975 *Self-Directed Learning*. Chicago, ILL: University of Chicago Press.

Koestler, A. 1967 *The Act of Creation*. Harmondsworth: Penguin.

Kolb, D. A. 1984 *Experiential Learning: Experience as the Source of Learning and Development*. New Jersey: Prentice Hall.

Krampe, R. T. and Ericsson, K. A. 1996 'Maintaining excellence: deliberate practice and elite performance in young and older pianists'. *Journal of Experimental Psychology: General*, 125, 331–359.

Kremer, L. and Perlberg, A. 1979 'Training of teachers in strategies that develop independent learning skills in their pupils'. *British Journal of Teacher Education*, 5(1), 35–47.

Kuh, G. D. and Pascarella, E. T. 2004 'What does institutional selectivity tell us about educational quality?' *Change*, 36(5), 52–58.

Kulik, C. L., Kulik, J., and Scwalb, B.J. 1983 'College programs for high-risk and disadvantaged students. A meta-analysis of findings'. *Review of Educational Research*, 53, 397–414.

Larson, R. W. and Verma, S. 1999 'How children and adolescents spend time across the world: work, play, and developmental opportunities'. *Psychological Bulletin*, 125, 701–736.

Lea, S. J., Stephenson, D., and Troy, J. 2003 'Higher education students' attitudes to student-centred learning: beyond 'educational bulimia''. *Studies in Higher Education*, 28(3), 321–334.

Leach, D. 1983 'Early screening techniques'. *School Psychology International*, 4, 47–56

Leat, D. 1999 'Rolling he stone uphill' teacher development and the implementation of thinking skills programmes'. *Oxford Review of Education*, 25(3), 387–403.

Leites, N. S. 1971 *Intellectual Abilities and Age*. Moscow: Pedagogica.

Leroux, J. and McMillan, E. 1993 *Smart Teaching: Nurturing Talent in the Classroom and Beyond*. Ontario: Pembroke Publishers.

Lockhead, J. 2001 *Thinkback: A User's Guide to Minding the Mind*. London: Lawrence Erlbaum.

Lord, J. 1972 *Teacher Education and Training: The James Report*. London: HMSO.

Low, G. 1998 'The first rule in lifelong learning'. *Education 21*, April, 3–4.

Lucas, B., Claxton, G., and Spencer, E. 2013 *Progression in Student Creativity in School: First Steps Towards New Forms of Formative Assessments*, OECD Education Working Papers, No. 86. Paris: OECD Publishing.

Lunzer, E. and Gerchow, K. 1984 *Learning from the Written Word*. London: Schools Council.

Lykken, D. T. 1998 The genetics of genius. In A. Steptoe (ed.), *Genius and the Mind: Studies of Creativity and Temperament in the Historical Record*, 15–37. New York: Oxford University Press.

Ma, X. 2005 'A longitudinal assessment of early acceleration of students in mathematics on growth in mathematics achievement'. *Developmental Review*, 25, 104–132.

MacDonald et al., 1999 *Survey of Boys' Achievement, Progress, Motivation and Participation*. Slough: NFER.

Markušić, J., Sabljick, J., and Strossmayer, J. J. 2019 'Problem-based teaching of literature'. *Journal of Education and Training Studies*, 7(4), 20–29.

Martin, G. N. 2017 'A persistent misconception'. *The Psychologist*, April, 8.

Martin, L. 2019 'Video watching'. *Journal of Experimental Psychology*.

Marton, F. and Säljo, R. 1976 'On qualitative differences in learning. 1 Outcome as a function of the learner's conception of the task'. *British Journal of Educational Psychology*, 46, 4–11.

Marton, F. and Säljo, R. 1984 Approaches to learning. In F. Marton, D. J. Hounsell, and N. J. Entwistle (eds.), *The Experience of Learning*, 36–55. Edinburgh: Scottish Academic Press.

Maslow, A. H. 1987 *Motivation and Personality*, 3rd edition. New York: Addison-Wesley.

Mayer, R. E. 1992 *Thinking, Problem-Solving and Cognition*. Oxford: Freeman.

McClure, M. L. 2004 'Clarity bordering on stupidity/Where's the quality in systematic review?' *Paper presented at the Annual BERA Conference UMIST*, September 16–18.

McCoach, D. B., Yu, H., Gottfried, A. W., and Gottfiried, A. E. 2017 'Developing talent. A longitudinal examination of intellectual ability and academic achievement'. *High Ability Studies*, 28(1), 7–28.

McCombs, B. J. 1988 Motivational skills training: combining metacognitive, cognitive and affective learning strategies. In C. E. Weinstein, E. T. Goetz, and P. A. Alexander (eds.), *Learning and Study Strategies; Issues in Assessment, Instruction and Evaluation*, 141–191. San Diego, CA: Academic Press.

McCombs, B. L. 2002 Self-regulated learning and academic achievement. A phenomenological view. In H. Fry, S. Ketteridge, and S. Marshall (eds.), *A Handbook for Teaching and Learning in Higher Education*, 4th edition, 67–123. London: Routledge.

McGraw-Hill Publishing Company. 2019 *Power of Process: Process Wheel Guides* E mail Advertisement, November 23.

McGuinness, C. 1999 *From Thinking Schools to Thinking Classrooms*. DfEE Research Report No. 115 London: DfEE.

McIntyre, A. 1980 The contribution of research to quality in teacher education. In E. Hoyle and J. McGarry (eds.), *Professional Development of Teacher's World Yearbook of Education*, 295–307. London: Kogan Page.

McLeod, S. A. 2011 *Bandura-Social Learning Theory*. http://www.simplypsychology.org/bandura.html (Accessed 20/11/2019).

Meek, M. and Thomson, B. 1987 *Study Skills in the Secondary School*. London: Routledge.

Merton, R. K. 1975 'Thematic analysis in science. Notes on Holton's concept'. *Science as Culture*, 188(4186), 335–338.

Miller, G. A. 1956 'The magical number 7 plus or minus 2'. *Psychological Review*, 63, 81–97.

Milton-Edwards, B. 2015 'Case study 19.2 Teaching Middle Eastern politics using blended learning with a web-based project 283–285 In H. Fry.,S. Ketteridge and S. Marshall, (eds.) 2015 *A Handbook for Teaching and Learning in Higher Education*, 4th edition. London: Routledge.

Mish, F. C. (ed.) 1988 *Websters Ninth New Collegiate Dictionary*. Springfield, MA: Merriam-Webster.

Mongon, D. and Hart, S. 1989 *Improving Classroom Behaviour: New Directions for Teachers and Learners*. London: Cassell.

Montgomery, D. (ed.) 2000 *Able Underachievers*. Chichester: Wiley.

Montgomery, D. 1977 'Teaching pre-reading through training in pattern recognition'. *The Reading Teacher*, 30(6), 216–225.

Montgomery, D. 1981 'Education comes of age'. *School Psychology International*, 1, 1–3.

Montgomery, D. 1983a 'Teaching thinking skills in the school curriculum'. *School Psychology International*, 3, 108–112.

Montgomery, D. 1983b *Evaluation and Enhancement of Teaching Performance*. Kingston upon Thames: Learning Difficulties Research Project

Montgomery, D. 1993 Fostering learner managed learning in teacher education. In N. Graves (ed.), *Learner Managed Learning*, 59–70. Leeds: Higher Education for Capability/ World Education Fellowship.

Montgomery, D. 1994 The role of metacognition and metalearning in teacher education. .In G. Gibbs (ed.), *Improving Student Learning: Theory & Research*, 227–253. Oxford: Oxford Brookes University.

Montgomery, D. 1995a 'Subversive activity'. *Education*, 21(April), 16–17.

Montgomery, D. 1995b The design, development and evaluation of assessment strategies involving real and simulated problems to effect general and specific capabilities. In M. Yorke (ed.), *Assessing Capability in Degree and Diploma Programmes*, 123–142. Liverpool: John Moores University.

Montgomery, D. 1996 *Educating the Able*. London: Cassell.

Montgomery, D. 1998 'Teacher education and distance learning'. *Education Today*, 48(4), 39–46.

Montgomery, D. 2002 *Helping Teachers Improve Through Classroom Observation*. London: David Fulton.

Montgomery, D 2015 *Teaching Gifted Children with Special Needs: Supporting Dual and Multiple Exceptionality*. London: Routledge.

Montgomery, D. 2017a *Dyslexia-Friendly Approaches to Reading, Spelling and Handwriting*. London: Routledge.

Montgomery, D. 2017b Using classroom observation to improve teaching and prevent failure with the "Five Star Plan" and audit system. In J. P. Bakken (ed.), *Classrooms: Assessment Practices for Teachers and Students Improvement Strategies*, 143–170. Nova Science Publishers: New York E-Book.

Montgomery, D. 2019 *Dyslexia and Gender Bias. A Critical Review*. London: Routledge.

Montgomery, D. and Hadfield, N. 1989 *Practical Teacher Appraisal*. London: Kogan-Page.

Moore-Johnson, S. 2019 *Where Teachers Thrive. Organising Schools for Success*. Cambridge, MA: Harvard Education Press.

Mueller, P. A. and Oppenheimer, D. M. 2014 'The pen is mightier than the keyboard. Advantages of longhand over laptop note-taking'. *Psychological Sciences*, 25(6), 1159–1168.

Muilenburg, L. Y. and Berge, Z. L. 2007 'Student barriers to online learning: a factor analytic study' 29–48 | Published online: January 19, 2007. http://dx.doi.org/10.1080/01587910500081269 (Accessed 3/11/2017).

NACE, 2019 Seminar News Editorial E-Newsletter p1.

Naplačić, A. 2012 *Problem-Based Approach to Anna Karenina, Madame Bovary and A Doll's House. Master's Thesis*. Osijek: Filozofski fakultet Osijek.

National Commission on Excellence in Education, 1983 *A Nation at Risk: The Imperative for Educational Reform*. Washington, DC: United States Department of Education.

National Committee of Inquiry into Higher Education (The Dearing Report), 1997 HMSO, London.

NCC, 1991 *The National Curriculum*. National Curriculum Council: York.

Necka, E. 1986 On the nature of creative talent. In A. J. Cropley, K. K. Urban, H. Wagner, and W. Wieczerkowski (eds.), *Giftedness: A Continuing World Wide Challenge*, 131–160. New York: Trillium Press.

Necka, E. 1992 *Creativity Training: A Guide for Psychologists, Educators and Teachers* (Translated by R. Stocki). Krakow: Kazimiers, Jasieniak.

NFER. 1983 *Study Skills*. Windsor: NFER.

Nias, J. 1996 'Thinking about feeling: the emotions of teaching'. *Cambridge Journal of Education*, 26(3), 293–306.

Nicol, D. J. 1997 *Research on Learning and Higher Education Teaching*. Sheffield: Universities and Colleges Staff Development Agency. UCoSDA Briefing Paper 45.

Nicol, D. J. and MacFarlane-Dick, D. 2006 'Formative assessment and self-regulated learning: a model and seven principles of good feedback practice'. *Studies in Higher Education*, 31(2), 199–218.

Niehart, M. 2011 'The revised profiles of the gifted: a research based approach', *Keynote Address WCGTC 19th Biennial World Conference*, Prague, August 8–12.

O'Leary, M. 2013 'Expansive and restrictive approaches to professionalism in FE colleges: the observation of teaching and learning as a case in point'. *Research in Post-Compulsory Education*, 18(4), 248–364.

OECD. 1972 *Note by the Secretariat*. Paris: OECD.

Osborn, A. F. 1963 *Applied Imagination. Principles and Processes of Creative Problem Solving*. New York: Scribner.

Pachane, G. G. 2017 'Teacher education experiences: what can we learn from Brazil, Portugal, and the USA?' *US-China Education Review* A, 7(2), 108–117.

Paik, S., Wang, D., and Walberg, H. 2002 'Timely improvements in learning'. *Educational Horizons*, 80, 69–71.

Palinscar, A. S. 1998 'Social constructivist perspectives on teaching and learning'. *Annual Review of Psychology*, 49, 345–375.

Paris, S. G. and Gross, D. R. 1983 Ordinary learning: programmatic connections among children's beliefs, motives and actions. In J. Bisanz and R. Kall (eds.), *Learning in Children: Progress in Cognitive Development Research*. New York: Springer-Verlag.

Paul, R. W. 1990 Critical thinking in North America. In A. J. Binker (ed.), *Critical Thinking. What Every Person Needs to Know in a Rapidly Changing World*, 18–42. Sonoma: Sonoma State University.

Pentaraki, A. 2017 'Reducing drop-out rates in on-line degrees'. *The Psychologist*, November Letters, 5.

Perlberg, A., Kremer, L., and Lewis, R. 1979 'Towards new teacher education models'. *British Journal of Teacher Education*, 5(3), 263–281.

Perry, P. 1983 Career prospects in the 80s. Career development and job satisfaction from the teacher's point of view. Speech by the Chief Inspector for Teacher Training text reprinted with permission. Annual BEMAS Conference May 1983. In D. Montgomery (ed.), *Evaluation and Enhancement of Teaching Performance*, 4–5. Kingston: Learning Difficulties Research Project.

Piaget, J. 1952 *Origins of Intelligence in Children*, 2nd edition. New York: International Universities Press.

Pickering, J., Daly, C., and Pachler, N. 2007 *New Designs for Teacher's Professional Learning: Bedford Way Papers*. London: Institute of Education.

Pintrich, P. R. 2000 The role of goal orientation in self-regulated learning. In M. Boekaerts, P. R. Pintrich, and M. Zeidner (eds.), *Handbook of Self-regulation*, 451–502. New York: Academic Press.

Pintrich, P. R. and Zusho, A. 2002 Student motivation and self-regulated learning in the college classroom. In J. C. Smart and W. G. Tierney (eds.), *Higher Education: Handbook of Theory and Research* (Vol. 17). New York: Agathon Press.

Plucker, J. A. and Peters, S. J. 2016 *Excellence Gaps in Education. Expanding opportunities for Talented Youth*. Cambridge, MA: Harvard Education Press.

Pollard, A. 1997 *Reflective Teaching in the Primary School*. London: Cassell.

Poorthuis, E., Kok, L., and Van Dijk, J. 1990 A curriculum assessment tool, *Paper presented at the 2nd Biennial Conference of the European Council for High Ability (ECHA)*, Budapest, October.

Powney, J. 2017 'Unprepared undergraduates?' *The Psychologist*, 3.

Qin, Y. and Simon, H. A. 1990 'Laboratory replication of scientific discovery processes'. *Cognitive Science*, 14, 281–312.

Quinn, D. M., Desruisseaux, T. M., and Nkansah-Amankra, A. 2019 'Does 'the Achievement Gap' evoke a negative stereotype? What the research says'. *Education Week*, 39(16), 24.

Race, P. 1992 Developing competence. *Professorial Inaugural Lecture*. Glamorgan: Glamorgan University.

Race, P., Brown, S., and Smith, B. 2005 *500 Tips for Assessment*, 2nd edition. London: Routledge-Falmer.

Ramdass, D. and Zimmerman, B. J. 2011 'Developing self-regulation skills: the important role of homework'. *Journal of Advanced Academics*, 22(2), 194–218.

Ramsden, P. 1991 'A performance indicator of teaching quality in higher education'. *Studies in Higher Education*, 16, 129–150.

Ramsden, P. 1994 'Current challenges to quality in Higher Education'. *Innovative Higher Education*, 18(3), 177–188.

Ramsden, P. 1997 The context of learning. In F. Marton, D. J. Hounsell, and N. J. Entwistle (eds.), *The Experience of Learning*, 2nd edition. Edinburgh: Scottish Academic Press.

Ramsden, P. 2003 *Learning to Teach in Higher Education*, 2nd edition. London: Kogan Page

Rasch, L. 2004 'Employee performance appraisal and the 95/5 rule'. *Community College Journal of Research and Practice*, 28(5), 407–414.

Rayner, S. 2007 'A teaching elixir, learning chimera, or just fool's gold? Do learning styles matter?' *Support for Learning*, 22(1), 24–30.

Reis, S. M. and Renzulli, J. S. 2008 What is this thing called giftedness and how to develop it? A 25 year perspective. In J. Fortikova (ed.), *Successful Teaching of the Exceptional Gifted Child*, 8–36. Prague: Triton Press.

Reitinger, S. 2015 Personal and family experiences living in Germany since 1974 an interview.

Renzulli, J. 1977 *The Enrichment Triad Model: A Guide for Developing Defensible Programs for the Gifted and Talented*. Mansfield, CT: Creative Learning Press.

Renzulli, J. S. and Reis, S. M. 1985 *The Schoolwide Enrichment Model: A Comprehensive Plan for Educational Excellence*. Mansfield Center, CT: Creative Learning Press.

Resnick, L. B. 1989 Introduction. In L. B. Resnick (ed.), *Knowing, Learning and Instruction: Essays in Honour of Robert Glaser*, 1–24. Hillsdale, NJ: Erlbaum.

Revans, R. 1945 Plans for the Recruitment, Education and Training in the Coal Mining Industry, Extract reprinted in Revans 1982, chapter 7.

Revans, R. 1982 *The Origins and Growth of Action Learning*. Kent: Chartwell-Bratt.

Reynolds, R. E. and Shirley L. L. 1988 The role of attention in studying and learning. In C. F. Weinstein, E. T. Goetz, and P. A. Alexander (eds.), *Learning and Study Strategies; Issues in Assessment, Instruction and Evaluation*, 77–90. San Diego, CA: Academic Press.

Rhodes, J. 2017 *The Psychologist Guide to University Life*. Leicester: BPS Pamphlet.

Riding, K. and Rayner, R. 1998 *Cognitive Styles and Learning Strategies*. London: David Fulton.

Roderiguez, E. 2015 Case study 17.1 Projects that benefit the community 250–251 In H. Fry.,S. Ketteridge and S. Marshall, (eds.) 2015 *A Handbook for Teaching and Learning in Higher Education*, 4th edition. London: Routledge.

Roe, A. 1952 'A psychologist examines 64 eminent scientists'. *Scientific American*, 187, 21–25.

Roe, A. 1953 *The Making of a Scientist*. New York: Dodd, Mead, & Co.

Rogers, B. 2007 *Behaviour Management: A Whole School Approach*, 2nd edition. London: Sage.

Rogers, K. S. and Span, P. 1993 Ability grouping with gifted and talented students. In K. A. Heller, F. Monks, and A. H. Passow (eds.), *International Handbook of Research and Development of Giftedness and Talent*. Oxford: Pergamon.

Rosenshine, B. 2010 *Principles of Instruction*. International Academy of Education UNESCO. Geneva: International Bureau of Education.

Royce-Adams, W. 1977 *Developing Reading Versatility*. New York: Rinehart and Winston.

Rutkowski, D.,Rutkowski, L., and Plucker, J. A. 2012 'Trends in education excellence gaps. A 12-year international perspective via the multilevel model for change'. *High Ability Studies*, 23, 143–166.

Rutter, M. L., Caspi, A., Fergusson, D., Horwood, L.J., Goodman, R., Maughan, B., Moffatt, T.B., Meltzer, H.C. & Carroll, J. 2004 'Sex differences in developmental reading disability'. *Journal of the American Medical Association*, 291 9(16), 2007–2012.

Ryan, R. M. and Deci, E. L. 2000 'Intrinsic and extrinsic motivations: classic definitions and new directions'. *Contemporary Educational Psychology*, 25, 54–67.

Ryan, R. M., Stiller, J., and Lynch, J. H. 1994 'Representations of relationships to teachers, parents and friends as predictors of academic motivation and self-esteem'. *Journal of Early Adolescence*, 14, 226–249.

Sadler, D. R. 1989 'Formative assessment and the design of instructional systems'. *Instructional Science*, 18, 119–144.

Shachar, M. and Neumann, Y. 2003 'Differences between traditional and didactic academic performances: a meta-analytical approach'. *International Review of Research in Open and Distance Education* 4(2) 153. http://www.irrodl.org/index.php/irrodl/article/view/

Scheerer, M. 1963 'Problem-solving'. *Scientific American*, 208(4), 118–128.

Schools Council. 1980 *Study Skills in the Secondary School, Pilot Edition*. London: Schools Council.

Schultz, R. A. 2002 'Illuminating realities: a phenomenological view from two underachieving gifted learners'. *Roeper Review*, 24, 203–212.

Schunck, D. 2002 Social cognitive theory and SRL. In B. L. Zimmerman and D. H. Schunk (eds.), *Self-Regulated Learning and Academic Achievement. Theoretical Perspectives*, 2nd edition, 125–151. Routledge: London.

Scott MacDonald, W. 1971 *Battle in the Classroom*. Brighton: Intext.

Scriven, M. 1986 'New functions of evaluations'. *Evaluation Practice*, 7(1), 21–30.

SED Scottish Education Department. 1978 *The Education of Pupils with Learning Difficulties in Primary and Secondary Schools. A Progress Report by HMI*. Edinburgh: HMSO.

Setren, E. 2019 'Flipped classrooms'. Education Week, 27/8/2019. ssparks@epe.org

Shayer, M. and Adey, P. (eds.) 2002 *Learning Intelligence: Cognitive Acceleration Across the Curriculum from 3–25 Years*. Buckingham: Open University Press.

Silverman L.K. 2004 'Poor handwriting: A major cause of underachievement'. http://www.visuospatial.org/Publications/ Accessed April 2007

Simon, H. A. and Chase, W. G. 1973 'Skill in chess'. *American Scientist*, 61, 394–403.

Simonton, D. K. 1997 'Creative productivity: a predictive and explanatory model of career trajectories and landmarks'. *Psychological Review*, 104, 66–89.

Simonton, D. K. 1988 *Scientific Genius: A Psychology of Science*. Cambridge: Cambridge University Press.

Simonton, D. K. 2005 Genetics of giftedness: the implications of an emergenic-epigenetic model. In R. J. Sternberg and J. E. Davidson (eds.), *Conceptions of Giftedness*, 2nd edition, 312–326. Cambridge University Press.

Simonton, D. K. 1984 *Genius, Creativity, and Leadership: Historiometric Inquiries*. Cambridge, MA: Harvard University Press.

Skilbeck, M. 1989 *School Development and New Approaches to Learning: Trends and Issues in Curriculum Reform*. Paris: Organisation for Economic Co-operation and Development.

Skilbeck, M. 1989 *School Development and New Approaches to Learning: Trends and Development*. Paris: OECD.

Skinner, B. F. 1953 *Science and Human Behavior*. New York: Macmillan.

Skourdoumbis, A. and Gale, T. 2013 'Classroom teacher effectiveness research: a conceptual critique'. *British Educational Research Journal*, 39(5), 892–906.

Sloboda, J. A., Davidson, J. W., Howe, M. J. A., and Moore, D. G. 1996 'The role of practice in the development of performing musicians'. *British Journal of Psychology*, 87, 287–309.

Soriano de Alencar, E. 1995 'Developing creative abilities at university level'. *European Journal for High Ability*, 6(1), 82–90.

Spearman, C. 1927 *The Abilities of Man*. New York: Macmillan.

Stephenson, J. 1988 *Inaugural Speech on the Launch of the Project on the Challenge of Higher Education for Capability*. London: Royal Society of Arts.

Sternberg, R. J. 2000 Creativity is a decision. In A. L. Costa (ed.), *Teaching for Intelligence II*, 85–106. Arlington Heights, IL: Skylight Training and Publishing Inc. 85-106

Sternberg, R. J. 1986 *Beyond IQ. A Triarchic Theory of Intelligence*. New York: Cambridge University Press.

Sternberg, R. J. 2013 'Creativity, ethics, and society'. *International Journal for Talent Development and Creativity*, 1(1), 15–23.

Sternberg, R. J., Lubart, T. I., Kaufman, J. C., and Pretz, J. E. 2005 Creativity. In K. J. Holyoak and R. G. Morrison (eds.), *The Cambridge Handbook of Thinking and Reasoning*. New York: Cambridge University Press 351–369.

Stoeger, H. 2006 'First steps towards and epistemic learner model'. *High Ability Studies*, 17(1), 17–41.

Stoeger, H. 2018 Self-regulated learning, *Keynote Address Biennial Conference of the European Council for High Ability (ECHA)*, August, Dublin.

Stoeger, H. and Ziegler, A. 2005 'Motivational orientation and cognitive abilities: An empirical investigation in primary school'. *Gifted and Talented International*, 20(2), 7–18.

Stone, C. L. 1983 'A meta-analysis of advance organizer studies'. *The Journal of Experimental Education*, 51(4), 194–199.

Stones, E. 1979 *Pychopedagogy*. London: Methuen.

Stones, E. 1983 'Perspectives in pedagogy'. *Journal of Education for Teaching*, 9(1), 68–76.

Strauss, A. L. and Corbin, J. 1990 *Basics of Qualitative Research*. Newbury Park: Sage.

Stroebe, W. 2016 'Why good teaching evaluations may reward bad teaching'. *Perspectives on Psychological Science*, 11, 800–816.

Stroebe, W. 2019 'Excellence or ease? Exploring student evaluations of teaching'. *The Psychologist*, 50–52.

Strong, M., Gargani, J., and Hacifazlioglu, O. 2011 'Do we know a successful teacher when we see one? Experiments in the identification of effective teachers'. *Journal of Teacher Education*, 62(4), 367–382.

Sullivan, T. 1979 *Studying*. Cambridge: National Extension College.

Sutton Trust. 2018 Oxbridge recruitment 2015-2017, Speech by Sir Peter Lampl, December 7.

Sutton Trust. 2019 'Elitist Britain', London: Sutton Trust Research, July 25.

Swartz, R. J and Parks, S. 1994 *Infusing Critical and Creative Thinking into Elementary Instruction*. Pacific Grove, CA: Critical Thinking Press and Software.

Taba, H. 1962 *Curriculum Development. Theory and Practice*. New York: Harcourt Brace Jovanovitch.

Taylor, K. (ed.) 1991 *Drama Strategies. New Ideas From London Drama*. Oxford: Heinemann Educational.

Terman, L. M. 1954 'The discovery and encouragement of exceptional talent'. *American Psychologist*, 9, 221–30.

TESTA. 2010 Transforming the Experience of Students through Assessment. http://www.testa.ac.uk/index-php/resources/best practice-guides/127-principles-of-assessment.

Thomas, L. F. and Harri-Augstein, E. S. 1975 *Reading to Learn Research Report*. London: Brunel University, Centre for Studies of Human Learning.

Thomas, L. F. and Harri-Augstein, E. S. 1983 *The Self-organised Learner. A Conversational Science for Teaching and Learning*. London: Brunel University, Centre for Studies of Human Learning.

Thouless, R. H. 1967 *Straight and Crooked Thinking*. London: Pan Books (Reprint, 2011 Hodder).

Tinkler, D. E. 1990 Constructivism in learner managed learning, Keynote paper. *35th International Conference of the World Education Fellowship and First International Conference on Learner Managed Learning*, London.

Torrance A. P. and Hall, I. K. 1980 'Assessing the further reaches of creative potential'. *Journal of Creative Behaviour*, 14, 1–19.

Torrance, E. P. 1963 *Education and the Creative Potential*. Minneapolis: University of Minnesota.

Turan, S., Demirel, Ö., and Sayek, İ. 2009 'Metacognitive awareness and self-regulated learning skills of medical students in different medical curricula'. *Medical Teacher*, 31. 477–483 https://doi.org/10.3109/01421590903193521 (Accessed 03/10/2017).

Tuxworth, E. N. 1982 *Competency in Teaching*. London: Further Education Unit.

Vygotsky, L. 1978 *Mind in Society*. Cambridge, MA: MIT Press.

Wallace, B. 2009 What do we mean by an 'Enabling Curriculum' that raises achievement for all learners? In D. Montgomery (ed.), *Able, Gifted and Talented Underachievers*, 2nd edition, 59–84. Chichester: Wiley.

Wallace, B. and Erikson, G. (eds.) 2006 *Diversity in Gifted Education: International Perspectives on Global Issues*. London: Routledge.

Wallace, P. 2005 'Distance education for gifted students: leveraging technology to expand academic options'. *High Ability Studies*, 16(1), 77–86.

Wallas, G. (1926/2014) *The Art of Thought*. London: Watts & Co.

Wang, M. C. and Lindvall, C. M. 1984 Individual differences and school environments. In E. W. Gordon (ed.), *Review of Research in Education II*. Washington, DC: American Education Research Association.

Ward, P., Hodges, N. J., Williams, A. M., and Starkes, J. L. 2004 Deliberate practice and expert performance. In A. M. Williams and N. J. Hodges (eds.), *Skill Acquisition in Sport*, 231–258. London: Routledge.

Weikart, D. 1967 *Preschool Intervention a Preliminary Report from the Perry Preschool Project*. Ann Arbor: Michigan Campus Publishers.

Weikart, D. 1998 Report of an international comparative study of pre-school education. 24 hour World News, Strasbourg, June 4.

Weiner, B. 1980 'The role of affect in rational (attributional) approaches to human motivation'. *Educational Researcher*, 9, 4–11.

Weinstein, C. E., Goetz, E. T., and Alexander, P. A. (eds.) 1988 *Learning and Study Strategies; Issues in Assessment, Instruction and Evaluation*. San Diego, CA: Academic Press.

Weisberg, R. W. 1986 *Problem Solving and Creativity: The Nature of Creativity*. Cambridge: Cambridge University Press.

White, F. W. 1959 'Motivation reconsidered. The concept of competence'. *Psychological Review*, 66, 297–333.

Wilding, J. and Valentine, E. 1997 *Superior Memory*. Hove: Psychology Press.

Wilshaw, Sir M. 2015 *Text of Speech by the Chief Inspector for Schools*. London: OFSTED.

Winne, P. H. 1996 'A metacognitive view of individual differences in self-regulated learning'. *Learning and Individual Differences*, 8(4), 327–353.

Winne, P. H. 2002 Information processing models of SRL. In B. J. Zimmerman and D. H. Schunk (eds.), *Self-Regulated Learning and Academic Achievement. Theoretical Perspectives*, 2nd edition, 153–189. Routledge: London.

Winne, P. H. and Hadwin, A. F. 1998 Studying as self-regulated learning. In D. J. Hacker and J. Dunlosky (eds.), *Metacognition in Educational Theory and Practice: The Educational Psychology Series*. Mahwah, NJ: Erlbaum.

Woodhead, C. 1998 The Radio 4 Today interview, 8.10 am, September 6.

Wu, R. 2013 'Learning from the learners'. *The Psychologist*, 26(2), 154–155.

Yorke, M. (ed.) 1995 *Assessing Capability in Degree and Diploma Programmes*. Liverpool: John Moores University.

Yorke, M. 2003 'Formative assessment in higher education: moves towards theory and the enhancement of pedagogic practice'. *Higher Education*, 45(4), 477–501.

Yorke, M. and Knight, P. 2004 'Self-theories: some implications for teaching and learning in higher education'. *Studies in Higher Education*, 29(1), 25–33.

Zanaty, H. and Kitama, E. 2015 'Enhancing local education for sustainable development through learning cycle instructional model'. *US-China Education Review B*, 5(6), 382–391.

Zembylas, M. 2008 'Adult learner's emotions in online learning'. *Distance Education*, 29, 71–87.

Ziegler, A. 2005 The actiotope model of giftedness. In R. J. Sternberg and J. E. Davidson (eds.), *Conception of Giftedness*, 2nd edition, 411–436. New York: Cambridge University Press.

Ziegler, A. 2005 The actiotope model of giftedness. In R. J. Sternberg and J. E. Davidson (eds.), *Conception of Giftedness*, 2nd edition, 411–436. New York: Cambridge University Press.

Zimmerman, B. J. 1990 'Self-regulating academic learning and achievement: the emergence of a social cognitive perspective'. *Educational Psychology Review*, 2, 173–201.

Zimmerman, B. J. 1998 Developing self-fulfilling cycles of academic regulation: an analysis of exemplar instructional models. In D. H. Schunk and B. J. Zimmerman (eds.), *Self-regulated Learning from Teaching to Self-reflective Practice*, 1–19. New York: The Guilford Press.

Zimmerman, B. J. and Kitsantas, A. 2005 The hidden dimension of personal competence: self-regulated learning and practice. In A. J. Elliot and C. S. Dweck (eds.), *Handbook of Competence and Motivation*, 509–526. New York: The Guilford Press.

Zimmerman, B. J. and Martinez-Pons, M. 1990 'Student differences in self-regulated learning: relating grade, sex, and giftedness to self-efficacy and strategy use'. *Journal of Educational Psychology*, 1(82), 51–59.

Zimmerman, B. J., Bandura, A., and Martinez-Pons, M. 1992 'Self-motivation for academic attainment: the role of self-efficacy beliefs and personal goal setting'. *American Educational Research Journal*, 29, 663–676.

Zimmerman, B. J. and Schunk, D. H. 2002 *Self-Regulated Learning and Academic Achievement. Theoretical Perspectives*, 2nd edition. Routledge: London.

Zuber-Skerrett, O. 1992 *Action Learning in Higher Education*. London: Kogan Page.

Index

Lightning Source UK Ltd.
Milton Keynes UK
UKHW022213281021
393024UK00008B/37